JOURNEY FROM TEHRAN TO CHICAGO

My Life in Iran and the United States, and a Brief History of Iran

By H. Dizadji, MD, FACC

ISBN: 978-1-4269-2918-2 (sc)
ISBN: 978-1-4269-2919-9 (hc)

Library of Congress Control Number: 2010903508

Trafford rev. 12/28/2010

 www.trafford.com

North America & international
toll-free: 1 888 232 4444 (USA & Canada)
phone: 250 383 6864 ♦ fax: 812 355 4082

To:

Madelyn Shirin Dizadji

&

The People of Iran

Contents

Introduction

I started to write this book mainly for my children with particularly my grandchildren in mind. My intention was to provide them some information about my beloved country, my place of birth.

I wanted to tell them about my childhood, education, my home, parents, siblings, and my friends.

As the work progressed I decided to modify my initial intention in writing this manuscript and expand it to include a brief history of Iran and some aspects of my professional life in the United States of America. I believe this book will be of interest to all readers interested in the history, culture, and lifestyle of people in Iran, which recently has been under relentless political attacks and accusations. The glorious history of Iran is a history of one of the oldest civilizations of the world. I am hoping to present the readers a true picture of Iran, Iranians, their culture and religion.

To describe the cultural, socio-economic, political, religious, and educational aspects of Iranians during my living in Iran, in isolation without describing the historical events leading to that period of time probably will lead to misunderstanding and misinterpretation. Therefore I decided to discuss briefly and systematically the history of Iran and the Iranians' origin. I started with the Medes, Achaemenid and Sasanid dynasties. Since Islam has been the major religion of Iran during the major part of Iranian history, I discussed the Islamic civilization and the influence of Islam in the Iranian culture relatively in detail. The discussion then is focused on the growth and dominance of Shiism vs. Sunnism and identification of Iranians with Shia's Imams rather than Sunni's Caliphs, and eventual adoption of Shiism as the official religion of Iran. Comparing the ruling dynasties before and after Islam helps to understand further the reciprocal influence of the Iranian culture and Islamic religion.

This is not meant to be solely an autobiography, even though I am talking about myself. Describing my professional life in Iran and in the USA and comparing the educational systems, the practice of medicine and interaction among people in Iran and in the USA, indirectly reflect the different aspects of life during my stay in two countries. Despite differences in socioeconomic and religious aspects between two nations, all aspects of human behavior, adaptive and maladaptive are essentially similar, in both countries

During this work one concept became clear that in human evolution for the past several millennia we have progressed technically in an unimaginable pace, evolving from a primitive culture living in caves and hunting for foods to DNA mapping, space exploration, computer, and wireless communication.

But how about our predatory instinct? Are we not still killing, destroying in a sophisticated fashion with superiorly sophisticated instruments and with justification and rationalization? Are we not using nationality, religion, freedom, and defense to justify and whitewash and cover up our aggression and the violence?

Since 1962, except for a short visit in 1972, I have not been in Iran and I have been residing in the USA and enjoying the privileges with a great deal of appreciation. However, a heart wrenching and omnipresent nostalgia has been my constant companion, nostalgia for my childhood, schools, family, the places I have lived in the past, Shahrak, Zanjan, Tehran, Bojnourd, and Arsanjan.

These nostalgias and memories, sad or happy, have been like powerful magnetic forces attracting me to the past, enticing me to relive my past life at the present. I had to counteract these forces of the past and give more meaning to the present by focusing on my work, my love of family and children and my devotion to my patients.

In preparation of this manuscript in addition to the books listed in the references I consulted Encyclopedia Britannica and if necessary, Webster's New Biographical Dictionary for spelling and pronunciation of the names and non-English words. When appropriate I have included Farsi pronunciation of the Iranian names and words.

PART I

A Brief History Of Iran

CHAPTER I

Geography Of Iran

At the present time the area of Iran is 636,300 square miles (18th in the world), located between the Caspian Sea in the north and the Persian Gulf in the south. It is bordered on the northwest by Armenia and Azerbaijan or Azarbaijan; on the north by the Caspian Sea; on the northeast by Turkmenistan; on the east by Afghanistan and Pakistan; on the south by the Persian Gulf and the Gulf of Oman; and on the west by Turkey and Iraq.

Iran's territorial size has been altered over a period of long history in relation to the major civilization.

Historically in around 500 B.C., Iran extended from the Mediterranean Sea to the Indus River and included modern Armenistan, Azerbaijan, Uzbekistan, Tajikistan, Turkmenistan, Afghanistan, Pakistan, Egypt, Iraq, Syria, and Turkey.

It has been a bridge between central and western Asia, linking Asia and Europe.

Iran is made up of plateaux, deserts and high rugged mountain chains.

The Zagros Mountain range about 550 miles long and 150 miles wide extends from northwest, the border of Armenia, to southeast ending at the Strait of Hormuz (Farsi: Hormoz) with the highest peak in Zard Kuh or Zard-e Kuh Bakhtiari (Yellow Mountain) of over 14,000 feet. In 1908 the first oil well producing oil in the Middle East, was established in Masjed-e Soleyman at the foothills of the Zagros Mountains. Only Saudi Arabia's oil reserve exceeds that of Iran. Oil deposits of Iran are mainly located in the Zagros and the Persian Gulf coastal plain.

Elburz, or (Farsi: Alborz) Mountain range, about 560 miles long, on the north, stretches along the world largest lake, Caspian Sea, toward Khorasan or Khorasaan, with the highest peak of Demavand (Farsi: Davamand), about 19,000 feet comparing with Mount Everest of about 29,000 feet. The fertile Caspian coast with abundant rain is the major source of rice and tea in Iran and it also grows cotton and citrus.

The great, salt crusted, arid desert, Dasht-e Kavir in north central Iran lies to the southeast of the Elburz Mountains and stretches to Dasht-e Lut.

Dasht-e Lut, to the east of Dasht-e Kavir, in east central Iran extends southeast with its sand dunes as high as thousands of feet and salt filled depressions, with the surface temperature reaching 159 degrees F, the hottest surface temperature on the earth.

Two large rivers, the Rud-e Karun or Karoun and Zayandeh Rud, both originate from Zagros Mountains, near Zard Kuh and empty in Arvand Rud (Shatt-Al Arab) and in a swamp northwest of the city of Yazd, respectively. The third river, Sefeed or Safid Rud originates from the Elburz Mountains and drains eventually to the Caspian Sea. These rivers combined generate hydroelectric energy, and are utilized for irrigation and navigation (only Karun River) purposes.

The geographic pattern of Iran, high mountain ranges, deserts, and sea-gulf, contributes to wide seasonal and local climatic variations. For instance temperature reaches 131 degrees F in Khuzestan or Khuzistan province near the Persian Gulf to a very low of –35 degrees F in the province of Azerbaijan.

The fertile region of the Caspian Sea with forests and rice paddies due to high precipitation contrasts with hot and dry seasons of southeast regions.

The great variations in the topographical features of Iran and its climate are responsible for the heterogeneity of the population density, settlement, and types of dwelling architecture. They also influence the occupations, tribalism, and nomadic life, as well as agricultural, industrial, and cultural developments, and even religious practice and political views.

CHAPTER 2

History

It is interesting to find out how far back in history humankind existed in the Iranian plateau. Pre-historic archeological stone artifacts of the lower Paleolithic period of the Stone Age and flint tools dating to the Middle Paleolithic or Mousterian Times of Stone Age, made by Neanderthal man (Homo sapiens neanderthalis) are found in Iran particularly in the Zagros Mountains slopes, indicating the Hominid activities in the area more than 100,000 years ago. During this long period there were adaptive and evolutionary changes and geographical variations in the physical structure of mankind as well as changes in the cognitive and psychomotor skills. But in general the humans were capable of standing on their two feet, using their feet to walk and migrate. As time went forward they progressively became able to reason, try to solve problems at hand, use their hands to make tools, hunt, gather food, and fight.

Over a period of time some of them such as Neanderthals became extinct, the others became our progenitors, and continued to endow their descendants by their genetic structures to proliferate the Homo sapiens sapiens in the Iranian land and all over the world.

The Homo sapiens sapiens continued to do the same things as their progenitors, eating, sleeping, mating, discovering, and of course fighting and killing the other species and each other, moving toward civilization. As we evolved all these activities became more sophisticated, and Homo sapiens sapiens added defense mechanisms such as rationalization, projection, and denial to their cognitive skills and became capable of blurring the distinction of bad from good, portraying evil as an angel.

The sophisticated descendants evolved further to use their doctoral degrees, diplomas, diplomatic skills, political conventions, and their rationalization capabilities to justify the mal-adaptive behavior against each other individually and collectively and to obscure their predatory instincts.

The excavation of earth ware utensils in western Iran dating back to 8th-7th millennium B.C. at the end of Upper Paleolithic period about 10,000 B.C. and the beginning of Neolithic period (last phase of stone age) attests to the existence of a progressive and widely spread culture including advancement in tool manufacturing, domestication of animals and plants, followed by a full developed animal and village farming, among people inhabiting Iran at the time.

These trends continued during the following millennia, until the Bronze age of 3500-1000 years B.C., when ceramic, copper or bronze tools and weapons were introduced, and extended to the Iron age, starting 1200-1000 years B.C. in Iran, before the beginning of Iron age in Europe, when iron became the main ingredient of tools and weapons.

During 2nd half of the 1st millennium B.C. corresponding to the Achaemenid Empire, in addition to the archeological evidence, the written history including written documents from Mesopotamia provided sufficient data, to verify the historical events.

Before starting to address the documented history of Iranian people, it may be helpful to briefly discuss some of the pertinent civilizations of the region, which existed prior to the recorded history of Iran.

CHAPTER 3

Civilizations Prior To The Recorded History Of Iran

Mesopotamia was an ancient fertile region, also called the Fertile Crescent, between the Tigris and Euphrates rivers, now part of Iraq, in broader terms west to the Zygros Mountains, and east to the Arabian plateau.

Ancient Mesopotamia was originally unclaimed fertile land easily accessible to people seeking water, food, pastureland, and habitat. The region, like the other regions of that part of the world was attractive and suitable for the life style and life cycle of those old days. It starts with a small number of people settling down, forming tribal community, leading to a larger communities, and directed by a strong leader, expanding in all directions and possibly building a kingdom, only to be destroyed by new hungry arrivals to repeat the cycle again. Burning to ashes, then rising from it as a Simourgh, the Iranian mythological bird.

SUMER

About 4000 B.C. a group of non-Semite people settled in Sumer, located in southernmost part of Mesopotamia in the lower valley of the Euphrates river in the area that later on is to be called Babylonia, now southern Iraq, toward the Persian Gulf.

These settlers later on were joined by other settlers, including Semitic people and started the earliest civilization including agriculture, trade, and basic industry. By 3rd millennium B.C. and after arrival of more people, probably non-Semitic, the small communities of Sumerians progressed to several independent communities of city-states structure such as Ur, Kish, and Uruk, some with their own religious temples and pilgrimage, recognizing and promoting theology and the various forms of Gods to deal with their anxieties and death. These large communities competed with and fought each other, the larger and stronger ones gaining more power, reaching the level of dynasty, only to become the target of external forces such as Elamites and later on Akkadians by their Semitic leader called Sargon, the Great, a Semite king, who spoke Akkadian, a Semitic language and unified Sumerian territory as a part of his dynasty.

The Sumerian language spoken then is preserved in pictographic and subsequently in cuneiform writing, still exists on the clay tablets, is the world's oldest written document.

These writings, as expected contributed to the advancement of all aspects of the Sumerian civilization, particularly to the birth and preservation of early literature.

The hero of Gilgamesh Epic, the oldest story in the world, is the legendary Sumerian king, and the epic, completed about 2000 B.C., includes a story about flooding similar to the biblical Noah's Ark flood.

Sumerians eventually lost their independence, but they maintained their recognition as a major contributor to the early culture and technology of the world such as language, literature, codes of law, pottery, first wheeled vehicles and buildings.

AKKAD

Was an ancient region of Mesopotamia, the northern division of ancient Babylonia, opposite to Sumer, the southern division of Babylonia. Akkad is derived from the city of Agade, the capital founded by Sargon of Akkad (reigned c. 2334-2279 B.C.), a Semitic conqueror, the leader of Akkadians, and founder of Semitic dynasty of Akkad, ruling southern Mesopotamia, extending to Syria, Anatolia and Susa, the capital city of Elam in western Iran.

The Akkadians, the early inhabitants of Akkad were Semitic and spoke Akkadian, the oldest Semitic language and written in cuneiform.

BABYLONIA

An ancient Empire in SW Asia, in the lower Tigris and Euphrates rivers valley with the famous Babylon as the capital. The term of Babylonia is applied to the combined regions of ancient Sumer in the SE and ancient Akkad in NW. At the beginning of 2nd millennium Amorites, Semitic people migrated from Arabia to the area of Babylonia and Syria and Palestine. They absorbed Sumerian and Akkadian cultures and started their own kingdom and ruled this area of Mesopotamia extending from the Persian Gulf to Assyria in the north for about four centuries, forming the great empire of Babylonia with leaders such as Hammurabi (c. 1792-1750 B.C.), the well-known promoter of code of laws, the collection of existing laws in practice at the time, including the ones derived from Sumer. The laws were related to family affairs, property, trades, and slavery and were carved in stone pillars and tablets for public observation. The captured members of the defeated armies were usually the source of slaves.

After 1600 B.C. Babylonia was ruled by the Kassite dynasty for an additional 400 years.

During this period of time Assyria gained independence from Babylonia; Elam ended the Kassite dynasty only to be beaten back by a famous Babylonian new king, Nebuchadrezzar 1 (1124-1103 B.C.).

Sometime after Nebuchadrezzar 1's death Assyrian ruled Babylonia for about two centuries until a Chalean ruler named Nabopolassar occupied Babylon and reestablished the Babylonian empire (New Babylonia) with much achievement in science, medicine, and astronomy. His son Nebuchadrezzar II (reigned 605-c. 562 B.C.) conquered Syria and Palestine and destroyed Judah and Jerusalem, and initiated Babylonian captivity, the period of the exile of the Jews in Babylonia, 597-538 B.C. He upgraded Babylon. In 539 B.C. Cyrus the Great captured Babylonia, handing it eventually to Alexander the Great for the final disappearance.

ASSYRIA

Was an ancient empire in SW Asia in northern Mesopotamia, southeast to Turkey now in the region of northern Iraq with capital of Ashur, then Nineveh. Assyrians with a reputation for cruelty received independence from Babylonia in 14th century B.C., during Kassite ruling of Babylonia, and began to gain power in the Mesopotamia region, intermittently ruling the area, at times extending from the Persian Gulf to Egypt. Ashurbanipal was the last ruler of Assyria.

THE ELAMITES

Although several observations point clearly to the existence of people with culture and tools in Iran prior to Elamites, a solidly documented significant civilization in Iran, probably started with Elamites. This civilization under a central and federated government with waxing and waning authority, started in the late 4ᵗʰ and early 3ʳᵈ millennium B.C. in Khuzestan and surrounding areas, collectively called Elam, located in the southwest region of Iran. The leadership of dynasty was located in Susa (modern Shush at the site of ancient Susa), the capital, at the slope of Zagros, and it was usually determined by inheritance arrangements. In addition to engaging in then current activities in Iran, the Elamite dynasties had intermittent peaceful treaties, and confrontational relationships with their neighbors, including Sumer, Babylonia, Assyria, and different regions of Mesopotamia. Over a long period the Elamites were culturally influenced by these nations, invaded by them and lost independence to them and faded to obscurity; or, invaded them and became a dominant dynasty with military power, political expansion, and glory. Although the level of cultural achievements, the precise nature of the language (s) and script (s), and the types of religions, if any, of Elamites have not been clearly identified, it is reasonable to believe that all of these trends had been variable and changing because of the impact of the surrounding nations. Different scripts, derived from or related to other languages such as Akkadian cuneiform or otherwise have been considered by the linguists to represent the spoken Elamite language during different period of the Elamite dynasty in Iran, it has not been proved, however, that these scripts are conveying the spoken languages of Elamites or others. The language might be related to Dravidian language (one of the world's major language families, spoken also in southern India and certain parts of Pakistan) or may be an isolate with no relation to other languages, it probably was one of the official languages of the Achaemenid dynasty and became extinct by the end of 4ᵗʰ century.

In 640 B.C., Susa was invaded by the Assyrian king, Ashurbanipal, ending the independence of the dynasty, later on to become a subordinate province of the Achaemenid Empire.

SCYTHIANS or Scyths also called Sakas were nomadic migrants of 8ᵗʰ and 7ᵗʰ centuries B.C., originating from Central Asia, related to ancient Iranians, settled in the area, now Crimea located at the southern Russian region. Crimea is a peninsula in the region between Black Sea and the Sea of Azov. Sakas were part of Scythians, which in addition to Sakas included other similar tribes.

Rich, powerful, and civilized Scythian Empire lasted for several centuries. The Scythians were brave worriers famed for their horsemanship. They fought with bow and arrows and Persian sword and they were paid in today's language a commission fee for presentation of the heads of their enemies.

CHAPTER 4

The Kingdom of Medes

The years of about 750-550 B.C. of the Iron age III correspond to the Median period. Documented in the cuneiform script, the Medes one of the two major Indo-European Iranians (the other major group being the Persian), had moved along the southern border of the Alborz Mountains to the eastern Zagros Mountains and the region of the ancient city of Ecbatana (Greek) or Aghbatana (Iranian), and were moving toward western Zagros. Ecbatana, Median capital, founded, according to Herodotus, by the first king of Media (Deioces, ruled 728-675 B.C.) or, according to modern scholars, by his son Phraortes (ruled 675-653 B.C.). The Median tribes of the region rather than acquiring the title by force or inheritance probably elected the first king. Ecbatana lies at the site of modern city of Hamadan (the site of Avicenna's Monument). Later on the Persian followed the Medes path, but eventually moved to southwest of Zagros, the area of Elam and modern Fars.

During their westward travel the Iranian of that time, Medes and Persian, not only encountered resistance from endogenous local settlers, but also confronted by the foreign competitive forces such as Assyrians and preexistent Elamites in a competition over the land.

The Median kings had to fight against a major power, the Assyrians to conquer and keep their share of the land. Assyria an ancient empire at the time extended from the Persian Gulf to Egypt.

The Medes had also to deal with large numbers of Scythians in western Iran at the time. The Scythians were a part of nomadic warriors migrated from central Asia to southern Russia in 8th-7th centuries B.C. and formed a strong empire at the Black Sea area, now a part of Russia. The Scythians along with the Medes were the source of serious threat to the Assyrians. Both confrontational and cooperative relations between the Medes and Scythians have been described. Phraortes or Fravartish, king of Media, died, reportedly during a battle with the Assyrians. After his death, Scythians for many years ruled Media (653-625), until the Medes killed their leaders. Then under Cyaxares (ruled 625-585 B.C.) the son of Phraortes, the Scythians visibility decreased, they probably left the western Iran or more likely assimilated with the Medes forming a united confederation ruled by Cyaxares. With a strong and organized army Cyaxares faced the Assyrians and captured Nineveh, the large and populated city of the Assyrian Empire. Then with the assistance of his temporary ally, the Babylonians, he expelled the Assyrians to Syria, ending the Assyrian dynasty. At the time Cyaxares was controlling the western Iran in totality, extending in all direction to Tehran, Fars, and Anatolia. Because of this wide authority the Babylonians were apprehensive; but the apprehension did not linger, because very soon Astyages (ruled 585-550) the successor of his father Cyaxares and the last Median ruler, faced Cyrus II, or Cyrus the Great.

CHAPTER 5

The Achaemenid Empire or Hakhamanishian (550-330 B.C.)

The large group of Iranians traveling to the province of Fars (Pars) eventually formed the Achaemenid Empire, a tolerant and just empire. The name probably is derived from Haxamanish (Hakhamanish) or Achaemenes.

The lineage of Cyrus II or Cyrus the Great (Iranian Kurosh-e Kabir, 559-529 B.C.), the fourth ruler of Achaemenid, was traced to Hakhamanish through Cambyses I, the son of Cyrus I, fathered by Teispes (Chispish), who was the son of Hakhamanish.

Teispes and Cyrus I, both ruled Anshan (Anzan), a region of Elam. Herodotus, 5th century Greek historian, believed that Cambyses I married the daughter of Astyages, the last king of Media (ruled 585-550), and Cyrus the Great was their son. Cyrus II, after taking his father's position openly rebelled and fought against the Medes, defeating them in 550 B.C., changing the Median Empire to Persian Empire. Pasargadae (Pasargad) was his capital and is his eternal resting place. It is about 27 miles from Persepolis, in Fars province.

Cyrus the Great innovated new strategies to spread the Achaemenid Empire; he united different Iranian forces within Iran, including Medes, Persians and other Iranians; he approached his competitors and enemies one at a time, rather than engaging them in different fronts simultaneously; he identified and assimilated with conquered nations, was benevolent and merciful toward them, treating them as a partner rather than subjugated enemies. The besiege of Babylon, the greatest city in the Middle East at the time, illustrates Cyrus' skills in the long range planning.

In dealing with Nabonidus, the unpopular king of Babylon, he initially approached him diplomatically, and then after taking care of a more urgent issue, defeating the Lydian army, he confronted Nabonidus militarily and conquered Babylon, in 539 B.C.

Babylonians mistreated by their king, identified with Cyrus and accepted him as a liberator rather than a conqueror and one of their own. He was tolerant and supportive of all existent local religions. Cyrus freed the exiled Jews from captivity, and returned them to Palestine. The Jews were originally deported to Babylon in 586 B.C. from Jerusalem by the Babylonian king Nebuchadrezzar.

Cyrus was killed in 529 B.C., fighting the other conquerors in the far northeast region of Iran.

His vast, the first, the just, and his greatest empire in the world at the time, extended from the Aegean Sea to the Indus River.

Cambyses II (Kambujia II, 529-522) replaced his father Cyrus the Great, but the story, whether true or somewhat mixed with myth, reveals that Cambyses did not follow his father's tenets and during his reign, the Achaemenid Empire of his father lost some of the glorious reputation. Cambyses had his popular brother, Bardiya, killed before engaging in a battle with Pharaoh; although he defeated Egypt, his following related fights had been reported to be rather failures.

While attempting to control a revolt initiated by an imposter claiming that he was the Cambyses' slain brother, Cambyses died of an accident related wound infection or, as some have surmised, he committed suicide because of emotional instability and depression.

Darius I or Dariush I, Darius the Great (522-486), probably did not trust the historians, inscribed his own history in three languages interpreted to be Babylonian, Old Persian, and Elamite. The inscription is on the rock at the root of the Zagros Mountains in the village of Bisitun or Bisotun, near Kermanshah.

He described his methods of killing the imposter claiming to be Cambyses' brother, Bardiya, and his own ascendancy to the kingship. The imposter and usurper served, if any, only for a few months. Darius' great grandfather was Ariaramnes, the son of Teispes and the brother of Cyrus I.

Darius I had the personality and characters of Cyrus the Great and followed his ruling styles. Darius began his construction of Persepolis, improved the existent roads, built new ones, and introduced gold and silver coins for the first time in Iran.

Persepolis (city of persis or Parsa derived from the ancient Iranian tribe of Parsua), the modern Iranian name is Takht-e Jamshid, about 30 miles northeast to Shiraz. It was the ceremonial capital of Achaemenids (used mainly during spring) and was founded during Achaemenid Empire. The first stone of Persepolis was laid by Darius the Great between 514 and 512 B.C. Before Persepolis the royal family were resting in the cities of Pasargadae (the burial place of Cyrus the Great), Takht-e Suleiman or Soleyman, Susa (for administrative use and during winter), and Ecbatana (Hamadan, the summer capital). In 330 B.C. Alexander devastated Pesepolis and burned and destroyed the palace of the great kings. By the end of the Seleucid dynasty the city had declined to ruins. The Sasanid dynasty selected the nearby city of Istakhr as the center for their empire.

After securing peace within the Empire, Darius attempted to expand or maintain the Iranian territories stretched from east, Indus River of northern India, toward west to the Aegean Sea, in Greece.

Extension to the west involved a series of fights initiated with the Greeks of Ionia, the ancient region west of Asia Minor, then gradually extended to larger areas. These wars were marked with victories and defeats for both sides.

Darius' defeat in the battle of Marathon, fought in the Marathon plain in northeastern Attica, an ancient district of east central Greece, signaled the beginning of more serious conflict between the Achaemenid dynasty and the Greek city-state, the Greco-Persians wars.

In Marathon conflict the Greeks were victorious against the much larger Persian army. According to Greek historian Herodotus, the Persian lost 6,400 men vs. 192 Greek men. It should be noticed that Herodotus reports on the Marathon War and on several other historical events have been considered to be not verifiable and perhaps biased.

During the reigns of Cyrus and Darius, the Greats, the Persian Empire achieved the greatest empire and superpower status in history until then, ruling over a major part of the world.

Xerxes I (Greek), Khashayar (Iranian), Xerxes the Great the son of Darius I, Xerxes (486-465) was Babylon's governor prior to taking his father's place as a king. He controlled the Egyptian and Babylonian revolts, but in contrast to his father, he treated the rebels harshly and violenty. Xerxes I then pursued the task of his father, fighting the Greeks. He fought them in different fronts and in different times, including three battles of Thermopylae, Salamis, and Plataea, killing and destroying, including the burning of Athens.

Initially winning but mostly defeated by the Greek army, he did not realize the lack of organization and discipline in the Persian army, or was not able to correct them. The defeated Xerxes after returning to Iran abandoned the concept of extension of his territories and focused on personal pleasure and activities or dissolution; he was assassinated in 465 B.C., by Artabanus, in Persepolis.

Three relatively weak and ineffective kings followed Xerxes:

Artaxerxes I (465-425 B.C.) or Ardashir I or Ardeshir (Iranian) was the son of Xerxes I. Artabanus, the commander of the Guard or a vizier, after murdering Xerxes I, assisted Artaxerxes I to become the king, who in turn killed Artabanus. Artaxerses I controlled the revolt in Egypt, albeit with difficulty, signed a treaty with Athens in 448 B.C. ending the fight between Athens and Achaemenids. He was tolerant toward the practice of Judaism in Jerusalem.

His tomb is in Naqsh-e Rustam also spelled Naghsh-e Rostam, located about 7 miles northeast of Persepolis.

Xerxes II (425-424 B.C.) he was son of Artaxerxes I and was killed, 45 days after ruling, by his half-brother Sogdianus.

Darius II Ochus son of Artaxerxes I (423-404 B.C.) seized the kingdom from Sogdianus, his half-brother, then killed him and adapted the name of Darius. Upon ascension to the throne, he faced revolts in Asia Minor and Egypt. Formed an alliance with Sparta against Athens, recaptured Ionia, appointed his son Cyrus as the commander in chief of Asia Minor to support Sparta, rebuilt the Spartan fleet, and gave power to Sparta, weakening Athens.

During Spartan and Athens wars, lasting intermittently from 460-404 B.C., the Iranians objectives were not well focused and determined. based mainly on the expediency of the moment rather than a long-range strategy, reflecting the weakness of the central government of Achaemenid.

Artaxerxes II (404-359 B.C.) succeeded his father Darius II, during his tenure the Egyptian revolt erupted again and Achaemenids lost Egypt, which became independent. However he was able to control the revolt of his younger brother, who was supported by the Greek mercenaries and eventually was killed during a fight. The newly established small Spartan power not only continued to be in conflict with Athens, but also waged war against the Iranians over Asia Minor. In 386 Artaxerxes and the Greeks agreed on his proposed King's Peace agreement. The agreement was about the concessions favorable to Achaemenids, including the supremacy of Iran over Asia Minor. Eventually with the help of Iran, Sparta weakened, Athens was revitalized, and Asia Minor continued to belong to Iran.

On the religious matters, he digressed. In pre-Achaemenid time the Iranians were polytheists, like other Indo-European groups. During Achaemenid period, Zoroastrianism or modified forms of it was practiced, at least in the royal court, until the reign of Artaxerxes II, when he restored the worshiping of the statues of old Persian deities.

Artaxerxes III (359-338 B.C.) son of Artaxerxes II, an energetic king, probably used his energy to slay people; Greek sources note that Artaxerxes III assassinated most of his relatives, including eight of his half brothers to secure his kingdom. His first attempt to conquer the lost Egypt failed, but it caused rebellion in Sidon of Phoenicia in the regions of modern Syria, Lebanon, and Israel. On the second attempt in 343, he defeated Pharaoh of Egypt and appointed an Iranian satrap to govern Egypt.

Back in Susa Artaxerxes was poisoned by his minister, a eunuch and the real ruler of his court named Bagoas. He was succeeded by his son Arses.

Arses (Xerxes III, 338-336 B.C.) son of Artaxerxes III, became a king with the help of a court eunuch Bagoas, and was murdered by him.

Darius III (336-330 B.C.) was great grandson of Darius II. Bagoas, the eunuch who liked to murder, made him a king. Persepolis, the great capital of the great Achaemenid dynasty was captured by a Macedonian named Alexander. Darius III, the last Achaemenid king while attempting to flee, leaving his family, wife, and his mother behind was murdered by the Bactrian satrap. His offer to ransom his family and cede major part of the Achaemenid Empire for alliance with Alexander failed; but at least he forced Bagoas to poison himself by using the poison he had prepared to poison the king.

During the reign of these kings the Achaemenid dynasty had no major achievement.

The survival of the dynasty so long after Xerxes death until Darius III probably is related to the solid foundation laid by two great kings, Cyrus and Darius.

In addition to the continuation of hostile confrontations with the Greeks, the kings during this period of the dynasty had to deal with uprisings and rebellions in Egypt and other provincial governments. The fighting against these revolts was mostly non-decisive and repetitive skirmishes.

As the end of the dynasty was approaching, the internal conflicts in the royal houses were getting progressively destructive. Suspicions, murders, intrigues, manipulations by the eunuchs were infesting the royal courts. These internal mal-adaptive forces combined with weak and uncoordinated external policies were leading to the demise of the great dynasty.

Chapter 6

Alexander III, or the Great (356-323 BC)

He was born at Pella, Macedonia, king of Macedonia (336-323). In 336 his father was assassinated and Alexander succeeded him. Then he marched south to Greece. He was successful in the unification of Macedonia and the Greek states, promising them a democratic government and his support. He controlled all Greece by 335. Now he was prepared and wanted to start and spread the Hellenistic crusade and culture to the nations to be conquered. He incessantly and restlessly began to conquer. He moved toward East to attack Persia in 334 at the age of 22 for pursuit of glory. After crossing Asia Minor he won against the Persians at the battle of Issus, defeated Darius in 333, then advanced to Syria, Jerusalem, to Egypt, where he founded Alexandria, and by 331 he reached Susa, the capital of Elamites, finally Persepolis, the majestic capital of Iran, burned it to the ground. His soldiers violated women and killed the men. He then moved to the eastern border of Iran and eventually to India in 327. On his long journey from Greece to India some of the cities welcomed him out of fear of his revenge, and some of them showed resistance and faced his anger. Then they were tortured and killed. He included, old, young, women and children in massacre to revenge for their wrongdoings in the past, for their resistance, or perhaps for deterrence of their future resistance. The great king now was becoming a barbarian king. While in India his soldiers refused to follow him further, therefore he returned back, on his way back to Susa, he lost more than ten thousands of soldiers from starvation and thirst. By the time he had arrived at Susa the Barbarian king had turned to an insane one.

Alexander, as a teenager was studying with Aristotle, his father didn't want him to become a warrior, like himself; but Alexander's ambition to excel in warfare prevailed and he turned away from philosophy and abandoned the nurturing of his mind and intellectual life for building his body, and gaining strength for an adventurous existence. His attraction to physical activities, sports, archery, and fighting seemed to be uncontrollable. His preoccupation with his physical appearance and his desire to be admired were at a narcissistic level. His sexual orientation was not clearly established, despite taken several wives. Passion, ecstasy, volatile temper, and his aggressive behavior eclipsed whatever intellectual domain he possessed. His tendency for generosity, kindness, forgiveness, empathy, or expression of remorse did not prevent him from torturing, mutilating, and savaging his enemy warriors, particularly during bouts of inebriation, which was progressively increasing in duration and frequency.

While back in Babylon, after a heavy dose of wine and after several days of a feverish state, he died at the age of 33 at his zenith, ten years after leaving Macedonia. He died as Alexander the Great or perhaps as the semi-insane barbarian the Great or even the genius.

After living for several years in Asia, Alexander began to identify with the Great Kings of Iran and their style of rulings. He recognized the necessity of the Iranian participation in the development of a united culture, ruled not only by Macedonians-Greeks, but Macedonians-Greeks-Iranians, under leadership of one emperor acceptable to all.

He devised plans to achieve the homogeneity of the people within his realm. He married Iranian women himself, strongly encouraged his generals and soldiers to marry Iranians and provided financial incentives for mixed marriages. Established Greek colonies in Iran, adopted Iranian dress code himself. He even elevated himself to the level of deity; he became the supreme deity of Greece, the Zeus. Was this self-promotion an act for unification of his territories or a sign of delusion that he was no longer human and was identifying with Gods? Probably both.

CHAPTER 7

Seleucid Kingdom (312-64)

Alexander had no designated successor, and he left his vast empire to the strongest after him. After his death the empire became divided and the power struggle among the generals to control the divided empire erupted. One of the strongest generals named Seleucus, sympathetic to Alexander's ideas, with the collaboration of the Ptolemy I, first king of Ptolemaic dynasty of Egypt, seized Babylon in 312 and became its king, founded and consolidated the Seleucid kingdom and extended it from Syria to the Indus River, including Bactria and Babylon, ruling from 306-281 B.C. He was assassinated in 281, by the son of Ptolemy I and succeeded by his son Antiochus I and other Seleucid kings. The Seleucids promoted the Hellenistic culture, and implemented the Alexander strategies to unify the culturally diverse societies. The enthusiastic and cult-like promotion of Greek culture, at times, was leading to resistance and the alienation of heterogeneous groups of people. Gradually but steadily the influence of the Seleucids and effectiveness of their Hellenization attempt, particularly in the eastern territories decreased and the invasiveness of the nomads increased leading to the eventual uprising of the larger provinces or satrapies, such as Parthian, southeast of the Caspian Sea and Bactria, now northwest of Afghanistan. A serious decline and loss of control in the kingdom resulted in independence of many territories and the Roman conquest of rapidly disintegrating kingdom in 64 B.C.

CHAPTER 8

Parthian Empire, second Iranian dynasty

After the death of Alexander the Great, a horseman and warrior Iranian tribe of the Indo-European and Central Asia origin, called Parni, originating from southeast of the Caspian Sea moved south and invaded Parthia, a province roughly corresponding to the western region of present Khorasan in the northeastern region of Iran. The members of the Parni tribe adopted the name, the culture, and the language of people of Parthia, who had recently gained independence from Seleucids. The leader or head of the Parni tribe was named Arsaces I, founded a dynasty after his name, to be called Arsacid dynasty or Ashkanian. Arsaces I ruled probably from 247-211 B.C., part of this period he was a king. After gaining momentum the dynasty became the Arsacid Empire or Parthian Empire, overlapping with the Seleucid dynasty.

Arsaces considered the Arsacid dynasty as a successor for Seleucids in the Parthia region, and tried to achieve peace with Seleucids. The successors of Arsaces attempted to consolidate their dynasty and maintain their independence, and at times went on to expand their territories with variable success. With the ascension of Mithridates I, the Parthian military, political, and economic expansion and acquisition of new territories accelerated resulting in an open conflict with Hellenistic Seleucid kings. Mithridates I, who has been compared to Cyrus the Great, a virtuous and brave man, described in his coin the Great King, died in 137 B.C. During Mithridates II Parthians reached their summit, their world power extended to Armenia and eastern Asia Minor. Armenia became part of the Iranian sphere of influence. The Seleucids were confined only to Syria. Mithridates II established a direct communication and diplomatic relationship with then two great powers, the Rome and the Chinese Empire. As a vital economic and political link between east and west he concluded a treaty with the Emperor of China to encourage the international commerce and trade. He titled himself, the king of the kings, and the Parthian Empire became comparable to Achaemenid Empire; he played the role of Darius of the Achaemenid Empire within the Parthian Empire, he consolidated whatever had been acquired by Mithridates I.

CHAPTER 9

Wars with the Romans

Conflict with Romans dates back to the year of 66 B.C., during the ruling of Phraates III, the fourth Parthian king after Mithridates II. In this year Pompey, a Roman general and a member of the First Triumvirate (60 to 54 B.C.), with the other two members being Crassus and Caesar, reached a peace agreement with his contemporary Parthian king. However, shortly after the agreement, Pompey moved his army to the territory, which was under protection of Parthians.

In 53 B.C., again the army of Crassus, another Triumvir and the governor of Syria at the time, underestimating the power of Parthians attacked the Parthian Empire under Orodes rule (son of Phraates III). His army was defeated and smashed and Crassus along with his son was killed and the Roman army of 40,000 was destroyed. The attack of Crassus probably was motivated by his desire to receive military recognition in competition with his fellow Triumvirs, Pompey and Caesar and on expectation of a rich booty. After the Parthians victory and Crassus death and because of exigencies of Roman leadership a civil war ensued between Caesar and Pompey, lasting from 49-45 B.C., and resulted eventually in Pompey death in Egypt in 48 B.C. The civil war contributed to the destabilization of the Roman position in relation to Parthian Empire and further advanced the Parthian power.

After Pompey's death Julius Caesar became an absolute ruler of the Roman world and dictator from 46-44 B.C.

Caesar was assassinated in 44 B.C. prior to being able to compensate for and revenge Crassus' death, which he was contemplating.

In 36 B.C., one year after Phraates IV assassinated his father and took over, Mark Anthony, a general under Julius Caesar and a member of the Second Roman Triumvirate (43-30 B.C.), attempted to invade Parthia, from his position in Armenia, to materialize the wishes of Caesar, but he failed and lost 35,000 men.

Now Anthony defeated, and Parthia and its ruler Phraates getting more power, Octavian was ready to solidify his position and among other things to do, to face Phraates. He achieved a peaceful and respectful, but still a competitive relation with Phraates in about two decades B.C.

While the Parthians and Romans were in their peaceful co-existence, the savage and primitive power struggle and patricide within the Parthian ruling family continued.

The son of Phraates IV, Phraates V, replaced his father after killing him with the help of his mother an Italian slave girl, then marrying his own mother. After Phraates V, Orodes III, and Vonones the sons of Orodes II and Phraates IV, respectively, each reigned for 2-3 years.

After Vonones, Artabanus III, an Arsacid on his mother side and anti-Roman became a king with support of the Parthian nobility. He tried to unite and centralize the states and provinces of the Parthian kingdom by appointing his relatives to rule the states. However the central government authority did not last long, it began to weaken gradually and the kingdom divided to many smaller kingdoms. After Vonoses II (51), Vologases I (51-78 A.D.) revived the nationalistic feeling of Artabanus III; he compiled the Iranian holy book of Avesta, and issued coins with Pahlavi characters.

Pacorus II replaced Vologases I in 78, to be replaced by Artabanus IV from 80-81. During his ruling the Parthian kingdom continued to disintegrate, the nobility seeking inheritance privileges and independence, ignored the central government and the Roman constantly tried to agitate the internal conflicts within the whatever left from the Parthian kingdom.

In 110 A.D. Osroes replaced Pacorus II. During his ruling, in 114 Roman emperor Tarjan (Marcus Ulpius Traianus, reign 98-117) reversed Augustus strategy and invaded Armenia, conquered Babylon, Ctesiphon (Tisphoon in Farsi), the Parthian imperial capital, and other regions of Parthia with the goal of reducing Parthians to a vassalage state. His objective was not materialized and eventually he was defeated by the Parthians in collaboration with revolting provinces, with various ethnicities, against the Romans. Tarjan's successor Hadrian (Publius Hadrianus (117-138) returned the conquered area and initiated a peace agreement with the Parthians.

Osroes was succeeded by Vologases II (148-82), III, IV, V, ruling the region of kingdom corresponding to present day Iraq, and Artabanus V (213-224) ruling mainly southwestern Iran. During the reign of these kings, various invasions and counter-invasions, harsh and brutal attacks and counter-attacks between Parthians and Romans took place with variable outcomes, but without permanency. At the end the Romans failed their goal of reducing the Parthians to servitude.

The Parthians were tolerant of all religious practices, particularly of Judaism, and in general they worshiped three deities of varying degree by the various peoples, Ahura Mazda of Zoraostrianism, Anahita, ancient Iranian deity (Goddess) of mainly water-fertility, and Mithra, the ancient Iranian God of light, truth, and sun following the Achaemenid trend.

The Parthians started as a nomad tribe, over a period of centuries, striving to defend the sovereignty of Iran and the safety of its protectorates, reached the status of the great empire, representing the east faced another superpower, the Roman empire representing the west. The triumph of Parthia revived the national consciousness of Iranian comparable to the Achaemenid era, paving the way for upcoming of another empire, the Sasanid.

Chapter 10

Why Intermittent Glories And Failures In The Iranian Royal Dynasties?

First one might conjecture that these intermittent declines from a glorious and solid state of the Iranian empires into the bursts of disarray and deterioration of organization may be due to the combination of ineptness of the rulers, who inherited but did not earn the crown and the invasive external forces eager to plunder the lands of Iran. One also may surmise that the long duration of the Iranian dynasties may influence these waxing and waning observations. The time interval from the time Cyrus the Great started his empire until Darius III, the last Achaemenid king was murdered was 220 years. It elapsed 554 years from the time of Darius III before Shapoor I started his great Sasanid empire.

Historical observations indicate that maintenance of a plateau at a high level of achievement for a long period of time is extremely difficult if not impossible. At these levels further growth in power, property, or dynasty and empire cease and various uncontrollable events may have destabilizing effects and lead to the initiation of decline.

Climatic and evolutionary changes, technical, industrial, and agricultural growth, all will affect the economy, political state, peaceful or confrontational international relationship and eventually the goal and direction of the governing body for a better or worse.

It is more difficult, however, to explain the great discrepancy between the vacillating moral values from one period to another. How could one reconcile between Darius the Great's prayer inscribed in gold and silver plates discovered in the Persepolis palace asking God to protect the country from enemies, famine and falsehood, with the barbaric behavior by the future Iranian rulers of patricide, blinding, and castration of the present or the future challengers? These acts may be due to random deep-seated psychological disorders of one ruler or a personal vendetta; but they are not isolated events and they recur repeatedly in different periods of Iranian history. Savagery and cruelties were demonstrated and used by the rulers for the protection of power by any cost and were focused on potential real challengers rather than imaginary ones. This preemptive elimination of the opponents is not limited in time or space, they seem to appear universally and all the time, manifesting in different forms and disguise. These behavioral patterns were not considered to be against the law, because they were committed by the makers, judges, and the juries of the laws, by the rulers, and the killing by them was the law of the land. These rulers were acting within the dictates and reinforcement of culture-faith-belief of their communities. The identification with and adaptation of prevailing culture was a virtue irrespective of the consequences. Counter-culture behavior would have been perceived as an anomaly, indicating disloyalty to the community and a cause for rejection by the majority.

As adaptive attitude continued, cruelty such as patricide was no longer to indicate a lack of an elementary sense of decency, but interpreted as a sign of strength of the ruler, who began to act as the leader of a gang, not the ruler of a dynasty, ready to be murdered by the leader of another gang.

In 224 A.D. Ardashir the son of Babak from Persis (present day Fars) extended his father's possession of a city near Persepolis, conquered one city, annexed another one, united more, then challenged Artabanus V, who was killed in a battle and the leadership in Iran was transferred from Parthians to Sasanids. Despite the internal conflicts and external hostilities, despite of patricide and fratricide or because of them the Parthians extended their kingdom from India to the Roman Empire, attempting to upgrade the country to the level of Achaemenid era.

Chapter 11

Sasanid (sasanian in Farsi) Dynasty

Sasanid dynasty was named after Sasan also spelled Sassan, who probably was a prince or a noble man, probably from Istarkhr or Estakhr, located in the Persis province. Ardashir I, the founder of Sasanid dynasty, was the son of Babak, a local king, who probably was the son of Sasan. Ardashir succeeded his father as a king of Persis in 208. Gradually he began to conquer the nearby localities and later on provinces and to expand his territories, eventually defeating the Parthian army and slaying Artabamus V (224), the Parthian king. He conquered the Parthian capital, Ctesiphon and founded the Sasanid dynasty and acclaimed himself, the king of kings. (224-241). Ardashir I selected Zoroastrianism as the official state religion and attempted to unify it. He engaged in a series of battles and successfully fought his enemies at home before confronting Rome and starting war. Meanwhile he shared with and delegated his ruling authority to his son Shapur I, a few years before his death. Shapur I (241-272) replaced his father Ardashir I, and continued his father's trend. Shapur while expanding his empire soon faced confrontation with Roman Empire claiming victory over the territories in the eastern Roman provinces in the regions of present day Syria, Turkey, and Armenia. He used his knowledgeable and skillful prisoners for architectural and building purposes. Valerian, the emperor of Rome was one of his prisoners. He built Gondeshapur, a center of learning. In the religious front he supported Manichaeanism. The small and independent local Parthian dynasties were eliminated and large provincial leaderships were bestowed upon the kings, usually selected from the members of the royal family by the king of kings.

Conflict with the Roman Empire and Byzantine Empire (330-1453, eastern part of Roman empire, taken by Ottoman Turkish 1n 1453) over various territories including Mesopotamia and Armenia during Sasanid dynasty continued with intermittent victory and defeat for both sides. There were 29 rulers in the Sasanid dynasty ruling for 427 years, with varying duration in reign, from less than one year to decades, and with variable efficacy and popularity during peace and war, with long lasting legacy or no legacy at all.

For instance Shapur II reigned for a longtime from 309 to 379 (born king). During his tenure he smashed the Kushan Empire, which had invaded the Sasanian territories, in the eastern front. He began to expand the Sasanid political as well as cultural identities to east, spreading toward China. In the west he was involved in a protracted war with Romans, conquering and defeating in the both sides. Julian, the Roman emperor (361-363) was killed in a battle against Shapur II of Sasanid.

Bahram V, (421-438), the fourteenth king of Sasanids the son of Yazdegerd I (399-420), also called Bahram Goor (or Gur, meaning onager) famous as an adventurer in hunting, but also a poet and musician was a popular, legendary figure, favorite subject of the Iranian literature, favorite enough to be cited by poets such as the great Omar Khayyam. Bahram V reached an agreement with Rome, securing the freedom of worship for the Iranian Christians and protecting them against prejudice and mistreatment.

Khosrow (or Khosrau, 531-579), was named Anushirvan -e Adel (Immortal Just Soul), the twentieth king, reached peace with Justinian, the Byzantine emperor, was the most famous king of the dynasty and an orthodox Zoroastrian.

He enjoyed the unanimous support of the people, therefore he was able to focus in the development and restoration of villages, roads, and bridges; reforming organizational, legislative and administrative aspects of the government; introduction of more equity in the taxation system; reorganization and updating of military and defense system to match the foreign wars; and controlling the intruding nomads. In the war front he invaded Syria and Antioch, and extended the eastern front to Oxus. The just, benevolent king, the defender of people, the promoter of the Iranian civilization, power, art, and science died 50 years after effective ruling.

According to tradition Khosrow I, nicknamed Adel or Just had a dark streak in his character, he murdered his brothers during his struggle for the throne of his father. It is possible that his justice and benevolence was not rooted in a high moral value, but it was a part of strategy to prevent dissatisfaction of his people and secure his sovereign status. The ruthless behavior such as dismembering, murdering, blinding the members of their family of the rulers and kings, otherwise benevolent and healthy, might have been a part of the Iranian culture acceptable to kings and their subjects. In those days like in these days in our culture killing the enemies during war, not only were acceptable, it was a duty and even an honor. It is not difficult to understand how the rulers of those days, not dissimilar to the rulers of our days, by stretching a little bit their imaginative power, they extrapolated the justification of killing the enemies during war to justification the killing of enemies or potential enemies before the war, sort of preemptive killing of potential enemies such as the members of the royal family, hopeful to become the king of kings, or just a king.

As time went on, the political and geographical control took a religious tone. By the late 3rd century the Roman empire had become Christian and was extending to Armenia, and the rulers of Sasanid were promoting and consolidating Zoroastrianism, all leading to religious tension between two great powers. The rulers demonstrated a variable degree of interest in Zoroastrianism, at times were advocates of Zoroastrian orthodoxy, at other times gravitating away from Zoroastrian religion toward Mazda. The tolerance toward Christianity or any religion other than Zoroastrianism also varied among the rulers or even by one ruler within his tenure. The degree of tolerance became an important factor in gaining support and loyalty of the people necessary to stabilize the throne. After Roman Empire religion officially changed from Paganism to Christianity, during the ruling of emperor Constantine the Great (306-337), the political and social tolerance toward the Christian communities living in Iran gradually decreased and Shapur II and his successors engaged in persecution of the Christians.

Khosrow II called also Parviz (591-628), the grandson of the famous Khosrow I was the last great king of Sasanids. During his reign, the Sasanid army regained its previously lost territories and in addition occupied Egypt and moved to the border of Ethiopia. He reached Chalcedon opposite Constantinople, extending the frontiers of Iran to those of Achaemenid era. Khosrow II was assassinated during a battle against the Roman.

The last king of Sasanids was Yazdegerd III, the grandson of Khosrow II.

Now weakened and asthenic because of prolonged wars, the Sasanids were facing the aggression of an emerging power, the Arabs. In a military confrontation with Arabs, Rostam (or Rustam) the commander of the Iranian army was killed, and the Iranian defeat in the Battle of Nehavand (642) during the rule of Caliph Umar (634-644), near Hamadan, signaled the collapsing of the dynasty. The king Yazdegerd escaping from one territory to another eventually was assassinated in 651 A.D., in the vicinity of Merv, ending the life of the Sasanid dynasty.

Despite of significant variations in the goals and objectives and styles of the rulers of the Sasanian dynasty, in general the Sasanids collectively reformed and advanced permanently the social structure of Iran. The kings functioned with supreme authority as the head of state, delegating the administrative, political, diplomatic, military, financial, and judicial functions to deputies knowledgeable and competent in their field of assignment or the members of nobility. The nobility, landowners and the religious leaders were a major part of the leadership, at the time. They and the great landowners were influential in the direction of Iranian society, because they owned lands and they inherited power, and elected the kings. The governors or rulers of provinces or satrapies, usually selected from the royal family, were replacing the local or petty kings and were accountable to the central authorities and of course to the king of kings, who also, at times, used to act as an advocate on behalf of his people, ruled by these leaders. The people included, all other citizen, merchants, artisans, workers, and of course the peasants.

Two branches of the government, both army branches, received much more attention during Sasanids and underwent detailed organizational changes.

The military army with large cavalry, infantry, and elephants and taxation army with an abundant number of tax collectors. The systematic reforms in both military army and taxation army were necessary to enable the former to fight and the latter to support the fight.

The Sasanid rulers preoccupations with the extension of the empire, dealing with Romans and Byzantines and religion, did not prevent them from advancing and promoting the various forms of art, such as painted decoration of palaces, frescoes, mosaic, and decorated ewer, plates, vases, and cups. The kings in action such as hunting usually were the subjects of decoration.

Limestone rock sculpture, distinctive of Sasanid period is abundant in the province of Fars in Iran. Some of these carved stones depict the kings performing different tasks, killing the lions, triumphing over the Roman emperors. Architectural remnants and constructions such as the royal palaces and fire temples characteristic of Sasanid period are also found in Fars, near shiraz, all indicating the interest of Sasanids in building and urban development. Decorative hunting scenes of Sasanid kings, coins with Pahlavi language inscription and depicting the face of the kings and fire temples, all attest to the high grade of craftsmanship of Sasanids.

The Sasanids did not stand still in the fields of economy, commerce, and trade.

Silk trade with China, silk industry within Iran, textile and clothing trades were promoted; Sasanid silver and copper coins were widely circulated; banking and monetary exchange systems developed highly.

CHAPTER 12

Zoroastrianism

Zoroaster or Zarathushtra or Zarathustra (about 628-551 B.C.), the legendry creator of the monotheistic religion of Zoroastrianism of Iran was born in Rhages, an agricultural village at the time (present day Ray a suburb of Tehran, Iran).

Avesta is the sacred book of Zoroastrianism. The book contains the teaching of prophet Zoroaster. The five-volume Avesta was put together and compiled in 4th or in 6th century from the remnants of old voluminous scripture, and according to some scholars, after variable input from the Magi. The original scripture probably was burned by Alexander the Great.

Ahura Mazda, the wise lord, the supreme god, the creator of world and spirit, and law giver and judge directed Zoroaster, the prophet to offer moral and religious advice to polytheistic people, and propagate the truth, as revealed to him by the supreme deity.

Ahriman, the evil sprit and his followers contradict the moral value of Ahura Mazda such as justice and truth and teach the evil principles such as lies. Man has freedom of choice and he is responsible for his thoughts, speech and actions, and he will be judged and rewarded or punished by Ahura Mazda. The followers of the right path and truth will receive everlasting blessing and the followers of Ahriman will be condemned, facing everlasting darkness.

Magi is pleural of Magus, a member of ancient Iranian religious group, a priest serving the Zoroastrianism or perhaps several other religions and having in-depth knowledge of the religious issues.

During Sasanid dynasty Zoroastrianism underwent ideological and structural changes. The state collaborated with and supported the religious organizations. The religious domain was divided into districts with their own religious leaders, comparable to priests called then mobads, in turn supervised by a head priest. The religious organizations not only acquired a decisive input in the selection of successors for the kingdom, but also engaged in the legal and judicial affairs of the state.

Pre-Zoroastrian ceremonies of fire rituals continued in Zoroaster time and practiced more systematically by Sasanids. The worship of Ahura Mazda or Ormizd constituted the essential part of the religion with holy fire representing his manifestation on earth. The rules of fire temples guarded the purity and sacredness of the fire.

Mani probably from Babylon and influenced by its culture, is the originator of Manichaeism, claiming to be a prophet of God and influenced by Christ teaching emerged and preached his religion during the reign of Shapour I of Sasanid dynasty. Mani combined Gnostic Christianity and Zoroastrinism and some aspects of Paganism and Buddhism, to give an appearance of universality to his proposed religion. Shapour I did not object to Mani's religion, his brothers and one of his sons were among many Sasanids following Mani. During the reign of Bahram I, the younger son of Shapour I, Mani was executed, the Manichaeism legend, however continued until 7th century A.D.

Mazdak was 5th century Iranian religious and social innovator and leader, the founder Mazdakism, a dualistic religion-philosophy, a derivative of Manechaeism. In Mazdakism doctrine a mixture of two fundamental principles light or good and darkness or bad forms the essence of everything in the universe. Man can promote the good or constructive principle adhering to high moral conducts such as kindness, ascetic life, and pacifism, and avoiding greed, killing, and eating flesh.

Mazdak was also introducing a social reform toward socialism including the liberalization of marriage rules and regulations, and community of property and women.

The conversion of Sasanid king, Kavah I to Mazdak faith did not prevent the protestation of orthodox Zaroastrians and conservative clergy against the Mazdakism.

CHAPTER 13

Islam and Iran

The termination of the Sasanid dynasty and the invasion of Iran by the Arabs and the introduction of Islam had a dramatic effect on the Iranian and Islamic culture and also influenced the civilization of many nations. The Iranians and Islam interaction promised a new and changed era with a distinctive civilization and culture.

The Prophet Muhammad (Abu al-Qasim, 570-June 8, 632 B.C.), the messenger of God, the founder of Islam was born in Mecca, Saudi Arabia, one of two holiest Islamic cities.

In those days Mecca was one of the cities in the region of the Red Sea, recognized as a mercantile center for trading goods with the surrounding regions, particularly Mediterranean areas. Wealthy Meccan leaders were polytheistic pagans with their religious temples attracting numerous pilgrims, boosting their religion as well as controlling the business.

His father Abu Allah died prior to the birth of prophet. He was under the care of his mother Aminah until the age of six and paternal grandfather up to age of eight. After the death of his mother and grandfather, he was cared for by his uncle Abu-Talib, the father of Imam Ali. The Prophet was a member of Banu Hashim family of the prominent Quraysh tribe in Mecca. Prophet Muhammad met his affluent wife Khadijah, during one of the trading business trips that he used to take with his uncle. This highly successful marriage and partnership lasted for about 25 years until Khadijah's death. The prophet's success in his business paralleled his success in the marriage, reaching a highly respectable position as a businessman in his community. But he wanted to reach beyond a comfortable daily life; his high level of social consciousness, partly due to his childhood hardship created a demanding spiritual need to better himself and his community from a materialistic wealth toward a more meaningful existence. He began, away from the daily routine of business, contemplating, soul searching, and meditating to achieve tranquility and inner peace and perhaps discover answers for some of the questions. Then one day in perhaps around 610 in an isolated location at a tranquil moment, he extrasensorially perceived a forceful signal, directed by an angel, Gabriel, revealing to him a first massage from God. The words implanted divinely on his mind were describing to him God and the creation, and directing the Messenger of God (Rasul Allah) to disseminate and when necessary to explain them to people. The revelation of God, Allah, only one God, to Muhammad, a descendant of Abraham formed the core of a monotheistic grand religion of Islam (submission or surrender to God's will), starting in Mecca, then spreading and reaching the immense territories of the present day by the believers in Islam usually called Muslims. The prophet continued to receive these messages during his life. The Qur'an or Koran or Ghor'an, the sacred book and the ultimate authority of Islam are the compilation of these revelations recited by prophet, memorized or written down by his followers. After the death of the prophet the collection of chapters or Surah (s) were initiated during the reign of caliph Omar, then subsequently were evaluated, scrutinized, and verified by experts and completed and presented in an unsurpassed literary excellence, during the reign of Uthman, the third caliph. In a few years after revelation and securing some several believers and worshipers, mostly rich young men in conflict with the wealthy establishment, the prophet actively engaged in communicating the words of God to the people soon to become the believers.

The existence of polytheistic temples in Mecca and the monopoly of business by a few were antithetic to the teaching of the prophet. Therefore he selected a unique pilgrimage temple, in Mecca, called Ka' ba to represent the only one God revelation. Ka'ba was a very respected shrine, probably built by Abraham and his son and contained the famous black stone falling out of the sky. There is "no God but God" belief did not bode well with Mecca's business authorities, who envisioned that diverting tourists to Ka'ba and directing them to the life of piety will certainly result in their loss of income and authority. They attempted to bribe him, but they failed. Then they began to threaten him and his followers. After the death of Khadijah and Abu Talib in 619, the leaders of the Quraysh tribe intensified their harassment of the prophet and perhaps plotted to assassinate him. The prophet aware and disappointed of the wrong doings of the Meccans and the hardship placed on the Muslim decided to leave Mecca and encouraged his followers to do the same. Supported by his followers the prophet secretly left Mecca and was welcomed to Yathrib, an agricultural city 270 to 275 miles to north of Mecca. Yathrib eventually was renamed as the Medinah or the city of prophet. The prophet had already been invited by several tribal leaders to emigrate to Medinah and had already secured a respectful position as an arbitrator and judge to oversee the city's intertribal negotiation at the time of conflict among them. The rival tribal leaders of yathrib under the leadership of prophet completed a document to guide the future internal and external affairs of Medinah. The emigration of the prophet in 622 A.D. from Mecca to Medinah is called Hejra or Hegira in Latin and the date marks the beginning of the Islamic calendar, indicating the birth of Islam.

Muslims, Umma, are people with divine goals and a collective responsibility and political objectives and practical guides for daily living and religious rituals.

After Hegira, peace and Islamic unification were not achieved immediately. The dynamics of formation of a new religious community were at work. The assimilation of new arrivals from Mecca, the adjustment of Jewish groups and pagan Arabs to the new religion, the collaboration of pagan with Jews against the Muslim, the resentment of some leaders of Medinah of the prophet, all had to be addressed by prophet Muhammad. Leaders of the Quraysh tribe were still hoping to curtail or eliminate the activities of the prophet, and Muslims were trying to stabilize and expand the new religion. On several occasions armed battles erupted between Muslims of Medinah and the leaders of Mecca, both parties suspicious and anxious of each other and eager to fight with significant casualties on both sides. The repeated failure of Meccans, despite their quantitatively strong manpower solidified the credibility of the Islamic community under the leadership of prophet Muhammad.

The superiority and triumph of the Islamic forces were attributed to divine blessing.

The conversion of Arabs, city dwellers as well as Bedouins, continued to increase.

Prompting the leaders of Mecca to acknowledge the solidarity of the ever-expanding Islamic community within the Arabic peninsula. The Muslim of Medinah gaining momentum, and the leaders of Mecca standing still, now it was the right time for the prophet to march toward Mecca. After some preliminary diplomatic negotiations and planning the prophet accompanied by his Islamic forces moved to Mecca in 630. The Meccans submitted to and welcomed the Messenger of God with minor incidence and generally enjoyed his impartiality and generosity. Mecca joined Medinah; both became the centers of activities for trade, unification of tribes and internal and external propagation and expansion of Islam.

The pilgrimage was limited to only one temple, the temple of one God, the Ka'ba. The prophet, the Messenger of God, the statesman, and the founder of the Islamic empire, died in Medinah on June 8, 632, ten years after the Hejira. The successor could not replace him as a prophet, he was the last Messenger and irreplaceable; the successor as a leader had only to carry on the message given to the Messenger by God.

CHAPTER 14

Successors of Prophet Muhammad

After the death of prophet Muhammad (June 8, 632), Abu Bakr a popular, wise, modest man, and a loyal friend of the prophet, about sixty years old was selected to become his first deputy or successor, with a newly created title of Khalifeh spelled also khalifah or Khalifa, westernized as Caliph, to lead as the religious and civil head of the Islamic community with duties to be determined, ruling from 632-634. After several months Abu Bakr opposed and denounced apostasy and was able to prevent divergence from Islamic tenets and maintain the unification and strength of Muslims. He was succeeded by Umar or Omar Al Khatib. Omar was nominated for the Khalifate by Abu Bakr, his close associate. Physically Omar was a tall, large, and strong man with a towering body and a rough facial appearance. Both Abu Bakr and Omar were members of the Quraysh tribe in Mecca and advisers to the prophet, both accompanied him in his 622 A.D. journey (Hejira) to Medina, although initially Omar was not sympathetic toward the prophet and his teaching. His contribution to the expansion of Islam and its principles and doctrine paralleled his imposing body, but behavior wise he appeared unassuming, unpretentious, living modestly, and identifying with the poor. During the just, effective, and organized ruling (634-644) of Omar, the Islamic expansion to Iran was materialized, the Sasanid dynasty of centuries ended after about three years of war. The Muslims were not fighting for conquest of land and loot, but for the Islamic principles and justice for all, for the Islamic community, for themselves and not for the rulers.

After Omar assassination by an Iranian slave in 644, Uthman or Othman, spelled also Osman, 68 years old, rich merchant of the Umayyad clan of Mecca, a faction of Quraysh tribe became the third Caliph. He was capable of providing financial assistance to the Islamic community, when needed. Othman converted to Islam early, soon after the prophet Muhammad began to disseminate the message of God. After divorcing his two pagan wives, he married a daughter of the Prophet, when she died he married another daughter of the Prophet. The third caliph was a pious and a very religious man, rather insecure trying to follow similar policies as Omar, but without the strength and leadership aptitude of Omar. He was not assertive enough to govern a vast and organized empire of Omar with a multitude of administrative and managerial functions. He mostly was preoccupied with praying and reciting the Qur'an, and concerned with the judgment day. He showed interest in public work, built streets, road, canal, and irrigation system, but he also spent lavishly to build several thousands mosques. Othman had a tendency to favoritism, delegated undeserved authority to his relatives and friends. Old age of Othman, inconsistency in his administration, and the beginning of corruption by the abuse of power by his favorites led to dissatisfaction and resentment. On June 17, 656 he was assassinated by a group of rebels in his home. His death resulted in a major division and conflict in the Islamic religion.

After Osman, Ali Ibn Abu Talib, became the fourth caliph, ruling from 656-661. Ali, the son-in-law and cousin of the Prophet Muhammad is considered by Shiah branch of Islam to be only a true and legitimate successor of the Prophet. At the very young age, he was converted to Islam, to become the second Muslim after Khadijah, a hero and a devout follower of the Prophet, a highly admired figure in the Shiah community, participating and accompanying the prophet, with courage in the battles for the expansion of Islam.

Ali facing the religious disorders left by his predecessors attempted to revitalize and apply the Islamic principles justly and equally. Ali attempted to eliminate nepotism of Othman and corruption.

Not sharing his objectives, the Quraysh aristocrats in Mecca opposed him. The opposition supported by Mu'awiya. Mu'awiya was the governor of Damascus appointed by Omar and given more authority and territory by Othamn. He took the opportunity to exploit the Othman's assassination and to challenge Ali to punish his murderers. He was supported temporarily by Ayesha, the Prophet's wife, in Mecca. Ayesha vigorously sided with Mu'awwiya against Ali, delivering fiery speeches and asking for revenge, but eventually withdrew her support from Mu'awiya. The opponents of Ali continued to intensify campaign against him, even incriminating him in a conspiracy to murder Othman, trying to alienate his followers and turning them against him. Mu'awiya not only did not recognize Ali, but also claimed to be the rightful caliph. While negotiation, after initial armed confrontations, between Ali and Mu'awiya continued some of the more radical followers of Ali called Kharijites (departed), perhaps disappointed by Ali's moderate attitude toward Mu'awiya, rebelled openly against Ali and assassinated him. Ali was buried near Kufah, Iraq. The majority of Ali's followers, the Shi'i (singular), Shi'ah or Shi'a (pleural) remained loyal to him and formed the Shia branch of Islam. Ali became the first Imam endowed with divine power of the Prophet, the power to be passed on to Ali's descendents, the power of especial perception of God's guidance.

Imam Ali was more than a khalifa; the Shi'a believed he was endowed with a divine power because of his blood relationship with the Prophet as well as his own individual knowledge of God through the Prophet, thus capable of guiding the Muslims in the path intended by the Prophet.

Sunnis, the majority of the Muslim community believe in mainstream Islam of Abu Bakr and Omar following the Messenger of God's instructions and are the practitioner of the Prophet's way of living, his sunnah (traditional way of living).

A highly respected and intellectually well-written book, Nahj al-balaghah, contains the collection of Ali's political views, sermons, and his sayings.

The first four successors of the prophet are collectively called Rashidun, translated "the rightly guided ones". The death of Imam Ali ended one theological dynasty, and started the Islamic schism.

CHAPTER 15

Islam more than a doctrine

Revelations to the prophet continued long after the delivery of "no God, but God" and the tenets of Islam. As a civilized community of faith and belief, Islam is directed and guided by laws, rules, and regulations of divine origins to pursue a clean life compatible with health and happiness of the community as a whole. The individuals' way of life and behavior to be judged after life for reward or punishment.

Therefore it is mandatory to provide an unambiguous and trustworthy direction for the faithful to emulate. These directions must be explicit and encompass guidance for the required and expected daily rituals deemed necessary for the betterment of the life of the community.

Islam as a practical religion requires the performance of daily program and duties from the Muslims. The authentications of these requirements however must be verified by reliable sources to avoid the confusion and misdirection of the faithful.

Some of these obligations and duties such as "five pillars of Islam" do not need verification, because they are part of revelations and are documented in Qur'an, or had been practiced when prophet was alive and available for guidance. At the absence of such solid and established sources to show the right and true path clearly to the Muslims, the Hadith, a collection of words and deeds of the prophet, provides the right answer as intended by the prophet.

The Hadith, a document of Islamic tenets and a community living guide, taking form early after the Prophet, quoted by people close to the

44

Prophet and verified by the pious Muslims with profound knowledge of the Islamic doctrine and with impeccable credentials (ulama or ulema pleural of alim "learned person"), was organized and continued to amass during Abbassid period.

In the Islamic civilization ulama were among the leaders of the community, in addition to religion, they were adviser and influential in educational, judicial, and social affairs with no particular rank or title in the government; no other title would have been more respectable and would have surpassed their own title of ulama.

The Shariah or Shar'ia (a way or path), deriving from Qur'an, Hadith, and other verified sources, refers to all Islamic laws, which entails more than legality, it is a way or path of life, every aspect of it. Some variations exist among the four versions of Sunni sect shariah and also that of Shia sect sharia, but these variations are not the source of disharmony among the Muslims.

THE FIVE PILLARS OF ISLAM ARE:
1. Shahadat: Accepting no God but God, and Muhammad his Messenger.
2. Salat or Salah: Praying (Namaz) daily, while facing toward Mecca.
3. Zakat: Donating yearly percentage of income to poor.
4. Sawm: Fasting from dawn to dusk yearly in the month of Ramadan.
5. Hajj: Pilgrimage to Mecca, at least once in a lifetime, if capable.

The Islamic doctrine in general and the revelation of God to the Prophet in particular were more than introducing a new religious belief and guides; they introduced new ideology about the existence, life and death, science and philosophy. As the Islamic doctrine expanded, the revelation of the words of God, at times, challenged the preexisting philosophical and scientific ideas and beliefs. The Islamic scholars, when confronting these conflicts, although agreed in principles with the nature of conflict, proposed solutions, with varying degree of enthusiasm and logics, from conciliatory in nature or refuting any idea not in line with revelation, thus creating a new source of intellectual discussion regarding the will of God in the daily living of his creatures and the importance of scientific and philosophical studies in solving the puzzles of life.

The relationship between God and the believers in Islam was also analyzed from different perspective. Should the believer fear or love or both love and fear God? The believer firstly should know his God. Some pious Muslims believed that getting to know God requires a constant effort and sacrifice, one needs to exclude materialistic thing to get close to God and receive love from God. Sufis take the process of knowing God to a mystical level; they believe in order to know God and experience and appreciate the beauty of God, one has to live an ascetic and pious life, to choose poverty, to be content with simple daily diet, to wear simple clothes, to perform spiritual exercise in the form of prayer, to fight against the inner ego, to change fear of Him to love of Him. One becomes a Sufi, not by going to school or reading, or following some rules and regulations, but by a constant and continuous searching. One has to purify his soul, elevating it to the level of God, in order to be united with him.

CHAPTER 16

The development of Iranian-Islamic civilization

The end of the Sasanid period and the beginning of the Islamic era (651 A.D.) in Iranian history corresponds to the earliest part of the Middle Ages and the start of interaction between Arabs and Iranians over a period of centuries. This interaction, combining the Islamic teaching and the pre-Islamic Iranian culture created a unique civilization constituting a fascinating, and a very important part of Iranian history and culture.

Several factors intervened, delaying and facilitating, the acceptance, the unification, and the centralization of Islam in Iran. The vast Iranian territories divided by mountain ranges and deserts conducive to the establishment of local territories and provinces, far distant from each other with different customs, habits, and life style, was an impediment to the spread of Islam. Also hindering the progress of Islam was the behavior of the conquering Arabs, accustomed to the tribal and nomadic life style, leading to a relatively short but bitter and destructive encounter between Arabs and Iranians, including killing and sporadic and isolated massacre of the Iranians, usually in response to revolts. Discrimination against Iranians, burning their books, imposing poll and land taxes upon them resulted in resentment, resistance, and rebellion against Arabs and, by association, against Islam, calling for revenge and creating a vicious cycle.

On the other hand the desire of the peasants and other masses for a better alternative life style, the promise and advocating of Islam for human

47

equality and financial fairness were among favorable factors facilitating the propagation of Islamic doctrine.

The landowners and nobility used their usual survival tactics; they recognized and cooperated with the Arabs. Many converted to Islam to avoid poll and land taxes, and some converted to secure a position in the ruling government and the army.

After the completion of the conquest of Iran by the Islamic force, the Sasanid territories in the east joined the western Islamic territories, Syria and Egypt to form the Islamic empire.

Despite hindrances the spread of Islam in Iran was relatively expeditious.

The capital of the great empire initially was Damascus, ruled by the Umayyads, and later Baghdad, ruled by the Abbasids. The empire eventually expanded from the Indus River in the east to Spain in the west.

Throughout the reign of Abbasids, and despite their efforts to adopt and borrow the Sasanids administrative and military policies and methods, the Iranian rulers of local groups of people of diverse origin, but all with nationalistic objectives gradually gained more authority and autonomy, forming dynasties semi-independent and independent of Baghdad.

As the local dynasties acquired more power, they began to usurp the authorities of caliphs, reversing the caliphs' role from the rulers to subordinates, similar to the past when the conquered Iranians domesticated and subdued the invaders and controlled them.

While these leadership changes were evolving in Baghdad, the other fundamental cultural changes were in progress in Iran, toward unification and assimilation, and Persianazation of the Islamic Empire.

The Iranian-Islamic scholars-experts soon became sophisticated and excelled in Islamic language, Arabic, the language of the Kor'an, Holy Book, of Islam. They translated the texts written in different languages to Arabic, and edited, compiled, and published the texts in philosophy, history, geography, science, mathematics, astronomy in unsurpassed Arabic language, enriching the Islamic and world culture.

The emergence of young and new dynasties of the Arab-Iranian or Iranian origin gradually stimulated the revival of the Iranian language of Farsi and prompted the birth of the great Iranian national epic of Shahnameh (Book of Kings), devoid of the Arabic words, the legendary classical history of Iran to the end of
the Sasanid dynasty.

CHAPTER 17

Umayyad and Abbasid Dynasties

After the assassination of Ali, the leader of his opponents, Muawiyah or Moawiyah, then the governor of Syria, related to Umayyad merchants of Quraysh tribe of Mecca, became the first caliph (661-680) and founder of the Umayyad dynasty in Damascus with its fourteen successors ruling the Caliphate or Khalifate and Sunni branch of Islam. Yazid I succeeded his father Muawiyah from 680 to 683. Yazid with his organized army confronted a non-compromising Husayn a defender of justice and virtue, and his accompanying members of his family, children, elderly relatives and a few fighters in a very hot desert, torturing them by depriving them of water. Yazid's army murdered Imam's party one by one, decapitating Husayn and sending his head to Yazid.

He was responsible for the martyrdom of Imam Husayn in the battle of Karbala in 680. Yazid is remembered with contempt by the Shias.

During Umayyads, Islamic doctrine and army, Arabic language, scholarship, literature, coinage, and religious foundations continued to expand in all directions; and the religious aspects of Islam intertwined with political and social endeavors promoting Umayyads from a rich local tribe to a civilized Islamic Empire. The continuous expansion of Islam brought back revenues, which enabled the government to support the people, the umma, to expand the Islamic territories and enlarge the Islamic community. Although conversion of the people in the conquered lands was encouraged and it provided security to a newly convert Muslim, it by no means was forced upon; all talented people, when needed were invited to participate in business and professional affairs and enter the work force; but usually non-Muslims were required to pay poll tax, the tax imposed on people not being a Muslim.

The dynasty ended in 750, and its last caliph was Marwan II (744-750).

Abbasid Dynasty (750-1258) named after al-Abbas, a descendant of an uncle of the Prophet, of the Hashimite group related to the Quraysh tribe. The dynasty headed and formed by the first Abbasid caliph Abu al-Abbas as-Saffah "slaughterer" (750-754), with the help of Abu Muslim, an Iranian Muslim and a Khorasani general from the city of Merv in Iran. After the defeat of the last Umayyad caliph, Marwan II, in Mesopotamia in 750, the Abbasid dynasty replaced the Umayyads and ruled until 1258. All prosperities achieved doing Umayyads could not be maintained for all people and they were becoming privileges limited to the rich. Inequality, injustice, and poverty slowly began to erode in Islamic societies. These events and deviation from the teaching of the Prophet, created a faster resentment in the eastern Iranians of Indo-European ethnicity, remote from central Islam, already resentful of the Arab dominance, and intrusions in Iranian life. The Iranians malcontent and suppressed by Arabs identified easily with Shias and gravitated toward them, feeling victimized by the traditional Umayyads Muslims leaders.

The revolt led and organized by Abu Muslim, was supported by the Hashimite group, referring to Banu Hashim of the Prophet. It started in Khorasan in the eastern region of Iran, and it was an Islamic Arab-Iranian movement against the tyranny of Umayyads. Abu Muslim an effective and energetic Iranian Muslim and leader was considered to be a lower class by the Umayyads because of being Iranian. Inordinate taxes on commerce, lands, and particularly head taxes, paying taxes on being Christian, Jew, or even Iranian were among the contributing factors to the dissatisfaction of Iranians as well as Arabs. Fractionation of Islam after Uthman's murder relative to the rightful successor of Prophet, imamate vs. caliphate contributed to the movement, directing the dissatisfied people including Iranians away from the Umayyad caliphate representing the tradition or sunnah. Abu Muslim was appreciated and acknowledged and at the same time feared for his power by the Abbasid caliphs. Therefore the second caliph, al-Mansur deposed him and had him murdered in 755. The unjustified killing of Abu Muslim became an impetus to the future revolts against Abbasid dynasty, contributing to its downfall.

After Abbas, his brother al-Mansur replaced him. Al-Mansur built the largest city of the world at the time, the city of Baghdad.

Abbasid transferred their capital to Baghdad, Iraq. Baghdad remained the major capital, although not a continuous one, of Abbasid's, becoming an unparallel commercial city.

During the Abbasid dynasty, the caliphate selected a new path and identity, identifying with international, including Iranian, Islamic converted groups, rather than with only Arabs. Iranians, particularly from eastern land, Khorasan, who had supported the formation of the dynasty, continued to influence, promote, and consolidate the civilization within the realm of expanded dynasty. Abbasid Empire burgeoned and, at times, spiraled upward, and reached its zenith during the ruling of Harun ar-Rashid (786-809). Harun al-Rashid, the fifth caliph, the caliph of the Thousand and One Nights, was the son of al-Mahdi. When al-Mahdi died in 786 Harun succeeded him. Harun ar-Rashid was an educated man, knowledgeable in history, literature, music and the Islamic doctrine. His tutor was Ahya Barmakid, who in association with Harun's mother was responsible for the ascension of Harun, who appointed him as his vizier or chief minister. During Harun's regime, the industry and trade advanced greatly and Baghdad achieved the status of the center of Arabic culture. Harun had his share of several revolts in different regions of Iranian territories. Although these revolts were controlled by the central government, they were the precursors of demand for autonomy by the local dynasties in the future.

After his death a long and useless civil war started between his two sons dividing the empire, al-Amin ruled as the caliph of Baghdad, and al-Ma'mun controlled Iran. Two brothers invading each other's territory with a destructible effect on Iraq, particularly on Baghdad. The struggle between the brothers continued until the death of al-Amin, when al-Ma'mun became the caliph (813-833) and eventually moved to Baghdad. During al-Ma'mun reign although Baghdad, was politically and militarily in a downward slope, recaptured its position as the cultural center and the source of intellectual and educational products. After al-Ma'mun's reign as the time went on the dynasty took an up and then down spiral course, vacillating, intermittently symbolizing a great culture or displaying an anarchy and disorganization, eventually turning steadily downward. After the murder of Abu Muslim in 755, the local Iranian revolts, for different reasons, but mostly revolving around the death of Abu Muslim, had continued against Abbasids. Included among them were the uprisings of:

Sunbadh from Nishapur to revenge the Abu Muslim's murder; Ishaq, the Turk, claiming that Abu Muslim was a Zoroastrian prophet; Babak in Azerbaijan, the leader of Khorram-dinan (816-838), a subset of the Shia sect of Islam, but also believing in transmigration of the soul and the divine status of Abu Muslim and perhaps, Babak himself. Babak was captured in 837 and died in 838.

Iranian provinces in the eastern region of the empire along with the other provinces including Syria and Egypt functioned independently; disorganized, undisciplined, and disloyal army, disintegrating economy, and local revolts contaminated and disabled the empire, leading to the invasion of Baghdad by Buyids in 945, another turn in the direction of the Islamic empire, particularly in Iran, resulting in incorporation of the Iranian cultural and social identities to Islamic principles as well as prioritization of Shiism as an Iranian Islamic religion.

Like other dynasties, kingdoms, empires, and superpower nations, the cause of decline of the Abbasid Empire was multifactorial. One factor playing a significant role in the downfall of the Abbasid Empire, also applicable to other empires and powers, was the failure of the leaders to recognize their limitations. When the dynasty was small in size and territories, the leaders were able to organize and manage it and apply the rules and regulation effectively. However as time went on, and the Caliphate reached the empire status, it required more competence than the rulers could provide, and failing to recognize this incompetence, they continued to reign. In lieu of fundamental and qualitative changes in the organizational aspect of the leadership to meet the demands, they began to recruit more bodies to enlarge their staff for support and enforcement of policies. Not being able or not willing to recruit Iranians or Arabs, they recruited the members of their arm forces and bodyguards, who were converted Muslims descendents of Turkic slaves, emigrated from central Asia steppes. These Turkic-soldier-staff surrounded the caliphs, not only protected and isolated them, they were working for them and advising, and representing them, eventually running the government and acting like caliphs, and now ready to recruit their own Turkic soldiers from central Asia.

The newly created positions for the Turks encouraged more Turks to aggressively cross the border and land in Iran. These new arrivals, although converted Muslim nomads, did not receive any training; they were wild, destructive, and ready to fight and kill and take over the established powers, controlling and destroying the communities they entered.

CHAPTER 18

The Birth Of New Dynasties

TAHIRIDS DYNASTY (821-873) IN KHORASAN

After al-Ma'mun replaced his brother al-Amin and assumed his position as an Abbasid caliph, he appointed the chief of his army, Tahir ibn Husayn, as the governor of Khorasan, to express his gratitude for Tahir's assistance in defeating, his brother al-Amin in Baghdad and securing the caliphate for al-Mamun; but al-Ma'mun by sending Tahir to Khorasan also wanted to avoid the mingling of Tahir with the affairs of the caliphate. Shortly after arrival to Khorasan, Tahir founded the dynasty and began to rule independent of caliph. Tahirids selected Nishapur or Neyshapur in Farsi, presently a city in Khorasan province, as their capital, they ruled independently in northeast Iran with a nominal but loyal affiliation with caliphate in Baghdad. After Tahir ibn Husayn (821-822), they were four additional Tahirid rules; last one was Muhammad bin Tapir (862-873).

Alavids or Alavian of Tabaristan (864-928) were of Shia sect of Islam, descendants of Imam Hassan, they established the dynasty in Tabaristan (present Mazandaran), Iran and introduced Shia Islam to the region. The natives, who have been treated unjustly and with cruelty by some representatives of Tahirids, invited Hassan ibn Zeid of Rayy for leadership. Hassan moved to Tabaristan and founded the Alavid dynasty. Hasan and his three successors ruled until 928, when they were defeated by Sammanids.

53

SAFFARID (C. 861-1003)

Then there was Yaghub ibn Leys as-Saffar (Coppersmith), the founder of dynasty from a village of Sistan. People of Sistan at the time were not fond of their Arab conquerors. This enmity dated back to the caliphate of Uthman, when the Arab conquered Sistan a secluded and far off region of Iran. Since then the people of Sistan, witnessed the unjust and cruel behavior of the Sunni Islamic leaders, the behavior, they thought, was not in compliance with the teaching of the Prophet. The people expressed their dissatisfaction, which continued until the formation of the Saffarid dynasty with rioting, revolt, protest, demonstration, and with disobedience of the laws. Ironically similar to our present day culture, at times, it was difficult to discern the motives of the participants in these activities. Were all the participants fighting for justice and principles, or some of them were pretenders with real objectives of self-gain, looting and armed robbery? Yaghub was one the ardent participants. Intelligent, ambitious, generous, and well liked by his peers, he supported the leaders of discontent against the caliph and his representatives in eastern Iran, promoting himself to a high ranking army officer in the rebel force and eventually upgrading himself to the governor of Sistan at the southeastern border of Iran. Then, as a competent and capable army officer, from that position, nominally dependent on the caliphs of Baghdad, he proceeded to enlarge his territory, from eastern Iran (Sistan) to the south to include Fars and Khusistan, extending to Afghanistan and Pakistan. He replaced the Tahirid dynasty after conquering Nishapur and annexing Khorasan. He attempted to subjugate the caliph of Baghdad, but before achieving his final goal he died and was buried in Gondishapur, Khuzistan. After Yaghub seven other Saffrids ruled their territories. The last one was Abu Ahmad Khalaf ibn Ahmad. Khalaf died in the prison of Mahmood of Ghaznavid. In his personal life he was cited to be a pious man, intellectual, and lover of literature, but in ruling he performed like many other rulers perform. He engaged in deceiving and revenging his opponents mercilessly; he murdered and buried his own son, because, his son opposed his cruelty and sided with Mahmood of Ghaznavid; yet he was praised by his contemporary poets for his love of poetry. This cultural schizoid behavior has been commonly observed in the history of the rulers.

SAMANIDS (819-999) were getting ready to take over and succeed Saffarids. Saman was the name of a village, near Samarkand. One of the local rulers of Saman, called Saman-Khuda, a descendant of a Sasanid general, a Zoroastrian converted to Islam, during the rule of Asad ibn Abd Allah al-Qasri (Ghasri), the governor of Khorasan (723-727) became the founder of Samanids and named his son Assad after the governor of khorasan. His four grandsons were privileged and supported by the Caliph of Baghdad, al-Ma'mun, were engaged in authoritative positions to govern many eastern Islamic territories including Samarghand and Herat, providing security and protection for the merchants and traders. Ismail ibn Ahmad ibn As'ad ibn Saman, the grandson of Asad, first became the governor of Transoxania, then through a series of war, expanded his ruling domain and became the first Samanid Amir (892-907), replacing Saffarids in Khorasan in 900 and selected Bukhara as his capital. He was known to be virtuous and pious Sunni. The Samanids promoted industry, commerce, architecture, literature, and the unique Iranian Islamic culture and art including the pottery unique to Samanid period. The northeastern native Persian language, enriched by the Arabic vocabulary, was revived as a literary language.

Its rulers remained loyal to the Caliphs of Baghdad and treated them as the spiritual leaders. They safeguarded the eastern periphery of Islamic empire for the Caliph and maintained the supply of Turkish slaves or former slaves much needed then in Baghdad. The Samanids enjoyed the support of Sunni religious leaders of Transoxania and Khorasan, but were not able to secure the loyalty of the Shia sect of Islam.

The highly generous rulers of the dynasty were preoccupied with the need and the protection of the people, therefore not using their authority to the full extent in the governing. In actuality, the courtiers, the staff, the high-powered Turkish slaves of the court very often were in control of the government. The provincial governors and local rulers, and army chiefs generally were semi-independents of the Amirs of the Smanids.

These intrinsic structural weaknesses and shortcomings within the government and constant struggles for power among the competitors led to the gradual decline in Samanid power in contrast to the rising power of Muslim Turks in Central Asia and resulted in the reversal of Turkish and Samanid relationship. The Turkish force became dominant over the vulnerable Samanids.

After Mansur II (997-999) was deposed, Abd al-Malik II and Ismail II for a short period were Amirs of Samanid reigning only over part of the region.

Ghaznavids Dynasty (977-1186) a Turkish group started in Ghazna (present Ghazni in Afghanistan) in 962, by Alptegin, a member of the Turkish slave guards family, ascending to the level of commander in chief and governor of Khorasan during the Samanid dynasty. Later on son-in-law of Alptegin, Sebuktigin (died 997 in Balkh), also a Turkish former slave, and Mahmud or Mahmood (ruled 998-1030), the son of Sebuktigin began to rule Ghazna and Khorasan respectively, and eventually expanded their territories to a vast area. Their troops composed of various ethnic groups, daylamites, Kurds, Afghans and commanded by Turkish generals. Abul Qasim Mahmud ibn Sebuktigin during his first few years in reign confronted the internal problems of his dynasty, deposed Mansur II (997-999) of Samanids; settled his differences with his other competitors; forcefully controlled his challengers of Samanids, Saffarids, and Il khanids; after securing his position in Ghazna he then focused his attention in India.

By this time Mahmud was being addressed by his followers and staff as Sultan, a new title, which prior to him it was an Arabic title reserved for caliphs.

During his reign Sultan Mahmud repeatedly attacked India and Indian's wealth of gold, silver, and jewelry and victorious in his conquest, he returned with glory, and rich with all sort of abundant booty, some taken from the Indian idolatry houses with golden domes and full of priceless jewelry. After all Sultan was fighting the infidels in India.

Before his death Mahmud captured and liberated Ray, burned to ashes the library; but he also, as it was expected, took possession of a large sum of money and high price jewelry. Then he annexed Ghazvin and with the help of his son Masoud, he conquered Hamadan, Isfahan, all resulting in thousands of deaths.

Sultan Mahmud died of tuberculosis in Ghazna in 1030.

During his reign Mahmud demonstrated a remarkable leadership, competence, and, at times dictatorial, elevated the local ruling Ghaznavid in Ghazna to a vast empire including the major part of Iran and Afghanistan and extending to the heart of India; the dynasty reached its peak, and Ghazna, as a cultural center, rivaled Baghdad.

Under Mahmud's tenure, a man dedicated to Sunni Islam, and intolerant and persecuting the followers of the other religions, the dynasty changed from a pagan Turkic state to an Islamic dynasty promoting art, architecture, and education; he supported poets, historians, and philosophers. Ferdowsi, the star of poets of the time, completed his Shahnameh during Sultan's reign, in about 1010, but he was not enchanted with Mahmud's behavior toward him. Mahmud did not honor his promised reward of gold, changing it to silver, at the completion of shahnameh. Ferdowsi withdrew the dedication of his book to Mahmud and rededicated it to a local ruler with Iranian ethnicity.

DAYLAM-ZIVARID AND BUYID DYNASTIES
Daylam also spelled Dailam, corresponding roughly to the present Gillan province of northern Iran, was the land of daylamites, who because of the mountainous location of their land were protected from outside invaders, even majestic forces of Islam were not able to penetrate their land. Although they lived independently and protected their ancient culture, they were willing to conquer and rule the lands south to their territory at the time of needs and opportunity.

Mardaviz ibn Ziar or Zeyar and Ali ibn Buyeh, the founders of their respective dynasties were from these people, anxious to move to south, toward the lands held by Samanids.

ZIYARID DYNASTY OR ZEYARID (ZIARIAN OR AL-ZIAR) was
founded by Mardaviz ibn Ziar (ruled 927-935) in Gorgan and Mazandaran (Tabaristan). Mardaviz or Mardavij reigned from Rayy and eventually expanded his territories to Hamadan and Isfahan, and Azarbaijan, involving armed confrontation with the forces of the caliph of Baghdad. Mardavij had remained loyal to Zoraostrianism, therefore, resented the caliphs of Baghdad and his intention was to revive the glory of the Sasanid dynasty. By wearing a crown with inlaid jewels and sitting in a golden seat he was imitating the glorious kings and he was dreaming to be one of them. At one occasion during his last year of ruling, in preparation for the coming of new year, he ordered his staff to organize festivities, ceremonial firework, and celebration; finding the preparation short of his expectation, Mardavij felt neglected and belittled by his staff and he ordered to reprimand his Turkish slaves, who fearful of their life preemptively killed him while he was taking a bath.

The Ziyarids overall, were supportive of arts and literature. The great al-Biruni for many years was associated with the court of Qabus or Ghabus ibn Voshmagir (978-1012). Ghabus was the fourth and the most famous ruler of the Ziyarid dynasty. He was a scholar, generous, and supporter of literature and poetry. However, he was easily provoked to anger and had a tendency to revenge and punish his subservient to death, thus creating a constant fear among his staff and army personnel. He was killed by the leaders of his army in 1012.

Abu ar-Rahman al-Biruni, born 973 in Khwarezm, Khorasan (now in Turkmenistan) died in 1048 in Ghazna (now Ghazni, Afghanistan), an Iranian intellectual, scholar, and scientist, linguist, of Shia Islam faith, expert in several scientific fields including mathematics, astronomy, physics, medicine, and history. He was the author of several books in his field of interest.

Keykavus the great son of Ghabus authored Ghabus-nameh (Book of Qabus or Ghabus) to advise his son in the princely behavior. The book is one of the masterpieces of Iranian literature in Farsi.

Gonbad-e Qabus or even a better Farsi pronunciation of Gonbad-e Ghabus, a baked brick tower built by the order of Ghabus in 1006, located in the central part of the city of Gonbad-e Qabus, Golestan province. The tomb of Qabus, is a tall cylinder, capped by a conical roof, a total of 236 feet high.

The Ziyarid dynasty ended in 1043, the last ruler was Anushirvan ibn Manoucher.

BUYID DYNASTY (945–1055) is characterized as an Iranian-Islamic-

Shia dynasty of northern Iran (Daylam, Gilan) origin, named after Buyeh or Buwayh, the fisherman father of three brothers, the founders of the dynasty, Ali (Imad ad-Dawlah), Hassan (Rukn ad-Dawlah), and Ahmad (Mu'izz ad-Dawlah). All three brothers with honorific title of ad-Dawlah given to them by Abbasid caliphs in Baghdad confirming their sovereign status in Iran and Iraq.

Three brothers, possessing different personalities and behavior and all three without adequate experience, collectively ruled a politically Iranized government in western Iran, extending to Isfahan, Fars, Rayy, Hamadan, Khuzestan, and Kerman, and as an Iranian-Shia dynasty assumed a supremacy status in Iran. The sons of Buyeh collaborated with Mardavij, the founder of Ziyarid dynasty. After the death of Mardavij, the Sunni descendents of Ziyarids allied with Samanids for their own protection and confrontation with Buyid brothers, who continued the policy of Mardavij to conquer and expand.

The youngest son of Buyeh, Ahmad moved from Khuzestan and occupied Baghdad in 945 and a few days after declaring an oath of loyalty to Caliph al-Mustakfi, Ahmad arrested him and appointed a new caliph, minimizing the political power of Abbasid Caliphs to a symbolic and ceremonial level, however maintaining the spiritual leadership of caliphs, despite of Buyids being of Shia faith.

Like the caliphs they continued to recruit Turkish slaves, training them, using them as bodyguards and introducing them to their administration.

During the reign of Adud ad-Dawlah (949-983), the son of Hassan, the dynasty reached its peak. The dam he built on the Kur or Kor River (Band-e-Amir), near Shiraz, still remains. The dynasty selected the city of Rayy, or Rey or Ray, as its cultural center to rival with the dynasty's other cultural center in Baghdad. In 1220 the great city of Ray was destroyed by the Mongols, and the population massacred, the survivors moved to Tehran. The modern city of Ray, Shahr-e-Ray several miles southeast to Tehran, is built near the ruins of the old ancient city of Ray.

The dynasty encouraged public works, including building hospital, schools, observatories, and libraries. It supported poetry and poets, including the great epic poet Ferdowsi, whose stories from his Shahnameh (the Book of Kings) are illustrated in the artistic pottery works from the Buyid era. Organizationally, the Buyid dynasty was divided to three major branches of Daylamites ruling from three cities of Shiraz of Fars, Baghdad, and Rayy; each branch ruled by an Amir, one of the three original brothers or their descendents, and all three Amirs in turn nominally accountable to one of them, in order to keep unity among them. Although they were rough people, the Daylamites were too few in number and depended on Turks in order to govern a vast country. This dependency, however, transferred the authority and decision making from Buyids to Turks, who in return used their authority to control Buyids and eventually to take over.

In 1055 Seljuks deposed Abu Nasr al-Malek ar-Rahman, the last ruler of the Iraq branch of dynasty and the authority of the dynasty in Baghdad ended.

The reign of the Buyid dynasty was for a relatively short time, but historically it was very important in establishing the Iranian sovereignty and their reign from Baghdad during the interval from the end of Arab occupation to the beginning of Turks invasion of Iran.

During and after the Buyids tenure some members of Daylamite group or non-Daylamites formed small and local dynasties and principalities varying in duration and strength and the degree of achievement for the Iranians. Most of these groups were submitted to Seljuqs or were terminated by them.

CHAPTER 19

The Seljughs or Seljuqs or Seljuks

During the 10th century of the Turks migration from Central Asia, one of the migrating groups from Oguz (also Ghuz) Turk was headed by a man called Seljugh, settled in the southwest Asia. His grandson Toghril Beg proclaimed himself Sultan of Nishapur in 1038 and with the assistance of his brother Chagri or Chaghri founded the dynasty, which ruled over large section of western Asia during 11th-14th centuries. Seljugh descendants, sultans and their followers converted to and promoted an orthodox branch of Islam, the Sunni, in the area of their empire, which in addition to Iranian territories including Khorasan, Rayy, Hamadan, and Isfahan, encompassed Mesopotamia, Syria, Armenia, and Palestine. By espousing the Sunni branch of Islam the Seljughs gained advantage over the Shia Buyids in Baghdad with the Sunni Abbasid caliphs.

In 1055, after conquering several territories in the Iranian plateau, Toghril moved to Baghdad, where he was welcomed by the Abbasid caliph, replacing Buyids with Seljughs and restoring orthodox Islam under the Sunni caliphate. Caliph of Baghdad at the time was al-Qa'im or al-Gha'im, who married Toghril's niece and further enforced the unity of Seljughs and Abbasid dynasties. The Abbasids had begun to show interest mainly in the spiritual leadership and their endorsement of the secular rulers had become a ceremonial gesture. When Toghril Beg's wife died four years later he married al-Qa'im's daughter, a year later, after more than twenty-five years of ruling he died.

After the death of Toghril Beg (b. c. 990, d. 1063, Rayy), his nephew Alp-Arslan succeeded him. Toghril selected Soleiman, the youngest of his four nephews, sons of Chaghri to replace him. He bypassed Alp-Arslan, the oldest nephew. Soleiman' mother, the widow of Chaghri, had married Toghril. Alp-Arslan protested and did not recognize his younger brother a legitimate successor to Toghril, therefore, supported by the leaders of the dynasty, proclaimed himself as the leader, the Sultan.

After subjugating his contesters, consolidating his domain, and solving the problems at hand, Alp-Arslan began to expand his inherited territories to east and west, delegating the administrative responsibility to Nizam-e Mulk.

In 1071 Alp-Arslan defeated the most powerful Byzantine army and Romanus IV Diogenes was taken as a prisoner. Malik-Shah at the age of thirteen succeeded his father Alp-Arslan in 1072 with Nizam al-Mulk as a guardian.

Under the reigns, Alp-Arslan (1063-72) and Malik-Shah (1072-92) in collaboration with Nizam-e-Mulk (1019-92), the Seljugh's great minister (vizier), the empire advanced and organized, adopting the Iranian political system, culture, and language. The building of Islamic-Iranian mosques and schools (Madrassahs) prospered and propagated.

The Seljughs attempted to define the authorities, responsibilities, and duties within their government as well as to clarify the relationship between the religious and secular authorities.

Intellectual matters and organizational aspects of the empire were delegated to Nizam al-Mulk (b. 1018/19, Tus, d. 1092, near Nahavand). He is the author of the famous book, Siasatnameh (the Book of Government or Politics), born to an educated and cultured Iranian family, was promoted to the post of vizier by Alp-Arslan and became De facto administrator of the Seljughs. A young man, a Fedai of Assassins, dressed as a Sufi and pretended to be one of them, knifed him to death. Nizam al Mulk, the most renowned and effective vizier was a philanthropist and he promoted the public welfare and founded mosques and schools, including the famous Nizameyyeh School in Baghdad. Shortly after Nizam's death, Malik Shah was poisoned, allegedly by the followers of Nizam al-Milk suspecting Malik Shah in the plotting of the murder.

Intellectuals and scholars such as al-Mawardi, al-Ghazali, and Nizam al-Mulk attempted to address and delineate the secular authorities of caliphate-Imamate vs. the authorities of sultans and the possible conflicts between them and the necessity for the regulations and guidelines. Al-

Ghazali (b. 1058, Tus, Iran d. 1111, Tus), worked with Nizam al-Mulk, lectured in Nizamiyeh College in Baghdad, critiqued and analyzed the work of Avicenna. He was a scholar and a prolific writer in the field of jurisprudence, logic, theology, the Islamic doctrine, and mysticism. In 1095, relinquished his official post and discarded his wealth and adopted the Sufism (Islamic mysticism) to experience the truth, rather than to define and explain it.

During Malik Shah's reign, the Seljuq reached their territorial peak and the highest level of greatness.

After Malik's death in 1092, the ensuing internal conflicts, feud, war, and intrigues among the family members and descendents, the Seljuq Empire was divided to independent territories, Anatolia, Syria, and the Iranian territory.

Mu'izz ad-Din Sanjar (1118-57), one of the four sons of Malik Shah was the last recognized sultan and the longest ruler of all Seljuq sultans of Iran. His brothers before him had unstable and ineffective ruling from 1092-1118, over different parts of the Iranian territories. His capital was Neishapur. A number of rulers revolted against him, including, his nephew Mahmud II, the son of Sanjar's brother Muhammad, who had reigned prior to Sanjar. Mahmud proclaimed himself, the Seljuq's ruler of Baghdad. Sanjar ruled almost 62 years in total, including the ruling of Khorasan for many years, before ruling as the sultan of all Seljuq's territories in Iran for almost four decades.

Mahmud II started the Baghdad branch of the now divided Seljuq Empire, ruling from 1118 to 1131, followed by several rulers of western Iran until 1161, when Atabeg of Azerbaijan began to control this branch.

Atabegs were appointed by the Sultans as the guardian of young Seljuq princes designated to govern the different regions of the empire, but they needed guardians because they were too young to govern.

Eldeguzid Dynasty (1137-1225) was one of the Atabeg Turkish dynasties in Azerbaijan.

Shams ad-Din Eldeguz, a ruler of Seljuq province of Azerbaijan and originally a Turkish slave founded the dynasty.

In 1161 he was assigned as the guardian of Arslan, the infant Seljuq prince of the Baghdad branch of Seljuq dynasty. Emir Eldeguz used his Atabeg status to rule his territory, and extending it to Isfahan and Caucasus. The last sultan of the Baghdad branch was Toghril III, who was killed in

1194 during a battle with Khwazem Shah, and Eldeguzids continued to control Azerbaijan.

Kharezm or Khwarezm an ancient region by the Oxus River (present Amu Darya of Turkmenistan and Uzbekistan). It was conquered by the Islamic Arabs in 7ᵗʰ century A.D.

Khwarezm was under ruling of Khwarezm-Shahs or Khwarezmid or Khwarazmiam Dynasty from 1077-1231, followed by Mongols and Timurids.

Khwarezm-Shah Dynasty was founded by Anustegin Gharachai the governor of Khwarezm appointed by Seljuq Sultan Malik-Shah in 1077. The dynasty continued to act in this region on behave of the Seljuqs and represented them until the defeat of Sanjar by the northern China Qara Khitay or Karakitai in 1141A.D., when Khwarezmids switched their loyalty to the Chinese.

After Sanjar death in 1157, the dynasty freed itself completely from the authority of Seljuqs and replaced it.

Khwarezm-Shah Ala' ad-Din Muhammad (1200-20), occupying a large part of Iran attempted to free the dynasty also from the subjugation of Qara Khitay, struggled against other hostile opponents, his own army chiefs, and Genghis khan. Since he did not have the support of the caliph in Baghdad, he was not able to form a united front, and gradually lost his territories until his death, when he was replaced by his son, Jalal ad-Din a ferocious, fast moving fighter against the Mongols, had been labeled the savior of Islam from the Mongols. He died in 1231 and ended the khwarezm dynasty.

One of the adventures of jalal was to attack Azerbaijan and depose the Eldiguzds.

There were other smaller and less noticeable dynasties remnants of Seljuqs, in the different parts of Iran, including Qara Khitay of far eastern origin, Atabegs of Fars, contemporary of the great poet Sa'di, Atabegs of Yazd, and Greater and Lesser Lurs.

One of the important events during Seljuq period was the Assassins organization.

CHAPTER 20

The Assassins

An underground and terrorist organization of the Ismailiyah branch of Shia sect of Islam was founded, organized, and expanded during Seljuq' empire.

In order to understand the purpose and the make-up of this organization, it is appropriate to discuss its historical background and the related group of Fatimids.

Fatimid was a strong political and Islamic dynasty believing in Isma'ilites or Isma'iliyah, the extremist branch of the Shia faith of Islam. The Fatimids probably descended from Fatimah, the daughter of the Prophet Muhammad. The Fatimids as a dynasty ruled in North Africa and Egypt from 909-1171.

The Isma'ilites recognize Isma'il as a last and seventh Imam, rather than his brother, Imam Musa Kazem a true successor of his father Imam Ja' far Sadegh.

In 972 or 973 al-Mu'izz, the influential Fatimid caliph established Cairo, Egypt, as the new capital, central power of Fatimids. Al-Mu'izz succeeded his father at the age of twenty-two, and like the other caliphs ruled as an emperor and Imam, combining two authorities. His move to Cairo was the first step in the extension toward the East. Fatimids were the rivals of Abbasid caliphs of Baghdad, denying their legitimacy and considering them usurpers of authority.

During the remaining 100 years the Fatimids tried to achieve their objectives of ending the illegitimate ruling of Abbasids and protecting their own emperor, encompassing Egypt, North Africa, Sicily, Syria, Palestine, Yemen, and two very important cities of Mecca and Medina. One of the means of accomplishing this huge goal was the widespread use of missionaries, directed by the capital in Cairo. The missionaries were assigned to teach, recruit, and convert the faithful, overtly and secretly, and incite them to subvert against the Abbasids and their followers.

Hassan Sabbah (died 1124), an Iranian, a follower of the Isma'ilites branch of the Shia faith of Islam was the organizer and the leader of the Nizari Isma'ilites and the founder of the Assassins movement in Iran. The term of Assassins probably derives from the word of Hashishi (Hashshash in Arabic, pleural Hashshashin) meaning a person addicted to hashish; it is believed that the members of Assassin by smoking Hashish went to an ecstatic and mystic state of experiencing paradise and equating the murdering of enemies to martyrdom worthy of paradise. In 1076 Hassan for continuation of his religious study went to Egypt and after the completion of his training in a few years returned to Iran to disseminate his knowledge of Isma'ilites and implement their missionary duties. In 1094 a dispute over the succession of the Fatimid dynasty between two brothers created divisiveness in the dynasty, Hassan decided to follow the older brother, named Nizar, and established the Nizari Isma'ilites in Iran. Hassan opposed the Abbasids, but also deviated from Fatamids of Cairo concept toward more radicalism, considering the terrorism as martyrdom and a divine duty for the faithful, as a means of achieving the objective of defeating the enemy. A very secretive policy of the organization as to the location, numbers and identity of membership, created a secret police state helping the Assassins to terrorize the citizens.

Starting in 1090, Hassan accompanied with his convert disciples moved to Alamut, Daylam and began to rule from the Alamut castle located in the Alborz Mountains, near Ghazvin. Initiation, training, promotion, and graduation of members were at different levels, based on the qualifications of the members, who achieved different levels of knowledge, rank and responsibility. From the fortified places in the mountain chains the network of Assassins calling themselves Fedais (devotees), directed by their leader penetrated and influenced the surrounding communities in line with the mission of the organization, and were ready to kill or to be killed and sacrificed, when necessary, focusing in high profile people, particularly the Abbasid caliphs. After the death of Nizam-e Mulk and

Malik Shah, the members of Isma'ilites taking advantage of the relative disarray in Iran demonstrated a more aggressive attitude within the regions of their influence, particularly in Isfahan and Rayy, overtly criticizing their opponents and engaging in murdering and kidnapping people from their homes. The citizens of Isfahan, alarmed and angry reciprocated and burned a large number of Isma'ilites alive. Despite of all these confrontations the Suljuq sultanate was not able to eradicate the Isma'ilites or perhaps some of the Seljuqs leaders were not willing to eliminate them, because they could utilize them in fighting and murdering their enemies. Assassins strongholds were gradually eliminated by the Mongols and in 1256 Hulegu Khan, the grandson of Genghis destroyed Alumet and ended the organization. The Agha Khan followers of today are the remnants of Nizari Isma'ilites.

CHAPTER 21

Mongols' Invasion

Then there were Mongols, who attacked Khwarezm and fought with Khwarezm-Shahs dynasty, massacred innumerable people systematically and terrorized the world. In some regions the numbers of people murdered was so high, it took many days to count the dead bodies, although this seems to be an overestimation and biased. Mongols, a major branch of the Altaic peoples (Turko-Mongolian), were horse-riding nomadic pagan Turkic-related tribes originating from the plateau of eastern central Asia, from a region not suitable for cultivation but compatible with the life style of the Mongols. They organized and trained a military force to expand and conquer in all directions, under the leadership of Genghis or Chengis Khan (c. 1162-1227).

Genghis' original name was Temujin, born in Mongolia, his father a chieftain, was murdered when Temujin was nine. He metamorphosed from a little man, the leader of a small clan, composed mainly of his companions, conquered the other clans, formed a loose confederation of tribes. Then he adapted the name of Genghis Khan (Universal Ruler) in 1206, to become the most famous warrior and conqueror. He created a vast empire, extending from the Pacific Ocean to the Mediterranean Sea, out of small tribes in Mongolia. Chengis first invaded China starting about 1205 and captured a large territory. Then later on about 1219 directed his force towards Iran and began conquering. He conquered Transoxania, destroyed the great cities such as Bukhara, Samarghand, Tus, and Nishapur in 1220-21, razing them flat and murdering the people. This brutal behavior partly emanated from the desire to revenge the prior brutal treatment and killing of several hundreds of people in a trade mission, under Genghis Khan's protection, ordered by Khwarezm-Shah Ala' ad-Din Muhammad. Khwarezm-Shah by his juvenile action and behavior, risking his life and life of innumerable people, was intending to intimidate Genghis Khan and preemptively dissuade him from possible extension of his power to Iran. He fled to die within the vicinity of the Caspian Sea. The last Kwarezm-Shah, Jalal ad-Din Mingburnu (1220-31) was murdered in Kurdistan. Genghis khan died in 1227.

Now Iran was ready for more adventures. Hulegu, the grandson of Genghis crossed the Oxus, after eliminating the Assassins stronghold in Alamut, besieged Baghdad, and the last Abbasid caliph, al-Musta'sim, was executed in 1258. Hulegu assumed the title of Il-Khan, a representative of Khan, to rule the conquered territories in Iran.

Il-Khanid central ruling was established in Azerbaijan, Iran, to represent the Mongols with the intention of remedying the disorganization of the previous rulers as well as to eliminate the problems brought on by the Mongols. By destroying the Isma'ilite fortresses, and by not interfering with the Islamic religion and promoting safety, participating in trade and cultivation of lands the Mongols began to appease and regain the confidence of the people. Among the Il-Khans, Mahmud Ghazan (1295-1304) an intelligent man was the most effective. He adopted Sunni Islam and began seriously with the help of his vizier, Rashid ad-Din, to upgrade all aspects of Iranian society, including industry, agriculture, trade, finance, taxation, construction, healthcare, and military. By converting to Islam, and adopting the name of Mahmud, he facilitated the merging of Mongols with the rest of the population. The Mongols reigned almost 140 years, initially they destroyed, but later on they built from the ashes, they established trading roads, provided religious freedom, introduced the arts and science of the Far East, their capital Tabriz attained a leading center status. As it happened frequently in the history of Iran, his successors were not able to maintain and prevent the deterioration of his achievements. Members of the military, local governors and others on behalf of Il-Khans or on their own behalf established smaller local dynasties until a major event in the future.

After Il-Khan Abu Sa'id (1317-35) died, several additional local dynasties formed. Hassan Buzurg (Farsi Bozorg for Big) founded a Mongol tribe Jalayirid dynasty in Baghdad (1336-1432), after defeating Hassan

Kucuk (Farsi Kouchek for small), his competitor in establishing more Il-Khanids. Mobarez ad-Din Mozaffar established the Mozaffarid dynasty in Shiraz, Fars (1335-1393), and there were other minor dynasties all over, challenging each other. Uways I, the son of Hassan Buzurg besieged Azerbaijan in 1360, and began to intimidate and usurp the Mozaffarids.

Timur or Tamerlane or Teymoor or Timurlenk (Timur the Lame, Teymoor-e lang) was born in 1336 in Kish (now in Uzbekistan) and died in 1405 in Otrar (now Kazakstan),

He was a Turk, but not a Mongol, however, according to some writers he declared himself to be a descendant of Genghis Khan. In 1383 with capture of Herat, he began his Iranian adventures, taking the eastern Iranian territories, moving toward west conquering Fars, Azerbaijan, Mesopotamia, Armenia, and Georgia by 1394.

Ruthless repression of the revolts, destruction of the cities, massacres of the people mark Timur campaigns for expansions. In 1398, continuing his destructive invasion, he moved to India, ending up with the brutal destruction of Delhi. In 1401 invaded Damascus, massacred 20,000 people in Baghdad, and in 1402 invaded Anatolia. After his death in 1405, his body was returned to Samakand, his capital, to be buried in Gur-e-Amir, his famous tomb or mausoleum. Timur in addition to his competent and destructive campaign demonstrated a consistency in selecting and appointing his relative as his deputies, who fought bitterly after his death for his position.

It has been commonly stated that Timur had shown interest in Sufism, an Islamic mysticism, the practice of which may elevate the spirit and soul to the highest level of existence and purity, reaching the eternal truth, downplaying the material gain. Practicing Sufism by a man who had built columns made of human skull is not reconcilable; it sounds like a dissociative identity disorder; conquering, harming, killing, are antithetic to the Sufism and the Sufi. If this assertion is based on solid evidence and if the interest of Timur in Sufism is genuine, then the character and emotional state of Timur needs more in-depth evaluation. Probably it is in our trait that in groping for justification of our actions we take time from building columns using people's skulls to meditate and disguise ourselves as Sufi

After Timur, one of his sons, Miranshah, inherited the rulership of the west including Iraq and Azerbaijan; the other son, Shah Rokh (1405-47, patron of the arts) received Khorasan in the east.

Miranshah died in 1407, then Shah Rokh, a pious Muslim with controlled temper in contrast to his father, united his brother's holdings in the west with his own territories in the east, extending and stabilizing the empire. During Timurids, Herat (now in Afghanistan), their capital was elevated to an intellectual and artistic Iranian center, particularly in miniature painting.

After Shah Rokh's death, the internal conflicts were resumed, Kara and Ak Koyunlus, also spelled Qara and Aq Qoyunlus, challenging the Timurid Abu Sa'id, who was killed in 1469, resulting in further retreat of Timurids to Khorasan. Notable and renowned Iranian poet Jami and painter Behzad were contemporaries of the last Timurid ruler, Husayn Bayqarah (1478-1506). After the Timurid dynasty, Zahir-ed-Din Babur, a Timurid started the Mughal emperors in India in 1526.

Turkmen they were Sheep dynasties, the federation of Turkmen tribes, Black Sheep, Kara Koyunlu (Ghara Ghuyunlu in Turkic Azari) and White Sheep, Ak Koyunlu (Agh Ghuyunlu in Turkic Azari). The leader of the Kara federation, Kara Yusef, seized Tabriz, helped sultan Ahmad of Jalayirid to gain the throne, but after Ahmad was killed in 1410, during a battle with him, Yusef replaced him in Baghdad. Yusef was hostile toward Shah-Rokh, and he was killed in 1420, while fighting against Shah-Rokh. His son Eskandar (1420-37) was a tyrant, the shrewd brother of Eskandar with the help of Shah-Rokh replaced him and reigned from 1437-67 and he was killed during an expedition against Uzun Hasan (for tall in Turkic Azeri), the leader of Aq Qoyunlu and within two years the Qara Dynasty was submitted to Aq Qoyunlu. The territories located in Azerbaijan and Iraq were ruled intermittently by Shia Qara Qoyunlu, from 1375 to 1468, extending to Fars and Isfahan, confronting the Timur army and competing with Aq Qoyunlu dynasty, a rival Turkmen federation.

In 1469 Uzun Hasan, captured and executed Abu-Sa'id, and established himself the ruler of the Iranian territories, and in 1470 moved to Herat. His son Yagub reigned from 1478-90, during his reign Tabriz attained the status of the center of literature and poetry.

Northern Iraq, Azerbaijan, and part of Anatolia were ruled by Aq Qoyunlu, Sunnis, from 1378 to 1503.

The last ruler of Aq Qoyunlu, Murad was defeated by Esmail of Safavids (mainly Shia) in 1503, and 1508 the dynasty ended.

CHAPTER 22

Safavid Dynasty

The Safavid Dynasty (1502-1736) a native Iranian dynasty established by Esma'il I or Esmail I (ruled 1501-1524), head of Kizilbash group of Shia sect, and a Sufi of Ardabil in Azerbaijan. By adopting Shia sect of Islam as the state religion of Iran, he created a much needed, unified and independent national and religious identity, unique to Iran. Safavid dynasty was originated from Savaviyeh or Safawiyah, a Sufi order, tariqah, which was founded by an esteemed Shaykh Safi ad-Din (1253-1334). Isma'il the founder of the dynasty was the grandson of Junayd, who married the sister of Uzun Hasan of Aq Qoyunlu. Haydar the son of Junayd married Halima, his cousin, the daughter of Uzun Hasan. Haydar was killed in 1488, fighting Yaqub, the grandson of his uncle Uzun Hasan.

Isma'il was one the sons of Haydar and in 1499 at the age of 14-15, supported by local tribes including Turkmen, went to war and defeated Aq-Qoyunlu. After besieging Tabriz from Aq Qoyulu in 1501, proclaimed himself Shah, and Shia sect the official religion of Iran, ruling the major part of Iran, including the parts with Sunni population.

Adaptation of Shia Islam as the official religion of Iran by Isma'il, combining his power as a religious leader and his power as the Shah was achieved with no major problem; but it soon became a source of conflict not only between Isma'il and Ottoman ruler Sultan Selim I at the time, but also between Safavids and Sunni Uzbeks, of Uzbekistan.

The religious assaults in both sides became brutal. Isma'il defeated Uzbeks in 1510 at Marv, made a jeweled cup out of the skull of Shaybanic or Sheibanic, the Uzbeks leader. Selim, an opium addict, defeated Ismail in 1514, calling a large number of Shia heretics, and murdered them.

The conflicts and wars in two fronts against Ottoman Turks and Uzbeks continued and resulted in a continuous defeat and weakening of Iran, becoming more pronounced during Tahmasp I (1524-76), Isma'il's son. Tahmasp, not only lost the Iranian territories to Turks, he lost interest in ruling, secluded himself, tried to get away from the problems, moved his capital to further east, to Ghazvin and eventually to Isfahan. The condition deteriorated further until the reign of Abbas I. The savior and the greatest sovereign of the Savavids.

Abbas I (1588-1629), also Abbas the Great, took the reign in 1588. In 1590 with the help of an Englishman, Sir Robert Sherley, he reformed the Iranian army substantially and upgraded it from a tribal cavalry to a standing army in the European style. During his major offensives, he defeated and expelled the Turks and Uzbeks and recaptured the lost territories, and besieged Baghdad in 1623. Now free of external threats he focused on organizing and improving the domestic issues and well being of the people, such as expanding trade, and fostering trade with Europe, upgrading roads, industry, and architect, and promoting art. Shah Abbas I built fascinatingly beautiful mosques and monuments, theological colleges, magnificent boulevards and squares. He showed particular interest in beatifying his capital, which he had transferred from Ghazvin to Esfahan or Isfahan. During his reign, not only Esfahan was internationally acknowledged in beauty and architectural grandeur and became the center of trade, diplomacy and art, but Iran also reached the status of great power, under the great Shah. Shah Abbas died in 1629, after which the Savfavid dynasty began to decline. Hossayn I or Husayn I or Shah Sultan Husayn (1694-1722) was the last independent ruler, and appeared to be ineffective and short of judgment, logic, and courage. In 1722 Mahmud of Afghanistan, a former subordinate of Safavids captured Esfahan, the Safavids capital and proclaimed himself the ruler of Iran. Shah Sultan, confronting Mahmud, abdicated and submitted to Mahmud and was murdered by him. Husayn was succeeded by his under age son Tahmasp II (1722-32), who controlled the northern provinces of Mazandaran and Gillan. After his initial support, Nader Shah, deposed him. Now two great powers were taking advantage of the downhill course of the Safavids and invading Iran, Russian Peter I, the Great from the north and Ottoman from the west, partitioning their occupied territories. It was time for Nader Qoli or Gholi Beg to interfere and take action. He deposed Abbas III (1732-1736), the symbolic little king and ended the Safavid dynasty and changed his name from Nader Qoli to Nader Shah of Iran.

CHAPTER 23

*Nader Shah (1688-1747), King (1736-47)
and Zand Dynasty*

Also spelled Nadir originated from Turkish Afshar tribe of northern
Khorasan, a tribe supportive of Safavids.

In 1726, Nader with his organized followers supported Tahmasp II, by
defeating Mahmud of Afghanistan. Mahmud, a former Safavid vassal and
from Qandahar, attacked and captured Isfahan in 1722, he had usurped
the throne from Shah Soltan or Sultan Husayn, the father of Tahmasp II
and murdered Sultan Husayn, proclaimed himself Shah of Iran, succeeded
by Ashraf, his cousin. Nader fought against Ashraf and Afghans at several
battles, Ashraf was killed in 1729, and Tahmas II became the king. Later
on Nader not satisfied with the performance of Tahmasp II and his
ineffective dealing with Turks and losing territories to them, deposed him
and appointed Tahmasp's infant son Abbas III to the throne and himself
as his Agent, only to depose him later in 1736 and proclaimed himself
Shah and formed the Afsharid dynasty. In 1722 Russians, under Peter the
Great, from the north and Ottoman Turks from the west invaded Iran
and partitioned their invaded territory in competition, and ostensibly to
protect their territories from each other. Both invaders were ousted from
Iran by Nader.

Nader Shah was successful in mounting a large and effective army, including competitive Iranian tribes with their chiefs as the commanders, such as Qajars and Bakhtyaris, and his own Afsharid tribe.

Nader shah with this newly organized army and his newly developed navy forces began his expeditions, annexed Bahrain and besieged Oman. Then he extended his foray to the Mughal Empire of India, moving as far as Delhi. He returned to Iran rich with the Peacock Throne and the Koh-e noor diamond, and Mughal's treasure, which temporarily helped the Iranian economy. After controlling the Uzbeks, his expanded empire appeared to rival the ancient Iranian empires.

Nader Shah probably believed that by extending his empire and conquesting the other nations' land he was preemptively preventing the assaults of his enemies.

Nader paid a high price for his military success; tens of thousands of people were killed during his constant military interventions and invasions, which also affected gravely the economy of the country. As he aged, his ruthlessness augmented alarmingly. In 1741 he blinded his son on suspicion of being accomplice in the attempted assassination of Nader. His ever increasing brutality toward people and torturing and executing them caused resentment and anger leading to revolts against him, resulting in his assassination by Afsharids in Khorasan in 1747, at he age of 59.

The co-existence of a troubling character disorder such as greed, cruelty and ruthlessness in an individual, who has achieved a superpower status in the military, politics, or even in religion, is not surprising and it was not unique to Nader Shah of Iran.

History is replete of such figures, prior to Nader and long after him. The question is what factors are contributing to this co-existence. "Power corrupts" is a popular saying, but it is a cliché and not an explanatory idea. It is possible that the co-existing erratic behavior causes the individuals to excel in acquiring superpower. It might be conjectured that trying to reach a glorious and powerful status by individuals might also be a disguised personality disorder and as such it is linked to other character disorders, all genetically determined and transmitted.

Misconstruing the actions of individuals causing the perishment of tens of thousands of humans in wars, as a glory worth of divine admiration is a common observation in all societies, past and present. It is also part of all cultures to call the punishment of a stealer of a loaf of bread, the administration of justice.

These are not answers; they are questions, which the intellectuals, philosophers, and deep thinkers of all times have been trying to answer. After Nader's death, his grandson, Shah Rokh or Shahrokh (1748-1796) succeeded him as the leader of the Afsharids confined to a local region in Khorasan, while in the other territories of Iran including Isfahan, Azerbaijan, and Fars local rulers and tribal chiefs such as Bakhtiyari, Qajars, Afghans, and Zands were attempting to build their own provinces. The new leadership and power passed to Zands in the central and southern Iran.

The Zand dynasty of southern Iran with Shiraz as its capital, founded by Karim Khan-e Zand (1750-79) of a small tribe. One of the generals of Nader Shah, Zand was a modest man, and a regent (Farsi, vakil) for one of the descendents of Safavid (infant Isma'il III). Karim was not Shah and did not act as such, he established a warm relationship with common people with their best interest in his heart; he avoided warfare; he restored peace and concentrated in agriculture, trade, art, and architect. He united Iran under the Zand dynasty, except Khorasan, which remained under control of Shah Rokh of the Afsharid dynasty.

After his death in 1779, discord over successions started again. Within ten years several rulers of Zand succeeded him, the last one was Loft Ali Khan, who became Shah from 1789-94 and he was defeated by Agha Mohammad Khan of the Qajar group, ending the Zand dynasty.

Chapter 24

Qajar (Ghajar) Dynasty (1779-1925)

The dynasty started with Agha Mohammad Khan, the founder of the dynasty. He was castrated in childhood, by the order of Adil Shah to unable him as a future rival. His name although was pronounced Agha, meaning Mister or Sir in Farsi, spelled differently, to portray him as a eunuch. The former chief of the Qavanlu branch of a Qajar tribe, Agha Mohammad Khan had been for many years a political hostage, by a rival chieftain in Shiraz before escaping and returning back to Qavanlus in Astarabad in 1779. Once freed Agha Mohammad began to search for Loft Ali Shah (1789-94) the last of the Zand dynasty and located him in Kerman, at southeastern Iran in 1794, and executed him. Then in 1796, he besieged Khorasan and murdered; the blind Shah Rokh of Afsharid in Khorasan, and proclaimed himself a King or rather a Shahanshah (King of Kings, 1796-97).

His legacy was cruelty, not uncommon findings among eunuchs of that era. He tortured Shah Rokh to death to find out the where abouts of the Afsharid treasure. At least he was torturing for a reason; he was not torturing because he was able to torture. He was assassinated by his own servants in 1797.

He was succeeded by Fath Ali Shah, his nephew (1797-1834). Fath Ali Shah's tenure is marked by the accelerated interaction, diplomatic and military confrontation between Iran and Europe as well as rivalry among

Europeans over the resources of Iran. He lost Georgia, Armenia, and northern Azerbaijan, during his reign, to Russia.

His grandson Mohammad Shah succeeded him and died in 1846, to be replaced by his son Nasser od-Din or Nasser ad-Din.

Nasser ad-Din (1848-1896) enjoyed the highest achievement in the Qajar dynasty. Iran began to accept and adopt western culture, including science, technology, and educational style. His chief minister, Mirza Taqi Khan (1807-1885), better known as Amir or Emir Kabir, an advanced reformer founded Dar-ol-Fonun. A reform oriented monarch, Nasser od-Din Shah established telegraph and postal services in Iran, engaged in building roads and publishing first Iranian newspaper; but he created resentment against himself by granting concession rights to foreign countries for allegedly personal gains. His fifty-year Tobacco concession was the most detrimental factor leading to the national boycott of tobacco and the withdrawal of the concession.

Nasser do-Din Shah was assassinated in Tehran in 1896 and his son a longtime crown prince, Mozaffar od-Din (1896-1907), succeeded him and ruled until 1907.

His reign witnessed a historical change in Iranian history, establishing a constitution and restructuring of monarchical power. His constitutional movement initially supported by the British, but not favored by the Russians, began in 1906 and rapidly took momentum. The Constitutionalists, the leaders of the constitution, were supported by a large number of urban and rural people. The Shah initially underestimating the revolutionary movement, reprimanded the leaders by imprisoning them, but not being able to control them, he capitulated. In 1906, he convened a National Consultative Assembly (Majles) to write a constitution, which was written in two months in line with that of Belgium, and ratified by the Shah.

He was not considered a very effective and competent ruler to be able to manage the financial crisis and imbalanced budgetary income and expenditure. He was not able to eliminate the corruption of his administration, and he continued to grant economic privileges and political concessions.

After his death of heart attack, his son Mohammad Ali Shah (1907-09) ruled for two years. He was incited by Russia to repeal the constitution. Mohammed Ali Shah tried, but he failed. But Russians in collaboration with the British were in the process of expanding and consolidating their sphere of influence. They directed Mohammed Ali Shah to attempt a second attack against the supporters of the constitution, he obliged, and he ordered the Cossack Brigade to attack the Majles while still in session, in June 1908. This event, however, made the Constitutionalists more resolved in fighting, gaining the wide support of the Islamic clergy within and outside of Iran. The armed Constitutionalist and their followers moved from Tabriz, despite of the brutal interference of the Russian army, to fight and defeat, the Cossack Brigade. Mohammed Ali Shah fled to Russia and was deposed. His son Ahmad, eleven years old, was named Shah (1909-1925) by the Constitutionalists. Within a few years Russia invaded Tabriz and Meshed and occupied Iran within their northern sphere of influence until WWI in 1914. The British having a secure position in their southern sphere of influence, looked the other way, respecting its agreement with Russia and disregarding it's commitment to Iran again. Ahmad Shah was not mature, strong and efficacious to rule. The occupation of Iran during WWI, by Russian, British, and Ottoman armies further weakened and downgraded him and Iran. After the Russian revolution and the end of WWI, the British were militarily controlling Iran, probably planning to colonize Iran by implementing an Anglo-Persian treaty prepared by Lord Curzon. In February 1921 after a coup d'etat, Reza Khan seized power. In 1925 the Iranian National Consultative Assembly (Majles) deposed Ahmad Shah, who was vacationing in Europe, and elected Reza Shah to replace him.

INTERACTION BETWEEN IRAN AND EUROPE

In the beginning of the seventeen-century, during the first two decades, shah Abbas, the Great expelled the Portuguese from the Islands of the Persian Gulf. The Portuguese had invaded the Island of Hormuz since the beginning of the sixteen-century, a few years after their navigator, Gama arrived at Calcutta.

In 1615 at the request of the English East India Company, the Great Shah authorized the Company to trade textile and silk across the Iranian border. Soon the company with the permission of the king monopolized the export of silk from Iran. Soon after the East India Company was exempt from customs at the port of Bandar Abbas.

In 1763 at the request of the British, Karim Zand allowed the British East India Company to engage in monopolizing commercial activities in the Bushehr seaport. These unusual privileges were a prelude to the British influence in the southern region of Iran, particularly after the British East India Company was placed under the control of the British government in 1784.

During Nader Shah's reign the Iranian territories had extended to Georgia in the northwest region. After Nader Georgia had signed a treaty with Russia and had severed the relationship with Iran, and since then Georgia's alliance with Iran vs. Russia had been variable and relatively uncertain. Meanwhile Russian envious of the British activities and excited by their Pavlovian reflex, entered the scene again during Fath Ali Shah's reign, and annexed Georgia. This annexation resulted in war between Iran and Russia in 1804; after a period of victory and defeat, Fath Ali shah in 1813 endorsed the Gulistan agreement ceding Georgia and other regions to Russia. In 1815, a second Russo-Persian war erupted because of a dispute over the Gulistan agreement, ending with the defeat of Iran again.

The British government and East India Company in competition with Russia and with each other continued their intrigue during Fath Ali Shah's reign; particularly they were alarmed of the possibility of Napoleon of France in collaboration with the Russians, invading India via Iran. They persuaded Fath Ali Shah to agree with treaties hindering the alliance between Iran and France. Meanwhile Fath Ali Shah continued to grant more trading privileges to the British, including tax exemption, hoping to receive British support against Russians' hostile attitude.

After repeated French overtures for alliance with Iran, in 1807, Fath Ali Shah agreed to ally with France. But a new treaty between France and Russia, resulted in the capturing of more Iranian territories by Russia. Despite a treaty in 1811, between Iran and England, promising military and financial aid to Iran, when in 1813, the Russian attacked Iran and seized a large part of the Iranian territory, no such aid was received by Iran, since the British and Russian were already in good terms. Not being able to deal with the aggressive bear in the north, Fath Ali Shah moved further toward the British fox and went thru his usual rituals, signing another treaty, but during the 1826 war with Russia, Iran was deserted again by the British and lost the war, leading to a Turkmenchai treaty and loss of more territories. During the remaining years of Fath Ali Shah and his successor Mohammad Shah, the British and Russians solidified their position in Iran, expanding western civilization in the eastern territories.

The British and Russians continued to strengthen their sphere of influence in the southern and northern region of Iran respectively during Mohammad Shah's and Nasser ad-Din Shah's reign, both of them used their influence to obtain concession, and widen their tax-exempt status, leading to an increase in the trade import with a dwarfing effect on the Iranian manufacturing products and bankruptcy, resulting in the devastation of the cities involved. The manufactures and unemployed workers moved from smaller to larger cities for jobs, causing a further deterioration of the former and overcrowding of the latter.

The exports were limited to raw material including opium, the production of which markedly increased with the unwanted consequences. Nasser ad-Din Shah's hasty efforts to remedy the problems combined with the British and Russian intrigues created more problems. He granted the monopoly and authority of carrying out the new projects such as the construction of railroads and establishment of banking system to Julius Reuter, a German born, British citizen and journalist. But Nasser ad-Din retrieved the privileges shortly after and paid a large amount in compensation to Reuter, but later on allowing Reuter to found his Imperial National Bank of Persia.

A major problem developed when Nasser ad-Din granted all rights of tobacco industry in Iran to a British company in 1890. This in addition to his previous concession led to a national protest supported by the leading clergies, merchants, and educated class of Iran, forcing Nasser to the cancellation of the grant, but paying a large sum of compensation again.

The British and Russians, two major rivals then, continued to expand their power within their sphere of influence and to interfere with the internal affairs of Iran in a stubborn and relentless manner, each using a method comparable to their national heritage. The British approach was a mixture of sophisticated dishonesty and a superficial legal justification, and ruefulness; the Russians on the other had been openly coarse, loud and crude.

Pahlavi Dynasty

The economic, social, and political disarray of Iran had become more pronounced during WWI. The time was right for a power, particularly a military one, to rescue Iran, as in the past. Reza Khan, an officer of the Iranian Cossack Brigade was such a man. A son of colonel Abbas Ali Khan was born on March 16, 1878, in Mazandaran, in northern Iran. Reza Khan combined his military experience and power with the intellectual talent of Sayyid Zia od-Din Tabatabai, after staging a coup d'etat in 1921, he was promoted to the position of war minister of Ahmad Shah, establishing a solid military base. After becoming a prime minister, in addition to military power, he also seized the political power to depose his king Ahmad Shah in 1925, ending Qajar dynasty and starting the Pahlavi dynasty, and changing Reza Khan to Reza Shah.

PART II

My Life In Iran

CHAPTER 25

Childhood

ZANJAN, MY BIRTH PLACE

I was born in the city of Zanjan, which is the capital of the present day Zanjan province. Zanjan is 204 miles to the northwest of Tehran, the capital of Iran. I am an Iranian (Persian); I speak Farsi (Persian). Iran is located SW Asia, Caspian Sea to the north and Persian Gulf to the south, Afghanistan to the east, and Iraq to the west. About 636,000 square miles, and according to the 2007 census about 70,000,000 population. Iran is a land with a glorious past of Persian empire and benevolent and ruthless dynasties, land of the greatest poets, Hafez and Saadi of Shiraz, Ferdowsi, and Rumi; the originator of the pre-Islamic prophet Zarathustra (Zoroaster in Greek) and Zoroastrian, the religion of good and evil; and adopter of the great Islam with pious ulema and Ayatollahs. The land of the high Alburz or Elborz mountain chain, reaching up to 19,000-foot snow capped Damavand, stretching from west to east across the northern border and Dasht (desert) Kavir with sweltering heat. A bountiful land blessed and cursed with abundant energy resources. The land of Persepolis (ancient capital) of Darius the Great (522-486 B.C.) burned by Alexander the Great of Macedonia, and the shrine of the 8th Shiah Imam at Meshed or Mashhad. The country of Persian, Kurds, Azeri, Baloochi, Turkmen, all Iranians. Iran the land of diversities and paradoxes. Iran the "Pillar of stability" of President Carter (Jimmy); and the "Axis of evil" of President Bush (W).

I vaguely remember the large house in Zanjan, where I was born, it had many one-level rooms. One melted memory that creeps to my mind every so often and feels like a dim flicker of light in a blackened hall. We were yelling in anger or we were screaming because of fear, but certainly there were loud noises, harsh words, running, hiding, there were stones thrown to our house from somewhere we didn't know exactly where? Was a misguided soul doing this to us in the void of the night? Or mean demon, or even a ghoul with a mood for devouring us. What happened, what action we took? I have no idea.

SHAHRAK

I woke up and opened my eyes, found my mother, surrounded by many people including my two sisters, holding my arms and keeping me under cool water in a river, which was running through about three hundred feet in front of our house. What were these people doing to me? Was I dreaming or waking up from sleep? No I was coming out of a coma. How did I lapse into a coma? I was told later on, I had carbon monoxide poisoning. I recall early on that day my mother, siblings, and I went to a public bathhouse, which was the customary bathing facilities available to us. The first day of opening of the public bathhouse was exclusively reserved for my family out of respect for my father, who was the only religious leader in the village. I recall my mother washing my hair, using her usual harsh skill, with soap and water and asking me to stand still and close my eyes to avoid the caustic soap entering my eyes, the cause of our constant fear of taking a bath. I recall this particular occasion clearly because for many years to come my comatose state was a source of combined anxiety and humor. I was trying very hard to keep my upright position in order not to fall, it seemed an invisible external force was forcing me down, then I don't recall anything, because I went into coma, caused by inhaling odorless carbon monoxide generated by the malfunctioning heating system of this exclusive public bath. My removal from the bathing area and exposing me to fresh air probably were sufficient treatment to provide me enough oxygen to replace the poisonous carboxyhemoglobin. Had I received 100% oxygen my unconsciousness would have been much shorter in duration, but of course no oxygen was available in Shahrak, those days. In the river I began to recognize people surrounding me, they were crying and laughing, crying because they thought I was going to die, laughing because I didn't die. My father, who because of his religious status usually did not display fatherly affection, I remember, was cuddling me, while I was awakening

85

from my comatose state. Fortunately I recovered from the unconscious state with no immediate or late complication, or at least I presume so.

Going to public bathhouses as an adult in addition to body cleaning purposes was a social gathering event. They usually have all facilities for a through bathing, hot and cold water, dressing rooms and bathing areas of variable sizes and cubicles, a specially built large tub, and attendants to assist the bathers.

In some of the public bathhouses, the bathing area consists of a large hall with pillars and a domed and decorated roof, containing colorful glasses. The large hot water compartment or tub, a recessed segment of the hall, similar to an average size above the ground pool, with a heating system is separated from the hall by a brick wall. The bathers wrapped in a towel, after the completion of the cleaning process, move from their cubicles and enter the alcove (tub) (Farsi: Khazineh) for one final washing up and rinsing. Large bathhouses may also have a large dressing room, carpeted and decorated attractively with cushions to lean on. The customers use these halls in addition to dressing and preparation to enter the bathing area, for chatting, or gossiping, or simply relaxation. They also may be used as conclaves of the community leaders. Some of these public bathhouses, such as Hammam-e Sultan Amir Ahmad of Kashan, Iran, are the remnants of the architectural glories of Iran in the past. Gradually modern private bathing facilities at houses and outside have replaced the public bathhouses, but they have also lost the cultural values represented by them.

GOING FROM ZANJAN TO SHAHRAK

I must have been about seven to eight years old, in the middle of second grade, elementary school, in Zanjan. It was a dark night; we were crossing a large river also in Zanjan, called Qezel (Ghezel) Ozan Roud (Rud). The water was as high as the stirrup of the saddle of the horse I was riding. Frightened of being drowned or carried down the stream, I was bending forward, holding on to the pommel of the saddle. The vague and shadowy images and voices of the members of my family are still imprinted in the reservoir of my memories. We were leaving Zanjan, the city I was born, to go to Shahrak, a village I would live for a period of 2.5 years.

Reza shah was the king at the time, he was coronated in 1925. Before that he was the commanding officer of the Cossack Brigade (a part of the military force of Iran) designed by Russians in Iran during the Qajar dynasty, preceding immediately the Pahlavi dynasty, which was founded by Reza Shah. He wanted to modernize Iran, probably imitating the regime of Attaturk of Turkey, our northwest neighbor. He was against women wearing Hejab, to cover their face from strange men, who were not the members of the immediate family. The Uniformity of Dress Law, which passed around my birth date, was not limited to women; it involved men and the clergy as well. It exempted several categories of clergy including the ulema and mojtahids or mujtahids such as my father from adapting the western style suits. Ulema is a general term, pleural of alim or alem meaning authority knowledgeable in different aspects of Islam. The Mojtahids are scholars competent in Islamic jurisprudence.

A large portion of the clergy wearing the religious outfit acting as ulema or ulama, but without the credentials required for exemption, were required to take examination to be certified as a clergy, and be exempted from the dress code. The religious outfit usually consisted of imamah (amamah), a scarf wound around the head very neatly, very similar to a turban; a long wide sleeved gown, similar to a cassock, reaching almost to the ankles, buttoned in front; aba covering the gown, a long full garment open in front. Ulema wearing black amamah were sayids or sadat (pleural of sayid), descendant of the prophet, white amamah indicated otherwise. Ulema for being sayid usually received an extra respect.

Reza Shah wanted the religious leaders to follow the rules and regulations of his secular government rather than the traditional religious authority. He wanted to separate religion from the government and minimize the influence of the religion on the public policies and daily life of the people. His intention was to secularize the social affairs, which were previously within the domain of the clergy. This attitude toward the clergy stemmed from his desire for so-called westernization and modernization of Iran and centralization of power. The relationship between the Iranian Islamic clergy and the government relative to religion, education, politics, public policies, and all aspects of the social affairs is a complicated one and it is difficult to define it in a simplistic term. Over a period of centuries the relationship between the religious and secular authorities has been defined variably, at times two parties competing for power, at other times united and cooperating to solidify the Islamic religion, periodically the clergy has submitted to the government or government catered to the clergy.

My father in Zanjan My father at the time was one of the clergy (ulema) in Zanjan. He was considered to be an Alem or Alim (religiously knowledgeable). He was one of Zanjan's Mojtahids that is an authority in the interpretation of Islamic laws. Mojtahids were required to undergo educational training relative to the Shia branch of Islam in designated and reputable centers such as Najaf in Iraq or Qom in Iran. The holy and pilgrimage city of Qom or Ghom also called or Qum is located 97 miles southwest of Tehran, and it is the largest center for Shia scholarship and the site of the holy golden-domed shrine of Fatemah Ma'sume, the sister of Imam Reza (789-816 A.D.), the eight imam of the Twelver Shia sect of Islam. My father had acquired this knowledge and title during his study in Najaf (holy city, Iraq, the site of the golden shrine of Imam Ali ibn Abu Talib, the fourth Caliph). Many Iranian Shias have lands around the holy cities of Najaf and Karbala for burial purposes after death and some own homes for pilgrimage intents. The religious laws of Islam have been derived mainly from the holy book of Islam, Qur'an or Ghor'an, and teaching and saying of the prophet (Hadith). Like most ulema my father was or he wanted to be influential in the religious affairs or societal conduct of the community. He considered the ulema as the guardians of the Islamic laws. Religious duties of ulema included providing guidance in praying, social welfare, moral leadership, and teaching. Their civic duties, performed within the religious laws (shari'ah, also shari'a) involved arbitration, protection of trust funds, overseeing the welfare of orphans and widows, promoting donations and financial contributions, certification of documents (titles of property, wills, etc.) dispensing the religious funds.

Civil laws gradually, but steadfastly, were usurping the religious laws, not only minimizing the authority of the clergy, but also depriving the clergy of a much-needed source of income. My father's departure for Shahrak coincided with almost completion of the civil takeover of the religious laws.

He had become a religious leader to be followed and listened to; he was marja-i-taqlid, also taghlid, and the source of authority for Shia Muslims. He believed that ulema must have autonomy in the religious matters and be independent of the state and government in expressing their opinion. Reza shah attempted to secularize the rules and regulations of the Islamic Shia religion, or even to create government directed religious organizations to compete with ulema directed religious groups. Reza shah wanted to change the dress code as fast as possible, unveiling the women, frequently against their wishes, he wanted to westernize the educational system, regulate or even eliminate maktab (Islamic elementary school) and madrassah (traditional Islamic theological or secular schools-seminaries) and create western oriented modern schools, elementary (dabestan) and high schools (dabirestan) and colleges and universities. He wanted to transfer the educational activities conducted by the clergy to the government. Those days in Zanjan the government interferences could not be avoided. The clergy including my father had two choices, to confront and fight the government and accept the dire consequences including jeopardizing the welfare and future of the members of the family, or to cooperate with the government against their principles and accept the risk of being identified as disloyal to the religion they were supposed to guard. Therefore my father chose another direction, he decided to leave Zanjan for Shahrak, where there was a need for a mojtahid to lead smaller or less visible religious obligations and ceremonies in a village too small and too far to be scrutinized by the government. He was exiled to Shahrak. Some members of the clergy did not reject the secularization concept and continued to participate in religious affairs in harmony with and subordination to the government, this group of ulema, administratively and financially obviously had a better and comfortable life styles. Did my father make a mistake? Who can say? We follow our inner voices, our conscience; it is a wonderful feeling to have inner peace.

My father couldn't agree with these changes based on principles as well as financial aspect of living. The religious people of the community directly supported him, by their donations according to the religious mandate of the time. He was hojjatelislam, also hojjatolislam at the time, the second highest rank in Shia Islam after ayatollah. He had studied in Najaf, Iraq, the center for Islamic education. In order to be able to make a living, therefore, he had to move to a smaller, less regulated community in need of a religious leader to guide and teach the community. Thus we were moving to Shahrak.

Shahrak was located 15 miles west to zanjan.

Our house in Shahrak. Our residence in Shahrak, was old, one of the few large houses in the village.

The building was solid with thick walls, facing the river in which I was held under water to recover from carbon monoxide poisoning. There was no gate, but a graveled parkway led to a large courtyard in front of the house, which was located far back. The profile of the house in my foggy memory resembles a medieval castle with higher walls, shouldered by two tall and domineering watchtowers or observation decks built totally of bricks. A narrow door was the only means of entrance to the shaft and narrow staircase of each tower, going up to the observation decks surmounting the towers. These decks were designed as a fortress for security purposes to safeguard the property and the residents. To watch and survey the surrounding areas for possible intruders to the village and hide and shelter the members of the family, particularly the females in case of invasion of the village by bandits.

I recall that on a few occasions my two older sisters were taken to the towers for their protection against rumored invasion of the village by hoodlum tribes.

An inner gateway led the courtyard to a large hall and the several rooms surrounding it, all with high ceilings and situated at the ground floor.

The heating system in Shahrak was similar to that of Zanjan and other houses I would live in the future in Iran. Heating was provided by space heating facilities and there were no central heating furnaces. Fireplaces for heating or cooking, using various size of logs, or charcoal and at times coal were very popular and available. Kerosene (naft) heaters of various size and configurations were being introduced and becoming a major source of heating in cities and towns, but at that time they were not available in Shahrak. Of course korsi, the most popular and convenient heating facility was available all the time and in every place. Korsi is one of the traditional Iranian furniture-heater ensembles, used during cold weather by the members of the families to keep warm. Korsi consists of three parts: a low four legged wooden table or large stool; a heater, traditionally a brazier filled with charcoal or coal, placed under the table; a blanket or quilt covering the table overhanging the sides of the table. The people sit on cushions around the korsi, covering their laps with the overhanging parts of the blanket covering the korsi. Usually there is another decorated fabric, called ru-korsi spread on the blanket to protect the covering blanket or quilt from spills of liquids and particles of food.

During my stay in Shahrak, there was no electricity, at nights the light was provided by multiple attractive and variously designed lamps equipped with wicks and filled with kerosene.

In addition to fireplaces and korsis, the farmers in Shahrak, as a village, were enjoying their tanur also called tandoor. Tandoor is a cylandrical oven about four to five feet in length, three feet in diameter, built in dugout earth, and heated with charcoal.

MY LIFE IN SHAHRAK

How did I spend my days in Shahrak for almost three years? We did not have toy, bicycles; but we had many horses. Early on we were instructed by nokars (male aids) and learned horseback riding including the proper sitting, using stirrups, holding the reins, and mounting. At times horses well fed, beautiful, acted wildly and sensing our lack of control, galloped aimlessly going nowhere and everywhere. We kept ourselves busy inside the house, spending hours in cutting and folding papers in the shape of birds, horses, jackets, and pants. We used to make paper soldiers and assigned them duties ranking from a simple private to lieutenant, captain, and to higher levels of rank. We used to plan a strategy for imaginary war between two armies made of paper soldiers. The origin of this origami in Iran was unknown, but it was the least expensive, clean, and useful for our intellectual development. Shahrak had beautiful mountains, clean and cool air, plenty sunshine, it was a pleasure to climb the mountains and look down the valley and the river. At times teasing and running after the lizards was an enjoyable pastime.

CHAPTER 26

Shia vs. Sunni Islam

My father was a Shiah or Shia Musullman also Mosalman (Farsi for Muslim).

At that time as well as now Shias constitute only 10-15% of the total Muslims worldwide, about 1.5 billion. The rest are Sunnis (originating from the Arabic world Sunnah, meaning tradition). These two sects of Islam starting soon after the death of the Prophet Muhammad differ significantly in the interpretation of Islamic theology and laws, particularly in relation to the rightful successors of the Prophet Muhammad, their qualifications, spirituality, and their relation to Prophet Muhammad.

The majority of Muslims selected Abu Bakr, the father-in-law of the Prophet Muhammad, a Muslim and a senior member of the followers of the Prophet, capable of leadership in the religious and social affairs of the Muslims, to succeed the prophet as a first caliph or Kalif (632-634 A. D. d. in Medina) of the Muslims. The selection of Abu Bakr was by consensus and by no means unanimous. Some of the followers preferred another loyal follower Ali (full name Ali ibn Abu Talib), who also was the son-in-law and cousin of the Prophet (his wife is Fatimeh or Fatimah, the daughter of Prophet Muhammad). This group, called Shiah, also Shii, Shiite or Shia (some use Shia as plural of Shii) believed in and promoted the concept that the successor of the prophet must have more qualification than simply be a competent administrator and the leader as perceived by Sunnis. He can't be just an ordinary man; he must be a holy man sharing the spirituality and divine characteristics possessed by the Prophet. So they rationalized and believed that only the family members of the Prophet, inheritors of these qualities will be able to lead and protect the followers of the Prophet and Islamic community (ummah). Initially, the consensus prevailed and Abu Bakr, was selected as the first caliph, succeeded by Umar or Omar (634-644 A.D., killed in Medina by a Zoroastrian Iranian)), the Uthman or Othman (644-656 A.D.), and Ali (656-661 A.D., transferred his capital from Medina to Kufa and died in Kufa) as the second, third, and fourth Caliphs respectively, with total term from 632 to 661. With passage of time this divisiveness and conflict, not only did not disappear, but it progressively became more pronounced and frequent and eventually was contaminated with violence and hate. As the rift between Shiah and Sunni advanced the Shiahs more forcefully advocated Ali as a rightful caliph and true successor of and anointed by the Prophet. After the death of the second and third caliphs and the change in the authority of the succeeding caliphs, the Shiah-Sunni conflict accelerated, the Shiahs denounced the first three caliphs as rightful successors, and considered only Ali a legitimate successor of the Prophet. Thus Ali (his title is Amir al-Mu'minin, meaning commander of the faithful) became the first Imam of the Shiah Muslims, the larger denomination of Islam after Sunni. Shiah Islam is divided to three branches the largest branch (85%) is the Twelver branch meaning as the name implies, the followers believe in twelve Imams. Majority of Iranians are Twelver Shiah. The second largest branch is Ismaili branch and third is Zaidi. Followers of Twelver Shiah, consider the twelve Imams spiritual and infallible successor of the prophet Muhammad, their words guide the faithful followers. Husayn was the brother of second Imam, Hassan ibn Ali. Commemoration of the martyrdom of Husayn has become a major ritual in identifying Shiah Islam. All Imams were divine scholars of their time and they represent the prophet of Islam. The twelfth and final Imam, Muhammad ibn Hassan, titled al Mahdi or Mehdi, is alive, but hidden (Ghaem, occult) until his return on the final judgment day.

The Ismaili branch of Shiahs, the second largest branch of Shiah, believe that after the sixth Imam, jafar ibn Muhammad, his eldest son, Ismail ibn Jafar, who died five years before Jafar, is the legitimate seventh Imam, in opposition to the Twelvers, who believe that Musa ibn Jafar, the younger son of the sixth Imam is the seventh Imam.

When Ismailis consider the seventh Imam the last one they are called, the Seveners and they are in minority in the Ismaili branch. The majority of Ismailis believe that after Ismail ibn Jafar the Imamate continued in the line of Fatimid caliphs, which eventually split to 2 branches, Musta'li mainly in Egypt and Nizari mainly in Iran.

The third branch of Shiah is the Zaidi branch, the followers of which accept Zayd ibn Ali, the grandson of Imam Husayn ibn Ali as the fifth Imam, in lieu of his brother, Muhammad ibn al-Bagher as accepted by the Twelvers.

To Shiah in addition to superiority in religion Ali possesses unique and superior characteristics not achievable by other human beings. He is known for heroism and chivalry, devotion to the Prophet. In numerous and various buildings and houses the framed pictures of Ali mounted on the walls portray Ali with his sword called zulfiqar or zulfighar reminding the Muslims of his courage, strength, and determination in protecting Islam and its followers.

This dual perception and interpretation of Islam by two sects started a long period of hatred resulting intermittently in violence, aggression and revenge. Umar and Uthman were murdered and Ali as a new caliph assumed leadership facing the task of restoring the peace and preventing further disharmony among the followers of Islam in general and followers of Ali in particular. The governor of Damascus, a cousin of Uthman named Muawiyah, and his followers challenged Ali and his followers engaging in an armed confrontation, leading eventually to assassination of Ali by the people angry over the chaos created by the leaders of both sects. The fight between Ali and Muawiyah was called Fitnah (indicating sedition, civil war, or revolt). These events historically are important, because they initiated the formation of the Umayyad dynasty by Muawiyah, the dynasty that stretched from 661 to 750 C. E. Muawiyah remained the governor and accepted also the function of caliph despite the lack of qualifications. Thereafter and during the Umayyad dynasty, the caliph became both administrator and religious leader, seeking the consultation and guidance of the religious leaders or ulema, when necessary.

As time went on, Sunnis identified with caliphate and considered the role and authority of the rulers to secure civil welfare and order and protect the Islamic religion rather than acting as an expert relative to God, and delving in and dissecting the meaning of the religion. Sunnis focused in organizational and authoritative aspects of the community and expansion of land and power such as confronting and defeating the Iranian and Egyptian forces. For Sunnis territorial expansion and materialistic success was indicative of the success of their religious belief.

Shiahs on the other hand identified with and sought the protection of the holy and divine Imamate and were preoccupied with spirituality and meaning and divine aspects of the religion. For Shiah the piety and the strength of faith were priorities.

In Shiah Islam, the ulema achieve a different level of education based on their cognitive capability, duration of education, and the quality of the center of study. They also reach different spirituality and knowledge of truth, independent of education. The absolute truth is endowed by God to the Imams only.

Martyrdom of Husayn or Hosein, the third Imam, son of Ali, a favorite grandson of the Prophet, at the Battle of Karbala, attests to the continuity of conflict between Shiah and Sunni sects in general and unwillingness of Shiah to recognize the legitimacy of the caliphate system of Sunnis in particular. Karbala is located 60 miles SW of Baghdad, Iraq, the Shrine of Husayn is in Karbala, which is the holiest city in Islam, after Mecca, Medina, Jerusalem, and Najaf). The martyrdom occurred in October 9 or 10, 680 C. E. corresponding to 10th of Muharram (Ashura in Arabic), 61 A. H. of Islamic calendars. The Islamic calendar is a lunar calendar and has 12 months in a year of about 354 days, about 11 days shorter than the solar calendar year. Therefore Islamic holidays shift about 11 days earlier in each successive solar year. The lunar year starts from the date the Prophet Muhammad emigrated from Mecca to Medina (Hjira) and is designated by A. H., which stands for Anno Hegirae. The current Islamic lunar year is 1431 A.H.L., corresponding to 2010.

Husayn, accompanied with the members of his family and a small number of people from a town near Najaf, Iraq, courageously and with gallantry fought against a much larger army of Yazid of Syria, the second Umayyad caliph, replacing Muawiyah. Husayn was deprived from the source of water by a general of Yazid, named Shimr, a much-detested name in the Iranian Shiahs households. After several days of intense battle, eventually, all male members of his company and his family, except his ailing infant son, parched due to desert heat, were brutally murdered and decapitated. Husayn's head accompanied by his sister Zaynab, and Ali, his son was sent to Yazid in Damascus. Zaynab played a great role in defending the infant son of Husayn as well as promoting and defending the principle of Shiism.

Husayn martyrdom against the brutality of the Umayyad caliph gives credence to Shiism as a sect, defender of the religious believes and principles against unjust authority and aggressive forces against Islam. For Shiah the dramatic experience of Karbala symbolizes the people, who in a vulnerable state and suffering, isolated and deprived of livelihood, but with strong and unyielding belief in their just cause demonstrate resistance against tyranny in the centuries past and the centuries to come.

In addition to Imamate, a major tenet of Shiah, the commemoration of the martyrdom of Imam Husayn has become a major identity feature of Shiah Islam. For centuries, the 10th day of the month of Muharram in the lunar Islamic calendar, marks the day for reenactment of the martyrdom. On this day, called Ashura, a spectacular procession is held internationally within the Shiah communities. I had witnessed several processions during my high school years, one of them occurring in the southern section of Tehran might exemplify the religious ceremonies of the commemoration. The young to middle age men marching in rows of four-five men, behind a flag carried by a young man, the line extending the length of a block, was followed by women wearing head scarves or black chador, which is a trianangular shaped cloth women wear loosely over their head and body to cover themselves totally except their face, to display modesty. The flag consisted of a sturdy metallic or wooden staff, 8-10 feet high, decorated at the distal end with colorful soft fabric, and on the very top was mounted a silvery color artificial human hand. Five fingers of the hand were representative of Imam Husayn and his immediate family, the Prophet his grandfather, Fatimeh his mother, Imam Ali his father, and Imam Hassan his brother.

Some men were wearing black unbuttoned shirts, their chest exposed, and red and inflamed. Others were wearing no shirts, their shoulders bruised and stained with blood, due to self-flagellation using chains. Yet another group of the mourners had white shirt on with blood dripping down from their scalp wounds induced skillfully by the mourners using a scimitar (Turkish sword) like instrument. The mourners were moving ahead with measured steps, chanting willfully and rhythmically coordinated with raising their hand slowly and lowering them rapidly and forcefully striking their chest with open hands.

The self-mutilation displayed in the procession, not only expresses the deep sorrows for the suffering of the family of Imam Husayn inflicted by caliph Yazid, but it also emphasizes the willingness of the mourners to experience the actual suffering and prompt the spectators in turn to share and experience also the suffering of their beloved Imam.

The processions and ritual vary in content and action based on location, size of the communities, cultural background and the directions they receive from the ulema. They may include people to represent, the martyrs, the horses, and the replica of items used for defense during the confrontation.

Did my father condone these? Of course not, he emphasized that these practices are not in concordance with the teaching of the Prophet and the Imams. However he as well as many other religious authorities looked favorably for participation of Shiahs in mosques or in special places such as Husayniyas or Hosseiniyeh (not a mosque, but a congregation hall for a special religious rituals, mainly for remembrance of Ashura) to commemorate and lament the Ashura. He believed that Imam Husayn's unwavering determination to sacrifice himself and his family voluntarily confirmed his and his followers commitment to supreme morality and truth, a glorious victory for Islam. Therefore he suggested spiritual and moral victory aspect should be commemorated along with the suffering aspect. As a matter of fact in the religious sermons led and performed in mosques by the ulema, it is a common practice to end the sermon with describing one or two events from the Karbala battle and to lament and even collectively cry and mourn Imam Husayn or his family. All year long, during Islamic holidays, Fridays eve, fortieth day after the death of Imam Husayn, in funerals, the Shiah, in small or larger number, may get together, and participate in rozehkhani, when a member of ulema, with any status, performs a ritual consisting of prayers, discussing a religious rule, quoting and reciting from the Holy Book Qur'an and eventually ending it by a speech or rozeh with lamenting and mourning the Imam. The participants collectively expressing their sadness, bending their head, placing their hand on their forehead, crying calmly, or even sobbing. Rozehkhani may be held as a common gift to express gratitude. For instance a mother prays to God, for survival of her child from an illness, and vows a Rozehkhani if her plead with her God is rewarded.

After the Islamic conquest of Iran during Umar caliphate, the great majority of Iranian adapted Sunni sect of Islam, which gradually was replaced by Shiah sect of Islam. The differences in history, nationality, language, and ethnicity, of both Iranians and Arabs are among the factors contributing to this change and preference and a further augmentation of Shiah-Sunni rivalry. Arabs were Semitic, Iranians were considered to be Ajam (non-Arab) by Arabs. Iranians spoke Farsi a derivative of Indo-European languages, Arabs spoke Arabic a derivative of Aramaic. Iranians were witnessing the downfall of their Sasanids Empire and resented the conquest of Arabs in general and the conqueror caliph Umar in particular, in contrast Arabs under the influence of Islam were gaining more momentum and dominance and building the Islamic empire. Caliph Umar was perceived by Iranians to discriminate against Iranians in general and Iranian Shiah in particular. In general Iranians preferred Shiah Imam to Sunni caliphs and considered them more just, in contrast to caliphs.

Imam Husayn's wife, Bibi Shahbanou an Iranian, was the daughter of Yazdgerd III, the last king of the Sasanid Empire.

These differences were projected to the religious beliefs and modified the understanding and interpretation of Islamic doctrine by both sects of Islam, intensifying the ideological differences between them. At the sixteen century the Savavids dynasty, Shiah became the official religion of the country. In 1501 Ismail 1, a Shiah and Sufi himself, after defeating the Mongols, established the Safavid dynasty, a blessing for Shiah. The dynasty supported and promoted the Shiah to a prominent and official state religion within the Iranian culture. A religious empire and learning center was created in Isfahan (A historical and beautiful city in central Iran). In competition with the caliphate of the Sunni Ottoman Empire, this position continued, expanded and solidified. The ulema received higher recognition in representing the Shiah Imams and specially the twelfth Imam, the Imam of ages (Imam al-zaman), until he returns on the Day of Judgment. The mutual recognition and solid coexistence continued without a significant fluctuation until the regime of Reza Shah and then Iranian intellectuals and pseudo-intellectuals introduced the idea of modernization

On their part, the caliphs of Umayyad, and Abbasids centralized in Baghdad and ruled from 750-1258, continued to denounce the Shiahs, by words accusing them of heresy and blasphemy, or by force, killing them, torturing them and burning their homes and their mosques.

CHAPTER 27

Father's Occupation In Shahrak

Like almost all Iranian ulema my father was Usuli, meaning that in Shiah Islam he had authority not only interpret the Islamic law, but also to expand it and propose new opinions (Ijtehad), he was not Akhbaris, who follow only Qur'an and Hadith (The saying of the Prophet).

After the completion of his training in Najaf he had received recognition by the senior ulema as a scholar in jurisprudence, divinity, philosophy, logic, literature, and language (Arabic, Farsi, and Azerbaijani). In Zanjan prior to transfering to Shahrak, he was leading a large and educated Shiah congregation and his opinion was solicited on major and complicated religious issues. In Shahrak he advised his followers, who mostly had little or no education, in the basic rules of daily prayers, fasting, religious taxes, inheritance, harams (forbidden) such as eating pork or drinking alcohol or usury, and donations and charities. The clergies of lower rank could perform some of these functions. He also performed marriages.

The citizen of Shahrak provided him a mosque, actually it was a spacious hall with high ceiling and pillars and wall-to-wall Persian carpeted floor. In this mosque he led daily prayers, particularly on Fridays. On most Friday nights he also delivered an Islamic religious sermon (khutbah), sitting in top seat of his minbar or manbar (platform), a high seat chair with three steps to climb up and sit.

His speech included one or more of the following, based on the qualification of the audience, the level of their understanding and their needs: Duties of Muslims, basic interpretation of Qur'an, basic explanation of Hadith, conflict between Sunnis and Shiahs, the purpose of God in creation of life, and usually a story related to leaders of Islam, and almost always ending with a sad story about Imam Husayn and his martyrdom, the latter invoking wailing and crying in the participants. He had to address the audience in a simplistic manner in order to communicate with them. Although my father never complained, I knew these obligatory functions for survival during his exile to Shahrak, must have been very painful. I also believe his capability to endure this sort of hardship at least partially was due to self-deprivation, asceticism, devotion, and martyrdom that the Shiah religion promotes. Identification of Shiahs with the poor and downtrodden significantly contributed to his tolerance of the hardship.

Probably the brightest part of his occupation in Shahrak was his teaching a few younger theology students or ulema (pleural for alim or alem, meaning knowledgeable) who had the basic education in Islam, but they wanted to further their knowledge. Because of the discrepancy in the educational background of the students he used to teach one student at a time, the dialogue at times lasted much more than scheduled one hour. The subjects of teaching were selected to meet the need of each student, and initially included the discussion on administrative and theological aspects of the Islamic clerics, progressing gradually to in-depth analysis of Qur'an and Hadith, Nahj al-Balagha (Path of Eloquence, Imam Ali's sermon and letters). The discussions were not limited to the Islamic religion and scholars alone; Christianity, Judaism, Zoroastrianism and other religions were also discussed. Philosophical topics including Socratic, Platonic, and especially Aristotelian philosophy were discussed routinely. It was not unusual to hear the name of western philosophers and literary figures. The Divine Comedy of Dante, the masterpiece of Goethe, Faust were discussed from the Islamic point of view. Henry James (1811-82) and Francois Marie Arouet (Voltaire) were among the popular philosophers for discussion.

MY EDUCATION IN SHAHRAK

In the middle of the second grade of my elementary school we moved to Shahrak, where there was no school for me to enroll and continue my education. Actually there was no plan for my education, or at least I wasn't aware of any plan. Searching hard in my melted memory, I visualize holding a book and sitting on a stool in the kitchen, my oldest sister (four-five years older than me) sitting by the stove and talking to me (teaching?) She probably was able to teach a second grader, but she did not have official training; those days there was no official training for girls, at least in Zanjan or Shahrak. My older sisters, Fakhri and Badrieh Khanum had been tutored in the privacy of their home by female teachers. How did I learn to write and to read appropriately for the second grade? I can't recall, but I must have learned enough to pass my term examination at the end of each year.

At the end of my second, third, and fourth grade school years before the summer vacations for schools I was ready to take my one-day final examination. With the help of my mother I would put my best clothes on and with the help of our senior nokar (male aid) I would get on a horse, pull my shoulders back, my chest forward, and hold the reins, accompanied and encouraged by our wise, loyal, and Kurdish nokar. He was a Kurd, dressed like a Kurd, a small turban on the head, wearing a beard, a jacket and large pants.

We used to call him Karbalai because he had made a pilgrimage to holy city of Karbala.

The pilgrims to Mecca and Mashhad are entitled Haji and Mashhadi (Mashdi) respectively.

He used to limp. There was a rumor that he was shot in the foot by another villager; he used to suffer from a chronic wound located in his heel.

We had to climb a mountain and travel mountainous roads to go to Tekab. The roads were narrow, serpentine and covered with small stones or dirt. Tekab was another village, but larger than Shahrak. At Tekab, I used to stay overnight at the home of a friend of my father's. Tekab had an elementary school, where I was allowed to take my final few hours, yearly school examination. In all three final examinations, I passed with a grade point average of ten score. The highest score one could get was twenty equivalent to 100, and below 10 average one would fail the examination. I cannot recall, the location, the setting, and the type of my examinations. How I was allowed to take the final examination just with home schooling, who made the arrangement, and was this privilege extended to everybody or was exclusively given to me because of my father religious leadership in the this large community? I was not told, or I have forgotten. I have always cherished this event in my life, because it speaks well for my sister who supervised my self-learning, my father who in his own unpretentious way made all these arrangements, and the highly organized and coordinated educational system in Iran in those days. Otherwise I would have been three-four years behind in my education or even totally lost my educational endeavor and end up illiterate. This home schooling in Shahrak with a final examination in Tekab was the foundation of my self-reliance and self-education and my success up to this moment.

NICE MEMORIES FROM SHAHRAK

For some reasons or another some moments of my life in Shahrak have remained in my memory's storage room and are easily retrievable, for instant I remember how at the end of day during summer I used to look out the window, across the river at villagers completing their work of the day. They were, using a wooden pitchfork; lifting and pitching the bales of hay to build and store a haystack for the future feed of their sheep and goats. They treated their animals like their children, tenderly with love. I also remember with much nostalgia, the cattle returning from the day of grazing, led by young Shephard and watchful dogs, sheep following goats, all like the members of a happy family, looking forward for a peaceful rest after a day of hard but pleasant work. The members of this multispecies community seemed to take their assigned duty seriously. The dogs' watchful look mirrored their concern for the safety of the herd they were watching.

GOING BACK FROM SHAHRAK TO ZANJAN

After I finished my fourth year of elementary school home schooling, I completed my fifth year in a Dabestan in Zanjan, I don't recall my returning back from Shahrak to Zanjan, I don't recall how and why and who decided to send me to Zanjan. In my foggy memory I could visualize the silhouette of a chubby and well-dressed teacher standing in a classroom with blurred and indistinct structure, addressing me that I was not suitable to be in the fifth grade class and I should be demoted to fourth grade. His opinion for some reason or another was not implemented, probably due to my father's intervention and involvement in final decision-making. I was allowed to continue and complete the fifth grade successfully. At the time I was living in my uncle's (my mother's brother) house, in Zanjan. He had several businesses of his own; I remember one of them was ice making factory, a lucrative business those days with no refrigerators available. I vaguely remember the house, but I almost clearly remember my resentment of being corrected by my cousins on many occasions. My cousins, who were older than I was probably had my best interest in their hearts, or they were resentful of me stepping in their turf. It does not matter, I remember it. It was agonizing to wait for their correction "for my own sake," they used to utter repeatedly. I can't remember the type of the corrections, but I remember the feeling after the corrections.

CHAPTER 28

Azerbaijan, Azeri vs. Turkic; Persia vs. Iran; Persian vs. Iranian-Farsi

I was exposed to the Farsi language for the first time, when I started my first year in elementary school in Zanjan. My mother tongue was Azeri, or Azari. Iranian Azeris (Azerbaijanis) are usually bilingual, speaking Farsi and Azeri; but all members of my family at that time, at home in Zanjan as well as in Shahrak spoke Azeri.

The Azeri language spoken in Azerbaijan is Southern Azeri, it is also called Arzerbaijani or Azarbaijani or Turki; it is a branch of Turkic language family, spoken by Turkic people. The Turkic language family include Turkish proper, which is spoken predominantly in Turkey, it also includes Oghuz or Oguz branch of Turkic, which shares many features with other members of Turkic language family. The present Azeri language is a derivative of Oghuz language spread to the area of the Republic of Azerbaijan and northwest region of Iran or Iranian Azerbaijan in the course of medieval expansion of Turkic people across Central Asia into the Middle East, between 6th and 11th centuries in general. This gradual Turkification continued in the future and intensified during the occupation of Azerbaijan by the Seljuq (Seljugh) or Seljuk dynasty in 11th century, and eventually by Mongols. Azeri spoken in Iranian Azerbaijan has changed over a period of time by a host of invaders and conquerors and the influence of Farsi and Arabic languages. It is written in Arabic-Iranian script.

Zanjan and Shahrak were located in the Azerbaijan province. Presently Zanjan City is the Center of Zanjan province.

Azerbaijanis are Iranians, who live in Iranian Azerbaijan, and speak Azeri. Based on historical, cultural, archeological, and genetic studies it seems reasonable to conclude that the present day Azeris probably are descendants of ancient Iranians, including Medes, a group of the original Iranians (Aryan) settled at Northwestern region of Iran with other Iranian tribes, at the area of ancient Media, roughly corresponding to the Azerbaijan of today. The word of Azerbaijan is derivative of Atropatene after Atropates, former Achaemenid governor of Media.

The Medes established a large empire between 900-700 B.C., eventually united with Achaemenid Empire around 550-500 B.C.

Iranian Aryan (Aryan is derived from Sanskrit Arya [noble], Avestan Airya, and Old Persian, Ariya) or their descendants were ancient Iranians (single ethnic or multi-ethnic and nomadic groups), indigenous or settled in Iran after migration a longtime ago, probably 3000 years. They became more dominant and identifiable during the Iranian Iron Age (c. 1300- c. 550 B.C.), particularly during Iron Age III (c.750-c. 550 B.C.) The migration, according to people, who believe in it originated from Central Asia or southern Eurasia. Their language was Aryan, closely related to Indo-European languages family (at times used as an ancestor of and at other times as a synonym to Indo-European), including Indo-Iranian language (pertinent to Iran and India, a restricted, and eastern branch of Indo-European, probably no longer in technical use) and Indo-Aryan (a subbranch of Indo-Iranian, probably no longer in technical use). By 9th century B.C., two or more ruling classes emerged from these people. The Medes starting in the east established their dynasty in the northwestern region of Iran (Azerbaijan) and later on the Persian following the same path as Medes eventually settled in the southwestern part of Iran in the proximity of Elam, moving eventually to Fars (Pars), and establishing the Achaemenid dynasty of Cyrus the Great (550-330 B.C.) the largest empire the world ever had seen. However eventually Medes and Persians reconciled their differences and united, after Cyrus the Great defeated the Medes' army. This ancient Aryan should not be confused with the distorted word of Aryan, propagated by Nazis Germany's Government, denoting racial superiority of some people, particularly the people of Nordic origin, over the people of different ethnic groups, including the people of Semitic origin.

The term of Persia usually used in West is derivative of Pars or modern Fars, a southern region of Iran, where a fraction of Aryan people settled and eventually established the Achaemenid dynasty. This local term gradually applied, chiefly by western people, to the total Iranian land and became synonyms with Iran. I prefer Iran (roughly land of Aryan) and Iranian to Persia and Persian respectively; they are simpler and more appropriate and accurate. In 1935, the Iranian Government officially adopted the name of Iran in lieu of Persia.

Generally Azeris are not of Turkic tribe origin, but are linguistically Turkic and naturally over a period of time some Azeris have blended into a multiethnic group.

The Official and educational language of Iran together with its various dialects and accent spoken by the majority of Iranian is called Farsi by Iranians in Iran, and usually is called Persian in English speaking countries.

Farsi language is the Arabic modification of Parsi. Persian or Farsi is a derivative of Indo-Iranian branch of Indo-European family of languages, which evolves to:

1. Old Persian (an old Iranian language), spoken in the Iranian plateau (ancient Iran) during early Achaemenid dynasty (about 500 years B.C.). Old Persian was written in cuneiform script.

2. Middle Persian, spoken after Achaeminid dynasty, during Sasanid era, and one of the writing systems of middle Persian is Pahlavi script. Pahlavi writing is originated from Aramaic, which was adapted by Achaeminids for a written communication within the Empire (thus usually referred to Imperial Aramaic).

   Aramaic, derived from Phoenician alphabet, has had impact on the various Iranian languages.

3. New and Modern Persian (Farsi or Persian). Since Islamic conquest of Iran, a modified Arabic script has been used in written Farsi; prior to Islam, Pahlavi and Avestan alphabets were used.

   The script utilized in witting Farsi and Azerbaijani is Arabic alphabets with addition of a few additional letters to make it suitable for Farsi language and it is written from right to left, and it was introduced to Iran after the Islamic conquest of Iran in the seventh century, In addition to changing the script, numerous Arabic words have been introduced to the Farsi language.

Generally historically conquerors behavior in Iran initially might be disruptive, but over a period of time the logic prevails and the solid and more established culture survives, usually conquerors assimilate with the Iranian culture rather than imposing their own culture.

In the seventh century Islam was introduced to Iran and Iranian accepted the religion, but promoted the Shiah fraction of Islam. Shiahs believe in one god, his last prophet Muhammad, and his son-in-law, Imam Ali, and the 11 descendents of imam Ali, the last imam, Imam Zaman has disappeared, when he returns, the earthly life will end and the divine judgment will start.

CHAPTER 29

Early Studies in Tehran

I started my sixth grade of elementary school (Farsi: Dabestan) in Tehran, capital of Iran. The name of my Dabestan was Ansari. I was enrolled in the school because it was the closest school to the house my oldest brother lived. My oldest brother had the responsibility of my supervision. He had completed an Islamic theological college, majoring in the field of Ma'gul (intellectual sciences) and Mangul (transmitted sciences). The type of the degree would be equivalent to bachelor of Art, or to be precise, a bachelor of Art, majoring in philosophy and divinity. The college was supported by the Iranian Government, therefore it was recognized by the government and its graduates could be employed by the government. However the Islamic religious hierarchy, independent of the government, I believe, was not too enthusiastic in the recognition of the college as an authentic and solid Islamic educational endeavor. Irrespective of the field of study, my brother was solidly informed in the area of Islamic jurisprudence, and philosophy, literature, and social sciences. Later on he acquired a doctorate degree in the same field and was addressed Dr. Amin Dizadji since then. He was employed in different miniseries of the Iranian government and gradually but steadily was promoted to the hierarchy positions, reaching the level of Deputy minister of Interior. He was intelligent and highly motivated, reaching such a high-level position in the government of Iran attests to his capability. In a visit to the USA, he was hospitalized at Mercy Hospital and Medical Center, for surgery, operated on by Dr. Robert Schmitz, Chairman of the Department of Surgery.

At the age of 13, I graduated from the Dabestan-e Ansari, after passing the required National Examination, which was held in the famous Polytechnic School, Dar al-Fonun or Dar ol-fonun, also Dar ul-fonun, in Tehran. Dar ol-fonun, now the Amir or Emir Kabir University, was founded by Amir Kabir (1807-1852) the Prime Minister of Nasser ad-Din or Nasser od-Din Shah of Qajar dynasty. Amir Kabir was one of the early reformists in Iran. In addition to modernizing the army and establishing weaponry, textile, paper, metal, and sugar factories and balancing the national import and export, budget, revenue, and expenditure, he founded the first official newspaper in Iran (translated Current Events from Vaqa-yi Ittifaqiyeh or Vagha-yi Ittifaghiyeh). These essential and fundamental changes jeopardized the financial interests and influence of Britain and Russia as well as illegitimate internal financial arrangements and created unstable socio-political conditions, all resulting in dismissal of Amir Kabir in 1851 and his assassination in 1952.

When I enrolled in the Ansari Dabestan, my vocabulary in Farsi language was very limited and I had an Azeri accent, because prior to that time I had only a partial exposure to a Farsi speaking environment. This deficiency did not create a major problem; I had no problem reading in Farsi, because my previous elementary school textbooks were written in Farsi, and very rapidly I acquired fluency in speaking, as usually happens with children. We really didn't need very much speaking vocabulary, because we hardly spoke. We had to sit quietly, in a crowded classroom, and listen to the teacher. Every so often, I was called to the blackboard and answered the questions of the teacher. Terrorized and fearful, I would approach the blackboard with anticipation of a negative outcome and humiliation. If my answers to the teacher questions were correct, I would be awarded and commanded by a disdain and harsh voice "sit down". If my answers to the questions were wrong, I would be awarded by "sit down" again, except this time it was preceded by a ruler sharply slapping on my back. I would like to emphasize that this experience was not a common experience. It was an isolated experience limited to that year and that class and only that teacher. Who knows what the teacher was thinking; did he believe that physical punishment was a positive reinforcement method and by using it he was trying to get the best out of his pupils? Or was he copying his own similar unfortunate experience from his childhood and projecting it to his pupils in his sixth grade class? Or was he simply enjoying his maladaptive behavior? The sad part of story is not the experience itself, it has happened in the past, in every part of the world and undoubtedly will happen again and no nation is immune to it. The problem in my situation was that we, the pupils, accepted it as a normal event and as a part of modern training and teaching system; we did not complain, there was nothing to complain about, we were going through daily routine teaching rituals. Any complaint would have been construed as apathy toward education and perhaps we would have been labeled the problem children. On Fridays Iranian Sabbath (weekend), we were off. My worst nights during the year were Friday nights, because on the following day (Saturday) I had to go to school and tolerate the emotional tortures of the day. We had a class president or supervisor of the class in the sixth grade; the Farsi name for this position was Mobser.

He was much bigger and, I believe, older than the rest of the students in the class, therefore he was assigned to the last bench in the class. Every so often while the students were settling down and waiting for the teacher to officiate the class, the Mobser would target one student for no reason at all, tip toeing from the back of the class and suddenly like a tiger jumping and slapping the occipital region of the head of the student in a violent fashion. Was this behavior predatory and genetically determined? Or was it a learned behavior from that teacher, and the Mobser was thinking that he is doing a good job and participating and promoting the educational endeavor in the modernized elementary school? A few years after graduation from the elementary school by a chance I saw him, older and tattooed on both arms, unkempt, shabby as an assistant bus driver (shaguerd-e shoffer), standing on the step of the entrance door of a public bus, opening and closing the door for the passengers and collecting the fairs. I was told by one of my old classmates that our Mobser had secured this job after living as a Tehrani "laat" (hoodlum), rough and tough and lawless, usually a male person, uneducated and of a lower socioeconomic group. laats enjoy bullying and harming the individuals younger than their own age and if necessary they use knifes or other harmful tools and objects to intimidate the others. They were quit few Laats in Tehran, particularly in the southern part, those days. The Laats use their psychopathic behavior as their skill in making a living. At times other people or even the government officials to intimidate the opposition or even the competitors conveniently use them. They may be rogue but not too smart, therefore they can be manipulated and used and often abused. The Laats may also promote themselves, and gradually by creating fear become a dominant figure in the community. Not infrequently they become alcoholic, drug abusers, diseased, dissipated and fade away.

JUNIOR HIGH OR MIDDLE SCHOOL

Dabirestan Allameh consisted of three years, from seventh to ninth grade, was a junior high school or middle school. In the seventh grade my French teacher was also my first woman teacher, she used to call me Izadi, instead Dizadji. I never corrected her because I was afraid I might offend her. Our French teacher was a beautiful, intelligent woman, sophisticated, competent, and we all admired her. Dizadji in Farsi means from Dizadj, which is a transliteration of Dizah or Disah in Azeri. Dizah was a village a few miles from Zanjan. My father Ismail or Ismael (Biblical Ishmael, son of Abraham) was born in Zanjan. My grandfather Ibrahim (Biblical Abraham, a prophet of Islam), and my great grand father was Izhagh (Biblical Isaac, son of Abraham) both were born in Dizah. Before the establishment of modern statistics and birth certificates and last names in Iran, it was a common practice to use the place of birth as the last name with addition of i at the end. Therefore Dizah will become Dizahi or Dizai and in Farsi, Dizadj becomes Dizadji. Sometimes I wonder if Dizai of Azeri is not a transliteration of Indian Desai. My father chose Dizadji for his last name, after Reza Shah made the birthday registry and the last name obligatory.

The teaching Arabic language in the junior high school was obligatory. The script of Farsi is in Arabic alphabets, in addition there are plenty of Arabic words in all forms of Farsi, the written, spoken, legal, religious forms, that makes it difficult to communicate in Farsi without using those Arabic derived words. Plus the majority of Iranian practice Shiism, a second major sect of Islam.

I mostly enjoyed my junior high school. I had assimilated Tehrani's culture and slang of the Farsi language appropriate to my age. I felt more secure because I was living with my parents, nostalgia of the past and uncertainty of the future were no longer present. The teachers were competent, dedicated and civil, the classes were enjoyable and my classmates were compatible and all seemed to be studious. But were we all civil and treated everyone with respect, all the time? Not at all, I remember at one occasion, we all seven graders erred and committed an unforgivable act. Poor boy he was sitting alone in his bench far back in the class, holding his anxious face between his hands, his elbows resting on his desk. His school uniform was new, clean and nicely pressed, we all were surrounding him and without a pause, yelling, laughing and some spitting at him, because he was a Jewish Bahai. His father had been converted from Judaism to Bahai faith. I was familiar somewhat with Judaism, but I had never heard a conversation about Bahai faith at home. We probably knew that was a religion, but we did not know how to define it and what was the difference between Islam, Judaism and Bahai. Bahaism was founded by Mirza Husayn Ali Nuri (Bahaullah, 1817-1892), born in Tehran. In 1867 he implied that he was a divine figure and manifestation of God. He claimed he was a new and latest of a series of past and future divine revelations of God including the founders of great religions, Mohammed, Jesus, Zoroaster, and Buddha, as foretold by Bab, whom Bahaullah ardently followed. Bahaullah and his followers, the Bahais believed in the unity of religions, in universal faith, all teaching the truth and the brotherhood of humanity. He was deported to Baghdad in 1852, and finally ended up in Akka in Palestine, where he died. Akka eventually became a pilgrimage center for Bahais.

Mirza Ali Mohammed of Shiraz, who declared himself Bab (Arabic, "gate) in 1844, was the promoter of Babism.

According to Babism, the twelfth Imam of Shiah sect communicated with his followers through an intermediary agent, called Bab and Mirza Ali Mohammed initially considered himself to be that intermediary. However, eventually he gave up the title of Bab and proclaimed himself the hidden Imam. According to Babism doctrine God is divine and can only be knowable through his divine manifestations, the prophets in the past and in the future with no finality. At the practical levels, the followers of Bab proposed, in general, more freedom from the religious restriction such as fair treatment of women, children, and merchants, lifting the Islamic ban on interest of money lending, and less severe judicial punishment.

After his proclamation in 1944, Bab was mostly imprisoned until his execution in Tabriz, Iran, in 1850.

Worldwide Bahais are followers of Bahaullah, only a few Babis, the followers of Bab exist today. Started and confined to Iran, the Bahai faith eventually spread to the West, particularly to the United State in the late 19th and early 20th centuries. The headquarters of the Bahai faith is located in Haifa, Israel. Babism and the Bahai faith were considered to be insurrection by the government during Ghajar dynasty and their followers are considered heretics by the Shiahs. Many Iranians believe that the British used the Bahai faith as a ploy to create divisiveness among Iranians. During the term of Mohammed Reza Shah, the Bahais played a major role in the government of Iran.

We were humiliating a Bahai child because of his father's religious belief. The punishment or reward of children because of the beliefs or status of their parents is still a common practice in modern societies, in religious, academic, labor work, and all professional environments. Nepotism toward a child may be a deal for a possible future financial reward from wealthy parents, but extrapolating the parental ideology or misfortune to children can't be rationalized. It is a predatory behavior or sin and it requires punishment.

We were collectively acting like a predator, without realizing we were performing a sinful act for no reason at all and we were enjoying it. There was no apparent reason for this aggressive behavior; our behavior was not related to a prior anger or frustration; we were not imitating a similar act committed by the adults; we were not defending our territories; we were not punishing or revenging a wrong doing. This aggression was not to fight another aggression.

It seems our mind or our soul was contaminated with a virus, a metaphysical one, without our knowledge, and this infected mind was leading us to participate in a wasteful behavior of torturing a harmless soul. Some of the victims of this ailment may recover from the infection, but the recovery is not unanimous, a small number of the afflicted persons might continue the virus in their permanently damaged central nervous system and contaminate other people in the future. We were too young and too innocent to realize that we were infected with the virus of hatred of unknown origin. This destructive disease of mind and soul called hatred, was not limited to our junior high school, it was prevalent in the other schools, in all other professions, within the labor and management, within the rich and poor. It was not limited to Iran; it had penetrated all nationalities with varying degree. It was not confined to that period of time; it continues at the present time. It is not limited to religion; the virus infects all kind of people, tall, short, big, small, white, black, and brown, all ethnicities, all nationalities. The persons infected with this non-identifiable human hate virus (NIHHV) have a great need to hate, constantly searching for a victim; without hate they can't survive. The types of the victims of the hatred vary depending on the structure and types and socioeconomic states of the society, in which the afflicted persons live. The origin of the virus and the mode of transmission have not been identified. It is possible, but not proven, that some people may be genetically more prone to acquire this virulent virus. It is also possible that NIHHV might be the product of a spontaneous mutation of some genetic structure. Prevention of this hatred virus is difficult, if not impossible, because the real cause is not known. Some factors, such as physical and emotional stress, poverty, ignorance and naiveté, imbecility, misguided religion, materialistic greed, and insecurity may predispose to this virus, therefore the elimination or minimizing of these factors may be useful in the prevention of this disease.

THE REST OF JUNIOR HIGH SCHOOL

As we continued to progress I began to develop a need to compete. I enrolled in the succor team of the school, playing soccer for the remaining years of my junior high school. It preoccupied my mind constantly. There was no organized and systematic training for students, we were learning on the job. In our school, those days, the development of cognitive skills was emphasized, the athletic activities were categorized as psychomotor skills and generally believed these activities force the students to shy away from academic studies.

I liked soccer and was progressing well in the sports as well as in the academic studies until the end of the eighth grade, when I was told by my mathematic teacher that I had failed my geometry examination and playing succor had contributed to this failure. I was very surprised and disappointed, I had thought that I did very well in the subject and I had no problem in geometry class or at the final examination of the year. I did not want to question the teacher's judgment, like all other teachers in the school, he was doing his best to educate us, plus questioning a teacher was not a customary practice those days and it was not a part of the culture, and my father wouldn't have pursued the matter either, so I did repeat my geometry during that summer vacation and my final examination score was 20, equivalent to 100. During all my education in Iran, including medical school the highest score was 20, average passing rate for all subjects collectively was 10, and scoring less than 7 in one subject was considered a failure and that subject must be reexamined after the summer vacation.

Since we never established a cause and effect relationship between my geometry failure and playing soccer, I continued playing soccer; and even on a few occasions I played volleyball, reaching a conclusion that generally those days there was not any incompatibility between sports and books. I wanted to get involved more in an extracurricular activity. A classmate of mine and I decided to publish a weekly newspaper for our junior high school. We started a poster of 1.2 meter x 1.2 meters (40 x 40 inches) in size, and titled it Aughab (Eagle) to identify our paper with fragility and strength. The paper was divided into different sections including sections in political analysis, weekly news of our school, sports, religion and scientific and liberal arts quiz. In the religious section our goal was not to promote one religion vs. the other; we wanted to encourage tolerance and respect for all religions. Let the people worship their God in line with their religious tenets, upgrade their spirituality and morality, and when facing a problem seek the guidance of their religious leader.

Those days we couldn't type, or even if we could type there was no typewriter at our disposal at the school. Therefore each section was hand-written by us on a piece of white paper legibly and pasted on the poster, which was mounted on a stand and placed in a room designated for information and exhibits of the junior high school. My classmate and I listed us as publisher, editor, and manager of the paper. We worked very hard to improve the quality, grammar, and penmanship of the articles of the paper.

Within twenty-four hours of posting of our newsletter, many students of our school approached us and submitted articles of several lines. Our teachers expressed very encouraging and positive opinion about our capability of writing a newsletter for the first time in the history of our school. What factor or factors motivated us in that age to undertake this innovative project? Imitating weekly magazines probably was one of the factors. The instinctive need for recognition, achievement, affiliation with others, and instinctive curiosity may be cited as intrinsic motivating factors. We enjoyed and got satisfaction and avoided boredom by doing something more than ordinary and routines. Also it is possible that we were simply conditioned by the externally unnoticed events and culture to do things without any specific goal or purposes, and our free will did not enter into the equation. This weekly newsletter had a short life of only 2-3 months; it was our last year of junior high. I was a valedictorian of the graduating class and was accepted in a well-recognized and prestigious senior high school (Sharaf high school) in Tehran.

A Modir (director or headmaster) was the administrator of the junior high school. He was not a clergy, but a pious man. His outfit was very similar to a clergy outfit, except he did not wear a turban or an overall. When walking on his way home, he used to carry and read or look at the Islamic holy book of Qur'an, we never knew why.

Sharaf high school was only a few blocks away from our house. Therefore I did not need a public transportation to go to school. As a matter of fact during all my schooling years from elementary to high school to University of Tehran, I walked to and back from school. Very often during lunch break, I had my lunch at home. I used to knock at the door with an identifying rhythm indicating my presence and informing and reminding my mother to prepare the lunch tray.

Our house had two sets of rooms, the set close to the street consisted of a reception room and my father's room. The set in the opposite end of the yard belonged to my mother and children, who were not married and still were living at home. All rooms had high ceiling with flat roofs. Kitchen and bathrooms were located at this area. A large yard separated these two sets. High walls around the yard secured the privacy of the house. A pool, a common finding in the Iranian houses in those days, was built in the center of the yard. The pool was called "hoze", was not built for swimming, although occasional the children used to splash in it. It was used for washing hands and faces, but it mainly was for decoration. The rest of the yard was garden, full of all kind of flowers. During summer at nights we used the flat roofs to sleep. The roofs were like beds, on which we placed our quilted mattresses, pillows and blankets. Those days, in Iran, sleeping on the roofs, in the cool nights, free of pollution and clouds, looking at the skies full of innumerable stars shinning above and spiral galaxy stretching across the heavens are truly nostalgic and unforgettable. Our house was located in a kutcheh, a narrow cul-de-sac branching off a street. The Kutcheh was named Dizadji, after my father. There were several other houses on the both sides of the kutcheh, where there were open gutters or "Joobs" through which water was running periodically, allocated to our district for household use. The water was saved in a reservoir located in the basement, used when needed through a faucet. Drinking water, like fruit, ice cream, and ice were available and sold in the kutcheh by the vendors and hawkers.

CHAPTER 30

Economic And Political Events During My Junior And Senior High Schools (1941-1947)

Beginning of my junior high school (1941) coincided with the invasion of Iran by the Allied forces, then the only country in the world to be invaded by all three Allies. Reza Shah abdicated and his son Mohammad Reza Shah, twenty-two years old, was inaugurated on September 16, 1941.

Although the war, particularly the invasion of Iran had negatively and significantly affected the living conditions of all Iranians, I was too young at the time to be concerned about the economy. As long as I was not hungry, I was safe at home and healthy, and my books were provided for me, I was content and preoccupied with my schoolwork with no significant anxiety. The degree of support and attention we received from our parents, particularly my mother was significantly influenced by our interest in our study and achievement in school. Very often, I was exempt from chores performed by the other members of the family, therefore rendering me to some extent oblivious to the daily events of life. Although my father was the source of my educational aspiration because of his scholarship in religion and philosophy, my mother was acting as a true and grand coach supervising and directing my educational endeavors, protecting me from any event, which may distract me from my daily studies.

One day for some reason or another, I was assigned to purchase our daily needed Sangak, a popular Iranian flat bread or Na'n (Na'n-e Sangak), the experience of that day made me aware of the hardship imposed upon the people, including my family due to the scarcity of food items including bread, associated with a severe inflation, after the invasion of Iran. Sangak is flat triangular bread baked usually in a large dome shaped oven made of bricks and mortar, located in a bakery store. The oven floor is filled with small stones (called sangak in Farsi). The oven and stones are heated using charcoal or wood, or perhaps gas. A round fermented dough larger than a grapefruit is gently flattened on a rectangular rack of about 24 x 24 inches with a long handle, the rack and the flattened dough is introduced to the oven through an appropriate opening and stretched smoothly on the top of the hot and glowing stones, in triangular shape, and baked to a brownish color.

There were about 100 customers in the store, not standing in line, but forming rows of circular lines around the center of the store where workers and the bakers were preparing the bread. I can't forget the anguished, frustrated faces of the customers, of different age groups, young, old, but also children of 8-10 years. There was no regulation, no first come first serve rule, no numbers to take, and only wailing screams asking for bread.

The baker, enjoying his power, randomly was selecting the customers, based on his own criteria, perhaps including prior monetary bribes. The Allies with no consideration to the Iranians' need for food, particularly bread, monopolizing the transportation system of Iran, not only were transporting the wheat product to Russia, but whatever is left, they were feeding it to the large number of the Allied troops as well as Polish refugees living in Iran. The Anglo-Soviet liberators of humanity against the Nazis, delighted by their own achievement were considering themselves the model of aspiration for the Iranian children, hungry for bread. There was another alternative for the people to get bread, if they didn't want to undergo the indignity of obtaining sangak, they could get, albeit with some difficulty, a loaf or two of bread, containing roaches and hair, stored in silos, established with assistance of the Allies.

Despite their ideological differences, Russian and British were polarizing the country and utilizing the much-needed Iranian resources by any means feasible, irrespective of the consequences affecting the welfare of the people. The longer the war lasted, the more chaotic social order, economy, security in Iran became and the central government reached a near collapsing state.

Mohammad Reza Shah had married Princess Fawzieh Bint Fuad, daughter of king Fuad of Egypt and the sister of King Farough of Egypt, in 1938. The princess was not of the Iranian ancestry and the marriage was not in line with the Iranian law. The marriage ended with divorce, which was finalized in Iran in 1948. In 1951 the Shah married Soroya Esfandiary-Bakhtiari. This marriage also ended with divorce in 1958, because Soroya could not bear children. Finally the Shah married Farah Diba from 1959-1980, who remained with him until his death, and was named Shahbanu (Empress) in 1967. The Shah was rather shy, inexperienced, not engaging. Except for a disintegrating army, the young Shah like his father did not enjoy a solid support base or a long-standing and recognized historical root; but unlike his father, he lacked self-confidence, strength, and brutality. Mohammad Reza's objective of course was his survival as the Shah of Iran after his father's abdication. Therefore, in line with his objective he cooperated with the Allies. Portraying himself as a European trained intellectual with no political ambition. He did not and could not endorse his father's dictatorial policies, denouncing them, restored the policies favorable to Majles and the religious authorities, for instance lifting the regulation on the religious practices and dress code imposed by his father.

Although a large number of conscripts and many officers in the army had deserted after the abdication of Reza Shah, the army in general remained loyal to Mohammad Reza Shah, who in return extended his support and appreciation to the army and continued to rebuild and resolidify it; after all the Pahlavi dynasty wouldn't have survived without the army.

During Reza Shah's reign the ministers, Majles, and Shah worked in unison to accommodate the wishes of his majesty; but early on Mohammad Shah's tenure, this harmony was replaced by conflict.

The deputies of Majles were divided into different groups, representing the aristocrats, landowners, tribes, religion, business, intellectuals, liberals, and civil servants; each group was led usually by a prominent political figure with an honorary title bestowed upon him. Each group was identified based on the political objective of the members, their constituencies, the level of support to the present Shah, whether they were favored or punished and persecuted by Reza Shah. The deputies were also classified based on their relationship with Allied governments, whether they were Anglophile and cooperated with British, preferred the United States, or identified with the Soviet Union. The groups usually were represented by a host of influential, financially solid, and highly recognized newspapers, particularly when their editors acted in unison.

The Majles, now, actively participated in the selection of the prime ministers and the members of the cabinets. The prime minister was supported and selected by the fractions of Majles, based on his own ideology, but also based on his willingness and capability to implement the groups' agenda as well as working with the occupying Allies. Working with Allies now has reached a new dimension because of the gradual but progressive involvement of the United States, particularly in competition and rivalry with British and Soviet Union governments. In the planning and implementation of plans such as military and economic policies, the prime ministers, at times assumed a rivalry role and confrontational position with Shah over their authorities, each seeking the support and requiring the intervention of Allies to make the final judgment. The Majles dedicated more time and effort to lessen the power of the Shah and the army, the two inseparable forces in the history of Iran. However the support of the Shah and the army by the Majles waxed and waned depending on the development of events in the country. The events creating anxiety in the Majles such as the acceleration of conflict between management and labor, workers strikes or rumors of possible concession of oil to the United State or Briton vs. the Soviet Union usually enhanced the support for Shah and the army.

The deputies representing their respective parties at times allied with the opponents or drastically changed their positions to facilitate the passage of a proposal to curtail the expansion of the army or to support a strong military.

As the Pahlavi dynasty progressed, the election process for Majles became more complex and perhaps more democratic. Varying forces became the determinant factors in the outcome of the election. These forces included the provincial governors and their ideology, their relation to the Shah, prime ministers, and the Allies; influential foreign government, mainly Soviet and British with their territory of influence of north and south of Iran respectively, and increasingly the United States; the tribal chiefs and local land owners; merchants of bazaar; intellectuals; and of course the religious leaders. The very important role of the political parties can not be overemphasized, with a wide range of ideology and objectives, with a varying degree of pro or con positions toward military, Shah, religion, and foreign government involvement in the internal affairs of Iran: conservative, believing in educational, economic, military reforms; or moderate believing in nationalism and independence of foreign influence, such as Iran party supported and led by the European educated professional;

or a leftist party wishing a rapid and dramatic change toward communism, such as the Tudeh Party with Marxist agenda or Socialist party.

Dr. Mossaddeq, who will play a great role in the future of Iran and the founder of the National Front party was supported by the Iran party and elected for fourteenth Majles in 1944. Many leaders of Iran party eventually joined the National Front.

The issues addressed by the Majles during my enrollment in Sharaf high school reflect to some extent the interactions among the deputies of Majles, the Shah, the prime ministers, and the political parties:

Military reform was a frequent topic of argument, at times using harsh and accusatory words.

The necessity and usefulness, size, cost of the army, corruption within the army in general and conscription in particular, discrimination against non-Persian speaking Iranian minority and misuse of the army in terrorizing Iranians, particularly by the Shah, civilian accountability of the army vs. accountability to the Shah were addressed frequently.

One of the important events during my last year in Sharaf High School was the appearance of two autonomous governments in Tabriz, Azerbaijan and Mahabad.

It all started earlier in Isfahan, where a conflict arouse between the owner and management and the workers. The workers, locked out from a factory by the owners, forcibly entered the factory, they sustained injuries, receiving the support of other sympathizers and the Tudeh party, and all resulted in a general strike in the city. These events incited anti-Tudeh sentiment within the tribes, landowner, newspapers, and the Majles, where some pro-Tudeh deputies realigned themselves with pro-shah groups.

The realignment and the debate, at times contradictory and shifting, among the deputies escalated, and they continued their usual attacks against their opponents, the Shah, and the prime minister. Several months later, the rivalry over the concession of Iranian oil among pro-US, pro-British, and pro-Soviet deputies supporting their respective foreign countries rendered the debates more forceful and abrasive, at times exacerbated by demonstration and protests within the country.

The dysfunctional state continued, four prime ministers were appointed and caught in the political turbulence, not being able to function, then resigned.

The last prime minister before the autonomous government was Mohsen Sadr, an octogenarian conservative hard-liner pro-British judge, who implemented his anti-liberal policies in general and anti-Tudeh policies in particular, banned liberally oriented newspapers and imprisoned some of the Tudeh party's members, all leading to more reaction from opposing deputies, including boycotting the Majles. Meanwhile, a rejected deputy of the Majles, identified as a communist, named Pishevari, formed an organization, called the Democratic Party of Azerbaijan, in Tabriz with the objectives of making Azeri the official language of Azerbaijan, using Azerbaijani tax revenue for Azerbaijan, and creation of a provincial assembly. The organization received, not surprisingly, immediate support by the Tudeh party and the Soviet Union. The Kurdish nationalists followed the leader and established the Democratic Party of Kurdistan in Mahabad with similar objectives, of course supported by the Russians.

I, like the majority of Azerbaijanis, considered myself an Iranian patriot, born in Zanjan, Azerbaijan. My ancestors have been born and died in Iran for centuries, speaking Azeri does not change my genetic, racial, emotional, physical, and cultural make up. Plus if every province followed the Pishevari concept, Iran will be disintegrated and disappear from the map. This cannot be tolerated; I was offended and developed a dislike for people like Pishevari and his supporters including Soviet Union. Several newspapers, as well as many civil leaders and many members of the Majles echoed the same sentiments. As expected this event led to the resignation and replacement of the prime minister and solidification of the army.

The Soviet Union assumed a more menacing attitude, interfered with the function of the Iranian army and political and economic affairs of Iran, and threatened the sovereignty of Iran by refusing to set up a date for their evacuation from Iran. Meanwhile the Democratic Party of Azerbaijan, shamelessly, convened a National Congress and formed the Autonomous Government of Azerbaijan, followed by the creation of the Republic of Kurdistan by the Democratic Party of Kurdistan. The arrogance of Russians in the north was of a great concern to the United States and contributed to the disharmonious relation and tension between Washington and Moscow, and prompted the United States and Britain to demand the Soviet Union to withdraw from Iranian territory immediately. In addition Britain saw an opportunity to expand its sphere of influence and particularly fearful of the new competitor, the United States, proposed a combined meeting of Americans, Soviets, and British to solve the Iranian problem.

Facing this major national problem, the deputies of the Majlas like usual and like the other human beings looked for a man with a reputation for strength to help with the crisis.

This man was available, his name was Ahmad Ghavam, who appeared or was portrayed as a strong, decisive, reassuring, and practical man. He was selected as a new prime minister. In politics he was identified and perceived as pro-soviet and anti-royalist and threatening to the Shah at the time, therefore well-qualified to negotiate with the Soviet Union. The Soviets found him able and effective, although this perception and image was not a stable one and was changing from time to time. Ghavam had a love and hate relationship with the Pahlavi dynasty. He was a landowner, a Qajar noble with a long history of service to the Qajar dynasty in a different capacity with a major input in the drafting of the 1906 Constitution. He was a French educated man, yet a Farsi language scholar who was the prime minister of Reza Shah, before he was exiled by Reza Shah. Ghavam opposed Mohammad Reza Shah, worked with him, forced out of the country by him, came back and supported the Shah again. This vacillating pattern was also demonstrated in relation to the Soviet Union and Tudeh party and the British and right-wing conservatives.

Ghavam negotiated with the Soviet Union and welcomed by Moscow, reached an initial agreement including the following: Negotiation between the Iranian government and provincial government of Azerbaijan.

Formation of Iranian-Soviet Oil Company.

Evacuation of the Russian army from Iran.

Withdrawal of the Iranian complaint filed with the United Nations, against the Soviet Union.

Then Ghavam negotiated with the Democratic Party of Azerbaijan reaching a provisional agreement on the core demands of the Party.

He continued to lean to the left steadily, he eliminated all restrictions imposed on the Tudeh party by the previous cabinet, and involved the members of the Tudeh party in the cabinet and leadership roles. To my surprise most of these actions were supported and even praised by different groups of the Majles and the Shah.

At the time I was in the last year of Sharaf High School, focusing on biology and science in preparation for the entrance examination called concour (French: competitive examination) of the University of Tehran, Medical School. The political and social aspect of life in Tehran was not among my top priorities. However I was very much interested in the developments and outcomes resulting from negotiation between Ghavam and the Soviet Union. Like the vast majority of Iranians, I felt insulted and resentful against the people who in the name of Azerbaijani were proposing to separate Azerbaijan from Iran.

Was Ghavam winner or loser in this negotiation?

Did Ghavam sincerely believe that this agreement with the Russians was in the best interest of the Iranian people? Or was he pressured and threatened by the Soviet Union for far worse outcome, such as refusal to withdraw the Russian army from Iran or reoccupying Iran, should he not have compromised? Or was he validating his authority, leadership, power, and effectiveness in solving problems? Or he wanted to ease tension between the western allies and the Soviet Union by eliminating Iran as a source of tension and the cold war. Or did he want to be nice to Russian, because he was treated nicely by them, and maintain a balance between two great powers, give a little more to the spoiled Russians in order to pacify them, otherwise they might show a temper tantrum because the British, also spoiled, have received more in the past?

Was Ghavam, thinking by solving the problem, he will achieve an objective that the great powers were having difficulty to achieve, then by helping them and making their job easier he will be one of the four pillars leadership of then-world: Roosevelt, Churchill, Stalin, and Ghavam?

Or simply he didn't know what he was doing and he didn't care? All of the above possibilities were being discussed in varying degrees and with different styles in the daily papers.

This behavioral pattern demonstrated by Ghavam was not specific for him, neither was it limited to that period in Iranian history, it is shown by all kind of politicians, all the time, and all over the world, it is a political behavior, partially based on our genetic make up and partially it is a learned behavior. The word of politic legitimizes it. The political scientists elaborate on this behavior, but do not have a remedy to prevent it. It is a syndrome, called PAC, no it is not, Political Action Committee, it stands for Political Action Confusion, it means the politicians make a deal, which leads to a variety of interpretations and create a confusional state.

It is a political game, enjoyed by the player, the winning, even if it involves some cheating, is the goal, but it is not guaranteed.

It didn't take too long, there was a strong protest by the leaders of tribes, starting with Qashqai or Ghasghai Tribe, spreading to Bakhtiyaris and other tribes and ethnic minorities, all demanding not only the same privileges as Azerbaijan, but also limiting the activities of the Tudeh party. Not to our surprise, the military leaders and the British promptly intensified their engagement in supporting the tribal insurgence openly and covertly.

Ghavam promptly sided with the tribe and army, reversed his direction, negated all previous privileges he had bestowed on the Tudeh party, shifted his alliance to the right wing, wooed the leaders of tribes, worked closely with the army, received help from a magnate in Zanjan, Zulfiqari or Zolfeghari. Then the army moved to Zanjan, the city, where I was born, then within one-two days to Tabriz, dismantling the Autonomous Government of Azerbaijan and its flimsy (Poushali in Farsi) army. No protest by the Russian. Afterward, the Shah and Ghavam, in competition with each other, claimed credit for this high achievement and triumph! The Shah flew to Tabriz and he was received with enthusiasm. According to the Shah, His Majesty initiated and planned the invasion and led the army personally assisted by his staff. In any way he certainly attributed the withdrawal of the Soviet army from Iran, and disintegration of the soviet backed puppet autonomous Azerbaijani army to his watchful leadership, the PAC syndrome proved to be contagious.

In accordance with the Allied Treaty, the western Allies, Britain and the United States had withdrawn their forces from Iran prior to March 1946, but Russians were glued to the Iranian soil. Iran had filed complaint with the United Nations. In March, 1946 the Security Councils of the United Nations reportedly addressed the Iranian government complaint, Gromyko, the Soviet delegate stated that the Soviet forces would be leaving Iran in a few weeks, if no unforeseen events does not occur, the Russian troops left Iran in May 9, 1946.

Next year, 1947, the proposal of the Soviet-Iranian oil concession introduced by Ghavam to Majles was defeated. Had Ghavam predicted or even planned this outcome, and was he really a wise and shrewd politician? Who knows? Later on the same year, after his resignation, Ghavam traveled to Europe for medical treatment, and his immediate predecessor was reelected as a prime minister. The Shah backed by the army, which he has been expanding with significant input from the United States, began to change his image of constitutional monarch and metamorphosed in a few years to independent monarch above the constitution, the beginning of his despotic monarchy.

It was February 4, 1949, during my second year in medical school, the Shah was entering, the University of Tehran, he was shot and wounded in the face, but survived. The Shah's bodyguards killed the assailant immediately, but he was identified as a photographer working for a religious newspaper, and a member of a pro-Tudeh union. This was interpreted as a conspiracy requiring an immediate decisive action by the Shah. Decisive action was a routine one: Declaration of martial law, outlawing the Tudeh party, confinement or deportation of the political and religious leaders, and suspending publications critical of the Shah or his family. The divinely protected Shah promoted himself to the status of the shadow of God on the earth. He obtained the authority to dissolve Majles, thus the total control of the government. He convened the Senate, which was provisioned in the Constitution, but not yet activated since 1906, to solidify his control of the Majles. The Senate had to approve the bills passed in the Majles. The Majles and the third reelected prime minister after the fall of Ghavam, began to implement the Shah's desires including strengthening the army, curtailing the freedom of press, honoring Reza Shah, titling him Kabir (the Great), transferring the royal estates back to the Shah.

CHAPTER 31

University of Tehran, Medical School 1947-1953

Although Mohammad Reza Shah Pahlavi consolidated his throne in 1949, his problems did not end, as a matter of fact, he began to face the major problem he had encountered to that point in his reign. The problem was Dr Mohammad Mossaddegh, a 68 year-old man in 1947, an upper class landowner, a Swiss and French trained lawyer, and founder of the National Front (N. F.) Jebhe-e Melli (J. M.) in Iran. Mossaddegh was an ardent supporter of a true constitutional government, thus considering the Shah a ceremonial head; the Shah believing in a kingdom with autocracy and glamour, shall we say, perhaps similar to Cyrus the Great of the Achaemenid Empire of Iran or at least similar to his father Reza Shah Pahlavi.

N. F. started as a committee chaired by Mossaddegh and developed into a broad coalition organization. Soon other organizations, parties, and group sharing the same major goals as the N. F. joined the National Front, even though they may have had other additional objectives not shared by the N. F.

N. F. initially composed of prominent professional individuals including lawyers, journalists, civil servants, intellectuals, and religious leaders particularly Ayatollah Kashani supporting implementation of the Islamic laws. N. F. gradually extended to the merchants of the bazaar, shopkeepers, university and seminary students, and women. The objectives of the N. F. gradually widened to include, the implementation of constitutional laws, maintaining national political and economic independence, electoral reform, freedom of press, free expression of opinion, and initiating the reforms to achieve these objectives including reforms in landownership, the army, and aristocratic privileges.

In June 1950, the Majles was addressing the proposed new version of the 1933 Agreement of the Anglo-Iranian Oil Company. The small delegation of the N. F. in comparison to pro-Shah, pro-British, and independent groups of deputies, rejected the proposal and accused the Anglo-Iranian Oil Company of violating the sovereignty of Iran and vigorously demanding the nationalization of the Iranian oil. The protest of the N. F. led to the resignation of the prime minister and formation of a new cabinet on June 26, 1950, with Razmara, a physically small army general, as the prime minister. Razmara, although a military man and supporter of the Shah at the time but not trusted by the Shah. He was a polite man, portrayed himself as an intellectual, liberal, and democratic when addressing us in my third year of medical school at the University of Tehran. He was wearing a military uniform. Razmara supported the new oil proposal vs. naturalization of oil proposed unanimously by the leaders of the N. F. Razmara was labeled a British agent by Fedaiyani Islam, a radical Islamic organization. He was assassinated by a carpenter and a member of the organization in the Central Mosque of Tehran in March 1951. He was promoted by the American Embassy in Tehran and supported by the USA as a strong military man to fight communism and support the USA interest in Iran. He was not strong, his military uniform was given him the appearance of strength and confidence; he was indecisive. It was not unusual those days in Iran, to recognize the lost souls such as Razmara hiding behind uniforms, with shining boots and glittering medals and stars, representing the Iranian army, supported by the USA. Among the other high profile American listed as the supporter of Razmara was the USA Supreme Court Justice William O. Douglas, in office from 1939-1975, nominated by President F. D. Roosevelt. Mr. Douglas was traveling in Iran at the time and was in process of writing a book about Iran. Justice Douglas was not in favor of Mossaddegh, and considered him to be a communist. These sorts of support or disapproval by the individual Americans, were not uncommon in Iran, and were influencing the policies of the USA toward Iran and at times creating a confusional state, leading official and responsible American authorities to a wrong decision. I was in my fourth year of medical school. The new prime minister replacing Razmara, out of necessity had a better cooperation with N. F. and wisely did not oppose the nationalization oil approved by the Majles and Senate, and of course by the people of Iran in March 1951. Organized protests, in the oil industry region of Iran began to demand the implementation of the nationalization law, and after the police interference resulted in casualties, the local protests changed to national demonstrations and mass meetings, a martial law was imposed, and pro-Shah group blamed the Tudeh party for causing class warfare, and uninformed, and illiterate people for the crisis. The Shah addressing the people using his divine wisdom suggested the implementation of Islamic law as the remedy for the crisis.

The Majles selected Mossaddegh as the prime minister on April 30, 1951.

The Shah had had the army and generals with guns to support him during the crises; Mossaddegh will use the people as his loyal army and was supported by ulema equipped with divinity. He began to tackle with the first item in the agenda, the nationalization of oil; the leaders of N. F. and Ayatollah Kashani supported him. Within a few months, although reluctantly, the Anglo-Iranian Oil Company ceased operation, but the British government continued to threaten Iran by its navy and filed complaint against Iran in the Security Council of the United Nation. In October 1951 Mossaddegh addressed the Security Council, and filed his own complaint against British interfering with the internal affairs of Iran. Meanwhile the Majles continued to debate other issues. Mossaddegh and his colleagues were trying to bring about electoral reform and increase the number of deputies representing the N. F. in the Majles in order to effectively confront the opposition, particularly, Anglophiles and pro-Shah deputies. Rhetoric by N. F. deputies against the influential, rich, and corrupt upper class landowners vs. the poor, hungry, honest, and exploited majority became fashionable. The opposing groups were critical of the government concentrating much more on the socio-economic aspects of Tehran, the capital, and neglecting the provinces to their detriment.

I was in my fifth year of medical school, it was July 16, 1952, when a dormant power struggle between the Shah and Mossaddegh erupted after he resigned suddenly as a prime minister, just a few days after his reelection, protesting publicly against the Shah over His Majesty's refusal to accept the request of Mossaddegh to appoint a war minister. Now there was another crisis. Who will be able to handle it at the time? Who else, other than our faithful Ghavam, ready to serve again and show his strength? Mossaddegh supported by the Tudeh Party and Ayatollah Kashani, appealed to the people. The people responded immediately; Merchants of bazaars, people from all walks of life stopped working, and participated in mass demonstrations and strikes, gaining momentum each day, the protests were spreading to the whole country, reaching the peak on July 21, 1952.

The Shah appealed to his army. The army was ready for confrontation with demonstrators in Tehran. Moving toward the Majles, the army ordered the people to disperse, they did not comply, and guns were fired and many people were dead and many more injured.

The Shah called Mossaddegh to form a new cabinet. Mossaddegh proudly declared this day in the Iranian calendar, 30th of month of Tir (Siyeh Tir) Day of Ghiyam Melli (National Uprising Day), the day when the people of Iran stood, tall and chin-up against the tyranny.

Mossaddegh encouraged by the outcome began to restrict the authorities the Shah had been claiming in the past; by May 1953, my last year in medical school the Shah had become a constitutional monarch as was envisioned by the Constitution.

Mossaddegh also planned strategies to reduce the budget, manpower, and function of the army, the Ministry of War was changed to Ministry of Defense. Per his request he was granted the power to decree laws for the implementation of social, political, judicial, and educational reforms to upgrade the quality of life, not only for the upper ruling class of Iran, but for all Iranians. In July 1953, after he confronted resistance to his demands by the conservative deputies of Majles and Senate, he called for a national referendum. He received an unprecedented vote of confidence of the Iranians, after which he was no longer a middle class supported aristocratic prime minister, he became supreme civil leader of Iran, in the eyes of the people and some fractions of the N. F., but definitely not all groups of N. F.

Mossaddegh was supported by all Iranians, even the Tudeh Party, so he had to widen his objectives to represent all, but some of his and his ministers agenda was interpreted by the traditional members of the N. F. to be: too liberal and socialistic; accommodating to and lenient toward Tudeh Party; not in line with the Islamic laws; too harsh on the merchants of bazaar, and even the army. This split gradually became more pronounced and resulted in open criticism of Mossaddegh, the opposing groups of the N. F., including Ayatollah Kashani, began to distance themselves from the Front and denounce or leave it.

The supreme leader of the people, Dr. Mossaddegh was becoming another regular prime minister now.

Then it was August 19, 1953, the army, loyal supporter of the Shah, completed its planning for a coup d'etat to eliminate Prime Minister Mossaddegh.

It started after the July 21, 1952 uprising. Certain high ranking officers of the army, not impressed and not happy at the events, formed a secret committee, chaired by a retired and pro-Shah general, named Zahedi, who had been a lieutenant in the Cossack Brigade.

The committee received cooperation from the British secret service; Kermit Roosevelt of the American CIA; heads of Imperial Guards, gendarmerie, and secret police. It also obtained the support of the tribal heads by supplying them with weapons.

The members of the committee communicated with the leading Ayatollahs of the time as well as with the opponents of Mossaddegh in the N. F.

One of the influential supporters was a thug, named Shaban Jafari, and nick named Shaban Bi-Mokh (Shaban with no brain) from the south side of Tehran.

Now the committee was ready to go, supported by: Generals, politicians, police, foreign powers, thugs, and the Shah. On August 16, 1953, Colonel Nasseri, heading the Imperial Guards, attempted to deliver a royal decree to Mossaddegh at his residence, replacing him with General Zahedi as the prime minister, but his plan was aborted by the chief of the army, whose troops arrested him. The Shah, who supposedly was vacationing at the Caspian, flew to Baghdad, Iraq and then to Rome, Italy. Demonstrations broke out in the street of Tehran; the Tudeh party was identified as the culprit and blamed for disturbances, although the demonstrators were representing all kinds of people. Mossaddegh, trying to control the chaotic situation, after consultations, including the N. F. leadership and the American ambassador directed the army to fight the demonstrators.

After Colonel Nasseri failed his mission, General Zahedi himself using the army tanks, surrounded Dr. Mossaddegh's residence and captured him on August 19, 1953.

Meanwhile, in addition to the army, Shaban led a demonstration starting from southern district of Tehran, chanting anti-Mossaddegh and pro-Shah slogans.

Ironically Shaban was a byproduct of a relatively respected and popular pre-islamic athletic institution called zurkhaneh or zourkhaneh (house of power). Zurkhaneh is a popular gymnasium found all over Iran, usually in large cities, designed to promote physical fitness and emotional strength, a chivalrous attitude, and high moral values. In addition to the professional athletes, a variety of people including highly educated and wealthy customers participate in athletic activities promoted in zurkhaneh. An essential part of the gymnasium is a hall of varying size and capacity, with a square or octagonal shaped pit, a few feet deep and in average 25-35 feet across, surrounded by chairs for the spectators.

The professional barefooted athletes (pahlavans) and amateurs of varying ages, wearing their T-shirts and leather decorated breeches walk to the pit and begin to engage in a unique and systematic Iranian national exercise (varzesh-e pahlavani or bastani). They flex and extend their extremities and trunk to the rhythm of a drum (Farsi: tonbak) played by a professional man singing and chanting poetry at the same time.

This part of exercise is followed by push-ups for a period of time. Then the trade-mark of zurkhaneh begins. The participants pick up a pair of long-neck bottle shaped wooden clubs, in average about six-seven inches in diameter at the bottom tapering gradually toward the neck, and 18-20 inches in length. They hold them by the neck; swing them around their shoulders and with varying degrees of velocity, in harmony with tempos of the drum. The ritualistic exercise usually ends after the pahlavan athletes whirl individually as the other athletes look on.

Shaban was not a representative of any zurkhaneh in general, and his actions did not reflect the opinion of the members of his zurkhaneh in the southern part of Tehran in particular.

The Shah flew back to Tehran. Mossaddegh down and the Shah up again, supported by his army.

Major General Zahedi was appointed the prime minister, and Martial law was declared.

In addition to Mossaddegh, the armed forces arrested and sentenced to imprisonment up to several years: The supporters of Mossaddegh in the N. F.; the high-ranking pro-Mossaddegh army officers; and the ministers of the Mossaddegh cabinet.

The Shah and General Zahedi, by including other generals in the cabinet were assured that the army would direct their cabinet. Furthermore the Shah needed more generals to increase his power to control his opponents. He appointed Teymour Bakhtiar, a young, ruthless, military general to head a ruthless, brutal, and torturing organization acronymed SAVAK for Sazeman-e (Organization) Ettelaat (Intelligence) Va (and) Amniyat-e (Security) Keshvar (Country). It is believed that the groundwork for this organization began after the 1953 coup d'etat, and finally completed in 1957, under close direction of the CIA of the USA, and later on Mossad of Israel. Bakhtiar was dismissed in 1961, and was assassinated in 1970, by the members of SAVAK. He was succeeded by Hassan Pakravan and later on by General Nematollah Nasseri, both executed after the 1979 revolution.

The Shah solidified his political power, by manipulating the election process to the Majles. The election of deputies to the Majles became overtly unruly, the deputies were elected fraudulently and the voters were intimated, threatened, and bribed to vote for handpicked deputies. So-called elected deputies were rich landlords supportive of the Shah.

In addition to fortifying his defense force, the Shah, made every effort to eradicate his opposing forces.

The Tudeh party with communist ideology, and representing the USSR was a priority issue for the Shah and the USA, and it became their first target. Several thousands of its members were arrested. Some of the party leaders, who did not recant or did not or could not flee, were executed, some were tortured to death, and some were sentenced to life in prison.

At the time there were several hundreds of students of Tehran University including medical school, who were sponsored by the military, wearing the military uniform. Several students of this group, who were supporting and cooperating secretly with the Tudeh party, shared a similar tragic outcome as their civilian counterparts.

Late in 1953 Mossaddegh was tried in a military court, defending himself and the National Front bravely. He criticized the Shah and the supporters of the Shah, the USA, and the Great Britain. He was ridiculed prior to and after the trial, which lasted for 40 days. He emerged from the trial as an old respected leader. He was sentenced to 3 years in jail, and under house arrest in his village named Ahmadabad, the rest of his life.

Meanwhile the leadership of the Islamic religion was divided to two groups.

One group followed Ayatollah Burujerdi, the eminent Shiah leader, residing in Ghom, who believed in independence of religion from the secular government, and assumed a neutral attitude. Not surprisingly some Iranians would have preferred more involvement of the Ayatollah and were not happy with his silence during the unjust behavior of the government.

The other groups of the religious leaders were Ayatollahs working in cooperation with and at times promoting the Shah's regime. These leaders, although they had impressive titles such as Imam Jomeh (Friday's Imam), never reached the prestigious status of Ayatollah Burujerdi. The Shah promoted the latter group, and by participating in some religious rituals and attending the religious shrines, he tried to validate his commitment to Islam.

During this period of time Ayatollah Kashani had a falling out with Mossaddegh, opposing Mosaddegh's request for unlimited power. Ayatollah Kashani was not against the present regime therefore was perceived by some as cooperating with the Shah, he gradually became less active and not visible and died in 1962.

CHAPTER 32

Fatal Power Syndrome (FPS)

FPS is a syndrome of epidemic nature, it is diagnosed in all parts of the world, in all sorts of civilizations and social structures, it is a common finding in political life, in religions, in corporations, in professional societies and organizations, in the army and civil life, and even among the gangs and hoodlums. In my observation the syndrome starts insidiously, the affected individual gets the authority to manage or perform a task or administer the law. The power may be received through inheritance, or vested by other authorities, or it may be acquired by force, or it may be given by people who are desperately searching for a leader to help them deal with all kinds of disorderly life. Irrespective of the source, in some individuals with genetic predisposition, this power produces a pleasant feeling in the affected individual, the more the power is used, the more the degree of pleasure, until the pleasure is peaked. At that point the affected individuals seek more power, and unaware of, they try to assert their power in matters outside of their jurisdiction and turf, finding a new source of pleasure and encouraged, they widen the field of their influence, and gradually they develop a sate of euphoric somnolence, which could be maintained only by exerting more power. Now the addiction phase of the syndrome has started. This phase is followed by the manifestation of tolerance to power. The affected individual needs more power to develop a similar degree of pleasure. The people against whom the power is directed start to protest, not noticeable to the affected person, who now believes the power is a divine property of his/her, and depending on the status, the affected person begins to obtain and use a variety of effective means and tools to impose the power and even to protect himself or herself. The tool may be a knife for a gangster, or a gun, or jail, the police, or the military or the whole nation. The more and larger the utilized tools the more elated the ill person will become, eventually reaching a delusional and stuporous state and complete insensitivity, feeling no pain, the affected individuals began to induce pain on the powerless, torturing, poisoning them, and at times even being admired by some. The admirer may be stupid or highly intelligent. Some of the admirers of the individuals with FPS might have an SSS (smart-stupid-syndrome), with a high IQ using the standard tests, but juvenile in the practical aspects of life. We should not forget that all individuals irrespective of the level of intelligence are prone to suffer from FPS. The affected individual if not treated or not treatable eventually go to a comatose state and die, believing they are ready to go to heaven. Of course not all of the affected persons will share this final demise. Some of them helped by family and friends are saved before reaching the comatose state, but nevertheless they are suffering from an incurable disease and they must be followed very carefully and they should be under observation and scrutiny. It should be emphasized that some of the affected individuals are more realistic and they might know that they are not going to heaven after death and hell is waiting for them.

CHAPTER 33

Tudeh Party of Iran (Hezb-e Tudeh-e Iran) and Sharaf High School

In 1937, fifty-three men in Tehran were accused of and arrested for propagating Marxism and communism ideology in Iran. After trial they were imprisoned. After the invasion of Iran by the Allied forces and abdication of Reza Shah, some of the communist prisoners were released and became the core of the leftist ideology movement. They called a meeting in Tehran and founded the Tudeh party of Iran, chaired by Sulayman Iskandari, on September 29, 1941

Later on the rest of the 53 also were released and joined the party. The original members of 53 included a physician, teachers, students, mechanics, civil servants, lawyers, cobblers, a tailor, and an illiterate peasant, many of the members had European or University of Tehran education and the majority were from middle class families, but a few had nobility backgrounds.

The party gradually took an official format, solidified the organization, formed a provisional Central Committee, published the objectives of the party, and established new branches in the numerous cities in the country. Two newspapers, Mardom (People) and Rahbar (Leader) in Tehran and additional papers in major cities promoted the Tudeh's ideology and informed the readers of current events.

Not everyone joining the party, believed in the ideology of the party, many joined the party, because it became a fashionable trend; to be recognized as an intellectual it was necessary to be conversant about Marxism, Leninism vs. imperialism and colonialism.

On the other hand many members of the Tudeh party, were sincere and dedicated and believed in the ideology of the party like a divine mandate refusing to listen to any other concept for social reform and progress. Several of my classmates in medical school were members or sympathizers of the party. They considered the leadership of the Soviet Union highly dedicated to the ideology, and a divine implementer of Marxism-Leninism, which according to them was infallible and true savior of humanity in general, and the poor and working class, under the tyranny of imperialism, in particular.

The objectives of the party included the strategies to make the membership all-inclusive, and established the programs specific to the needs of various groups of the membership, workers, peasants, women, middle class, and landowners.

In the political arena, the party proposed democratic objectives such as maintaining the constitutional laws, human rights, fighting against imperialism, fascism, and colonialism. The objectives also included reforms appropriate to the socio-economic-religious status and needs of the Iranian people. Revolutionary radicalism was not among the objectives of the Tudeh party at the time.

In 1944, Tudeh convened the first Party Congress in Tehran representing more than 25,000 members. The Congress after receiving the feedbacks from the delegates and identifying the deficiencies, elected a new Central Committee, made organizational changes and approved a modified program to change the class structure of the Iranian society, the structure which was causing despotism and dictatorship; now the party was moving a little bit toward socialism. Following the first Congress and during the next two years Tudeh expanded the provincial branches and formed trade unions, particularly in the south at the area of the oil industry, published more newspapers and recruited more readers, the circulation of Rahbar the central organ reached 120,000. The number of demonstrations, rallies, and strikes increased, with the number of participants at times reaching up to 60,000 to 100,000.

Tudeh had become a large, well organized, and influential party of Iran, eventually sending ministers to the cabinet of Ghavam. This achievement attracted the attention of the people not believing and opposing the ideology of the Tudeh party and it became a matter of serious concern for the government and the Shah, and caused anxiety in the administration of the oil industry against which the Tudeh had organized the labor strikes. These forces worked in unison to form a potential adversary against the Tudeh. For the next several years until 1953, Tudeh will demonstrate a passive aggressive behavior depending on the external circumstances and forces of government, including the attitudes of the prime ministers toward the Tudeh Party or the relationship between the Soviet Union and Iran. When under scrutiny and attacks by the opposition Tudeh adopted a soul-searching attitude, tried to undo the past mistakes. The leaders of the party blamed each other for being too conservative bourgeois, or intellectual reformists, and less revolutionary and militant and not enough proletarian; or too Marxist, labor and mass oriented and revolutionary militants; supporting too much or not supporting the bourgeois government of Mossaddegh, which has shown a vacillating attitude toward the Tudeh Party. The most recent leaders criticized the former leaders, made organizational changes, eliminated the Central Committee, reinstalled the Central Committee, modified the objective of the party and the mode of operation from transparency and overt to clandestine and covert ones, created affiliated Societies and Unions with objectives similar to those of Tudeh. When the party was almost burned to ashes, the external conditions changed, and the party arose from the ashes and gained more than 25,000 members and a few hundred-thousand sympathizers, engages in political activities, organizing mass demonstrations 100,000 people, holding mass meetings protesting the government including the government of Mossaddegh, calling him a feudal landlord and an American stooge, and organizing strikes until the next bout of depression and underground operations and punishment and execution by the Shah.

CHAPTER 34

History of Iranian Oil

It started in 1901, when Mozaffar ed-Din or Mozaffar od-Din, a Qajar or Ghajar dynasty Shah, granted the Iranian oil, mainly a lightening and heating commodity at the time, concession to William Knox D'Arcy, a rich Englishman. The oil was discovered in Masjed Soleiman, in Khuzestan Province of southwest Iran. D'Arcy obtained an exclusive concession to explore up to 500,000 square miles of Iran for oil for a sixty- year period, and to give Iranians only 16% of the revenue. After several years of work and expenditure and help from Burmah Oil Company, eventually in 1908, sufficient oil was obtained, and the company was officially called Anglo-Persian Oil Company (APOC). A first lord of Admiralty in London, called Winston Churchill was an advocate of changing coal to oil as a source of energy supply for the British navy. He, therefore enthusiastically recommended APOC, as the provider of oil, to the House of Commons of England. The APOC needed money to function and establish a refinery in Abadan, Iran. The House approved that APOC provide the needed oil to the Admiralty, which was controlling the largest fleet in the world at the time, and the British government purchased 51% of shares of APOC. Therefore in 1912, Iranian-D'Arcy private company changed to a British-Iranian government entity without notifying Iran. During WW1, high demand for oil needed for air, land, and water combats, upgraded the oil from a minor heating commodity to a diamond level commodity in Iran. During the same period of time in the USA, the demand for oil for military and civil purposes much exceeded the supply, increasing the value of Iranian oil to even more than diamond.

After WW1 as years went by, Reza Shah ascended to his dictatorial power; in 1927, after Sir John Cadman (a professor of mining and petroleum technology at Birmingham University) assumed the chairmanship of APOC, disputes between the APOC and the Iranian government represented by Teymoortash, the Minister of Court of Reza Shah, became more intense. Not only the Iranian government was unhappy with the original agreement, which was dreadfully unfair, but also Iranian revenue continued to decline, despite an increase in the income of the Company. The amount of taxes paid to the British government much exceeded the revenue Iran received.

The operation of APOC was not only considered to be an unfair business arrangement, but also symbolized the colonialistic and imperialistic attitude of the UK and perceived as such by the Iranian nationalists.

In 1932, Reza Shah, apparently unhappy with the progress of negotiation, fired Teymourtash and ordered the cancellation of the concession. However the British rejected Reza Shah's order. But Sir Cadman sensing the political tension promptly visited Tehran and had meetings with Reza Shah, and using his experience gained from unsuccessful previous negotiations, proposed a new agreement. Reza Shah amazingly acquiesced to this new agreement, which was ratified by the Majles in May 28, 1933. The new agreement extended the concession up to 1993, augmenting also the Iranian revenue of the oil with minimum $750,000/year and decreasing the area of control to 100,000 square miles. The title of the Company changed to Anglo-Iranian Oil Company (AIOC) effective, 1935. The new agreement appeared to be slightly better, but it did not eradicate the unfairness and inequality of the previous agreement. The resentments of Iranians against arrogance and self-proclaimed superior attitude of the British continued forward in an accelerated fashion, making the transitory nature of the new agreement easily predictable.

The new development in the oil industry mandated the consideration of nationalization of Iranian oil. The oil producing countries around the world such as Venezuela and Saudi Arabia, were setting higher prices for their oil, the price approaching fifty percentage of the profit. These external events and the failure of the British to cease over-estimating their technological value in the Iranian oil industry, as well as the Iranian resentments of the British, perceiving them as shrewd manipulators and foxy politicians were leading to a decisive action. Therefore it was no surprise that on November 25, 1950, the members of the oil committee of the Iranian Majles, chaired by Mohammad Mossaddegh, rejected the most recent agreement (Supplemental Agreement of 1949), proposed by the British. The action of the committee and the continuation of the national demand for the nationalization prompted the AIOC to relent to a higher profit sharing agreement, but the committee did not compromise and voted for the nationalization of Iranian oil unanimously in early march 1951. Mossaddegh condemned the 1933 concession as, not only unfair and unjust, but also a bit fraudulent and imposed upon Iran under dictatorship. The supplemental Agreement did not fare better, if approved it would have led to subservience of Iran until its expiration in 1993. Mossaddegh's ideology, goal, objectives, and his methodology were transparent and sincere, not tainted with political games and manipulations. His approach to achieve his goals has attracted much criticism by main stream and conventional politicians, calling his approach emotional and short lived; on the other hand many experienced Iranian nationalists believed that Mossaddegh's activities had everlasting favorable effects in the direction of Iranian history and maintaining the sovereignty of the country. They believed a secretive political game and maneuvering played by some Iranian politicians may lead to a short-term gain for the country, but with a non-sustainable long-term results and disastrous consequences. They also believed the adherence to transparency and the highest standard of diplomatic conduct, although, at times, may delay the achievement of the goal, but it most likely results in a permanent beneficial outcome for the welfare of the nation.

There were also voices against the nationalization emanating mainly from pro-British sectors, although a few experts in the oil industry genuinely believed that the nationalization might result in a sharp decline in income from Iranian oil leading to the worsening of the already economic turmoil. The royalists considered the nationalization a victory for Mossaddegh consolidating his position against the Shah. Public enthusiasm and support for nationalization were so forceful and overwhelming that all objections, even if legitimate were not noticed by the vast majority.

On March 15, 1951 the bill for nationalization of oil passed by the Majles, despite the opposition of the Prime Minister Razmara, who had been assassinated a few days prior to the nationalization, and had supported the Supplemental Agreement of 1949. On April 30, 1951, Mossaddegh was elected as prime minister by the Majles, without any input from the Shah and replaced Hossein or Husayn Ala, who had become prime minister after the assassination of Razmara.

The nationalization, albeit for a short time, led to the unification of groups with diverse interest: The Tudeh Party, the coalition of National Front, the various tribes, and the religious sector headed by Ayatollah Kashani, all devotedly supporting Mossaddegh, giving him an extraordinary power. After nationalization Mossaddegh wanted to discuss and finalize the legal issues including the compensation directly with the AIOC and he did not see any need for British government interference. He wanted the documents and books related to the Iranian oil in the possession of AIOC be transferred to the newly formed National Iranian Oil Company (NIOC), but AIOC refused to comply. In early June 1951, the Board of Directors of NIOC moved to the central office of AIOC, cheers and jubilation and joy filled the air and the view of the Iranian flag signified the victory of Iran in regaining the sovereignty. The British government representatives, refused any cooperation, considered the nationalization illegal and unethical and mere stupidity. They were in favor of the British government intervention, including a military one.

The AIOC leaders began to sabotage the international market against the Iranian oil export, the tankers, including those of the United States refused to fill and carry the oil resulting in a drastic decline in the oil export and income. The British also sore at the gluteal muscles region, slapped by the Iranians, in the summer of 1951 took the nationality issue to the World Court in the Hague. Meanwhile the US secretary of state at the time, Dean Acheson, sent Averell Harriman to Iran in mid-July, 1951. Harriman failed to achieve a peace between the British and Iranians. The economy continued to deteriorate, inflation became rampant, the government income was failing to meet expenses, and the poverty was visible in the daily life of people. While some political leaders were debating the wisdom of nationalization, the vast majority of students of Tehran University had no ambivalent feeling. They did not want to be subservient to the British knighted politicians, who had been enjoying the colonialism and had felt no shame in robbing the lifeblood of the other nations including the Iranians. The students preferred the hardship and sacrifice to humiliation and they had the full support of their families. The resentment against the United States working in conjunction with the British was mounting. The American attitude toward Iran at the time was shaped upon the fear of Mossaddegh and the extension of communism as well as on the materialistic gains.

The British government did not stand still. In addition to the World Court, it filed a complaint with the United Nations Security Council against Iran and continued to interfere with Iranian internal affairs, such as the right for nationalization. The British also tried clandestinely to replace Mossaddegh. The popular prime minister in turn deemed it advisable to order the evacuation of the British nationals from Iran, no later than October 4, 1951 and planned to fly to New York, and address the Security Council. The Mossaddegh address to the Security Council on October 16, 1951, was eloquent, both diplomatically and legally professional, effective and triumphant. No action was taken in favor of Great Britain or against Iran, and suggestion was made to await the final recommendation of the World Court. On July 22, 1952, the World Court passed judgment favorable to Iran, agreeing with Mossaddegh, that AIOC had a contract with the Iranian government and the nationalization of oil was within the authority of the government. The Court recommended the payment of an appropriate compensation, which Mossaddegh had also agreed to pay. After addressing the Security Council, before returning to Iran, Mossaddegh met with President Truman in Washington DC, both warned each other of the peril of communism, should the alarmingly weak economic condition of Iran continue.

By this time because of an increase in the international production of oil, and because of an organized and systematic collaboration of the western oil companies in the distribution of the available oil, the need for the Iranian oil markedly declined, resulting in very insignificant revenue from the Iranian oil.

Despite of World Court confirmation of Mossaddegh's stand on the Iranian oil nationalization, the British government refused to meet with Mossaddegh in order to finalize a proper settlement. It continued to encourage the multinational imposition of embargo on Iranian oil and discourage the western countries of providing technical assistance to NIOC. It also refused to pay the royalties it owed to Iran. The British authorities were preoccupied with the their goal of ousting Mossaddegh and replacing him with a more flexible and cooperative prime minister, and they used all their manipulative skills to persuade the united States to agree with a military plan to oust Mossaddegh. In October 22, 1952, Mossaddegh terminated these deteriorating relations with the United Kingdom.

The loss of income contributed to and aggravated the preexisting conflict between the Shah and Mosaddegh and the subsequent fall and rise of both. In early 1953 political and economic downturn moved from bad to worse, when Ayatollah Kashani, the prominent religious leader and Dr, Mozaffar Bagha-i, an influential member of the N. F. coalition, decided not to support Mossaddigh. In May 1953, Mossaddegh sought, unsuccessfully, economic aid from President Eisenhower, who was elected to the office, in January 1953.

In August 1953, Britain, and American jointly overthrew Mosaddegh and reinstated the Shah. General Fazlollah Zahedi became the prime minister, and almost immediately obtained financial aid from President Eisenhower. Loy Henderson was American ambassador in Iran.

CHAPTER 35

Constitutional Revolution and Reza Shah

Political, social, and economical chaos in the country and corruption and financial disarray within the government of the Qajar or Ghajar Dynasty with weak, indecisive, and hopeless leadership, concessions to foreign powers, mainly Russia and England, causing an erosion in the sovereignty of Iran led to 1906 Constitutional Revolution, a major event, ending the Ghajar dynasty, which had been ruling Iran since 1781. The revolution heralded a new era and system, the constitutional monarchy, when the monarch is accountable to the people for the first time in the Iranian history.

Forces of the Islamic clergy of all ranks, merchants of bazaar, intellectuals, civil servants, conservatives, liberals, and students in Tehran as well as in the provinces joined together to reform the unworkable and deteriorating system. They protested, preached, published, closed the shops, and went on strike until the royal court and their supporters capitulated without significant bloodshed. In August 1906 the establishment of the constitution was signed by Muzaffar od-Din Shah. The first National Assembly of 156 elected members, or Majles-Shora-ye-Melli or National Consultative Assembly, or simply Majles opened in October 1906 and the constitution was declared. However the united forces of the reformists fizzled; the intellectuals tried to pursue their goal of secularization and minimizing the supervisory role of the ulema. For instance the enlightened thinkers (translated from the commonly used term in Iran, Roshenfekr), particularly the European educated and reform oriented individuals, began to criticize the clergy and merchants for their inclusion of a Supreme Committee to monitor the Islamic legitimacy of laws introduced to the National Assembly (without the support of ulema and bazaar probably the revolutionary efforts would have failed). Some members of the clergy began to support the royalists. The new king, Mohammed Ali shah was reluctant to endorse the documents of the Constitution and did not acknowledge and accept the signed organizational changes. The conflict escalated, eventually leading to Civil War, arm conflict and forcing the Shah to abdicate and take sanctuary in the Russian legation, and his twelve-year old son, Ahmad, assumed the kingship under the supervision of a royal regent, and the Second National assembly was called.

The second National Assembly assertively started to organize the leadership, remedy the financial disarray and reestablish the lost order and security. Good hearted and trusting Iranians assumed that finally they had reached their goal of individual rights and freedoms and collective peace and prosperity. However their hope and expectations were not long lasting, soon preexisting conflict and disorganization recurred. Disharmony and division among the members of the Assembly began after the formation of two parties. The Democratic Party with socialist-leftist ideology and the moderate party with a conservative, aristocratic, and middle-class supported agenda. Division was not confined only to rhetoric; it exploded in armed violence, assassination, murder of the opposing members and eventual confrontation among the members of the same party. Provincial tribes engaged in upheaval against the central government, and engaged in rivalry and warfare against each other. Salivating Russian in the north and British in the South began to interfere with the internal affairs of Iran, proposed and enforced with ultimatums and threats, a variety of unilateral exploitational agreements, and eventually moved to Iranian territories in order to share a piece of the pie. After the Russian Revolution of 1917, the regional autonomous governments, propagating Bolshevism and communism in the provinces of Azerbaijan and Gillan, backed by the Russian revolutionary government, were established. All these events weakened the central government and created a hopeless state again. The people of Iran now were ready for another dictatorship.

How did Reza Khan become Reza Shah Pahlavi?
Here comes Reza Khan

The word khan was introduced to Iran by Mongols, presently has several meaning including leader, ruler, and commander; in some localities in Iran, it is also used as synonyms with mister, addressing a boy or a teenager politely and trying to avoid mister, which sounds too formal. Son of a soldier father, born in the county of Savad Kooh, in the Mazandaran province, on March 15, 1878, died in Johannesesburg, South Africa, on July 26, 1944, and invaded Tehran in February 1921.

He joined the Iranian Cossack Brigade at the age of fifteen, as a stable boy. He had a domineering physical appearance, a tall and burly man, 6 feet and 4 inches, demonstrating an assertive and ambitious attitude. He enjoyed partaking in controlling and suppressing local skirmishes and tribal rebellions, and participation in patrolling the roads for safety purposes. These characteristics and occupations expedited his prompt promotion in rank to colonel, and then to a general and eventually to the Brigadier General of the Russian trained Iranian Cossack Brigade, an elite military unit in the Iranian armed forces, formed by Nasir od-Din Shah Ghajar in 1882. His rudimentary, if any, education was reflected in his casual conversation, mixed with profanity learned from his military mates. Reza Khan married four times and had eleven children, the second wife, named Taj ol-Molouk gave birth to four children, including twins, a boy to become Mohammad Reza Shah, and a girl to become the Princess Ashraf, playing a great role in the policies of her brother. Reza Khan used to wear a plain khaki military uniform, usually with no ornaments or medals, buttoned up to the neck. His military hat was a round hat with a projecting front brim with a heightened crown.

In February 1921 Reza shah moved to Tehran, with his Cossack Brigade of several thousands from the city of Ghazvin, about 93 miles west of Tehran. In this mission Reza Khan, was supported and aided by the British authorities, who were wishing to prevent the advancement of Bolsheviks to Iran and were concerned about losing the control of Iranian oil. Iranian Gendarmerie (a military-police non-urban civilian law enforcement unit) collaborated with Reza Khan, who also received assistance from a young pro-British journalist and reformist named Sayyed or Seyyid Zia or Ziya Tabatabai or Tabatabaee. Reza Khan with the blessing of Ahmad Shah, the last king of the Qajar dynasty, and after a successful coup d'etat, proclaimed a new government in Tehran. He designated himself as the Commander of the Army, Sardar Sepah, soon to become the Minister of War and then the Prime Minister, with the goal of alleviating all existing Iranian maladies. Using the method learned during his military career, he began to rule the country, as a military establishment with discipline and authority, fighting the enemy at all cost, not the enemy of Iran, but the opposing forces to his authority. He was the general and the Iranians were the army. He considered the Iranians the soldiers, undisciplined, poor, illiterate, with not enough food and water, clothes, or shelter. His obsession was to unify the soldiers, give them uniforms, and provide them with barracks, never mind the history, culture, religion, pride, or freedom. He succeeded for a short term but failed in the long run.

Reza Khan steadily solidified his position and consolidated the Cossack Brigade, army, and gendarmerie, merging them together, he formed a unified military. On October 26, 1923 Ahmad Shah was exiled to Europe and Reza Khan became Prime Minister of Iran. In early 1925, the Majles gave him the title of Commander-in-Chief of the Armed Force, a title reserved for the King.

While consolidating his military power, he sought the support of various existing Iranian political parties and groups with conservative, socialist, religious, anti-religious, and reformist ideology. With civilian and the newly formed army support, he fought against insurgent rebel movements, the tribal conflict, rivalry and aggression; he negotiated to retrieve the imposed and unilateral treaties and agreements between the British and Russian governments and Iran. Reza Khan was determined to prevent the restoration of the Qajar dynasty; therefore, he inclined to establish an Iranian Republic. However meeting a vehement opposition by clergymen and some leaders of the Majles, namely Hassann Modarres and Doctor Mohammed Mossaddegh, he deviated from his goal. Then in December 1925, a constituent assembly deposed Ahmad Shah and officially changed Reza Khan to Reza Shah, who crowned himself within a year Reza Shah Pahlavi, the Shahanshah (the King of Kings).

Some Iranian satirists may say "too good to be true."

He remained Shah until September 16, 1941, a few months after my graduation from elementary school of Ansari, when he abdicated a few weeks after the Allied forces invasion of Iran in August 1941.

After 16 years of his reign, some Iranian satirists repeated again "too good to be true".

WHAT DID REZA SHAH ACCOMPLISH?

REDISTRIBUTION AND SHIFTING OF POLITICAL POWERS

Reza Shah continued to consolidate and upgrade his newly organized army. Quantitatively he increased the Iranian defense budget, the number of men serving in the army, implemented and extended conscription, added tanks and even gunboats to the army.

Qualitatively, he augmented the prestige and standing of the army. He and his son, Mohammad Reza, the crown Prince, appeared in public in military uniform, upgraded the income of the military personnel and their standard of living, established officers' club for them. Military officers of different ranks, general (sarlashgar), brigadier (sarteep), colonel (sarhang), major (sargord), captain (sarvan), and lieutenants (setvans) became the elites and privileged members of society, wearing and displaying their chic uniforms in public, in ceremonies, in all kinds of meetings, medals and ribbons displayed on their chest, decorating the officers, and the officers in turn walking or standing proudly in the streets, decorating Tehran.

Reorganization of the administrative aspect of the government needed not only to make it more efficient, but also to eliminate the old fashioned administrative terminology and introduce the new and fancy and chic ones. New ministries (vezarat), provinces (ostans), counties, municipalities, and districts, with governors, mayors, administrators were established and structured to work in unison and be easily directed by the central authorities, the ministers (viziers or vazirs or vezirs), who with the prime minister were chosen by the Shah and received the blessing of the deputies of the Majles, who in turn were elected by the blessing of the Shah or even more conveniently selected by the Shah.

In addition to securing the support of the powerful people, Reza Shah augmented his own power, he amassed a large sum of wealth and by acquiring sizable lands and properties, he deserved the title of lord of landlords to compete with his other title of Shahanshah (Shah of Shahs). He erected statues of himself in different public places to symbolically remind the people of his omnipresence.

Reza shah treated the whole country as an army establishment, the Iranian citizens were similar to the manpower of the army, they were in the eyes of Reza Shah the officers, and soldiers. They needed food, shelter (barracks), uniforms to survive, and enough education to understand rules and regulations of the army. The obedience, punishment for deviation from rules were the essential part of his rule. Items such as freedom of speech, religious practice, cultural identity, choice of food to eat and place to live, the right to own land and property to cultivate, all desired by the Iranians did not interest the Shah. Furthermore discussing them interfered with his preoccupation with a reform appropriate to an army rather than a nation, a glittering handsome, and chic nation with not much substance and endurance,

ONE NATION UNDER THE SHAH

Reza shah was comfortable in leading the military, then why not create an Iranian nation akin to a military set up? A secular, homogenous, free of ethnicity nation, sharing similar culture, language, ideology, and even outfits, saluting one person, the King of Kings.

Then there we go:

To minimize or even eradicate the Islamic clergy, Reza Shah imported a European justice system to Iran, and established civil courts with new statutes and judges, and assigned them legal issues that used to be within the jurisdiction of and a source of livelihood for Islamic clergy. He transferred all lands and foundations endowed to ulema to civil authorities. He prohibited the Shiah religious rituals such as processions commemorating the martyrdom of Ashura, very dear to the heart of Shiah Iranians at the time. He discouraged the pilgrimage to Islamic Holy cities of Mecca, Medina in Saudi Arabia, and Najaf and Karballa in Iraq. The pilgrimage to Mecca is one of the five pillars of the Islamic religion. All these changes resulted in downgrading of political, social, and economic states of the Shiah ulema, whether it was a part of his original intention or not.

The tribes in different parts of Iran, with heterogeneous culture, dialects, loyalty, habits, and leadership were considered obstacles to the unification of the nation, therefore it seemed logical to Reza Shah to assimilate the tribe into the core nation or even eliminate them. He tried to achieve the goal by extending the army to the regions, inciting conflict among the tribes, supporting one against the other, or even confiscating their lands.

This is probably a method of unification by alienation.

Using the army as a role model, Reza Shah contemplated that the officers of the army wearing a nice outfit, they looked modern, why not the other citizens of Iran? Therefore he prohibited the regional and ethnic outfits; western style outfits including European felt hats were introduced and advocated. Except for qualified and registered clergymen, all religious style dress such as turban (immameh or amamah, a headdress made of a long scarf-like cloth, wound around the head and aba ,sleeveless cloak open in front, were outlawed. Women, irrespective of their age could no longer wear veil and chador, a light fabric hiding the hair and body configuration of women. Some Iranians, particularly some Iranian women considered the change in dress code of women a part of emancipation of women, but the others, particularly the older women felt deprived of their religious right. For these women forced to walk in the street without a chador was equivalent to walking naked. They did not feel emancipated, they felt violated and undignified. Like the clergymen, the forced national unification of women resulted in their alienation and disunity. This happens when a simple person, even with good intention, tries to solve a complex situation with a simple solution.

DOUBLE EDGED REFORMS OF REZA SHAH

Education: the number of elementary and secondary schools with modern curricula and enrollment increased markedly during Reza Shah tenure. Tehran University for higher education, the result of consolidation of preexisting colleges was founded in 1934, progressively increasing the number of colleges and enrollment. Higher education schools, such as medicine, law, engineering, teaching became available. Scholarship in higher education in European countries sponsored by the government began during Reza shah's reign. The government encouraged admission of women to teaching institutions, including Tehran University. Despite of these advances and even opening evening learning centers for adults, the literacy rate in Iran was low about 10%. Graduate students, depending on their level of education and competence were employed by the government. Before the education the students had a divergent social, economic, and ideological background; after graduation, they formed two groups of people: civil servants or self employed professionals. In both groups they had one common denominator, they were educated Iranians, they had become a roshanfekr (enlightened). They wanted accountability, security, and freedom.

INDUSTRY

Industrial growth started with construction of the Trans-Iranian Railway, which was completed in 1931, the railway connected the southern region of Iran to the northern part. In addition a railway connecting Tabriz from the west to Meshhad in the east as well as thousands of highways were completed by 1941.

Independent plants including textile mills, sugar refineries, chemical and tobacco companies, and the oil industry expanded. Smaller companies such as shoemaking, carpentry, and construction merged. The work force of the burgeoning industry in combination reached to more than 170,000 workers. These workers, originating from different parts of Iran, formed another group of urban citizen identified collectively as industrial workers, which most likely would not support a big landowner named Reza Shah.

POWER AND FORCE AND REZA SHAH

Reza Shah had enjoyed his power as the leader of an army Brigade; the Iranian society waiting for a powerful leader encouraged him in gaining more power. So he did. Power modified his behavior, he became more assertive, less inhibited, careless, insensitive to the perception of others and more desirous to control. Leaders with too much power may develop a confusional state of mind, eventually changing the leadership of a nation to the ownership of a nation, and do with the nation what they please. With this kind of attitude Reza Shah proceeded with reforms. He identified the various problems in the Iranian society and tried to remedy them as fast as possible. To achieve his goal, he used his power and force, unaware of or insensitive to the consequences. The reforms, which were intended to benefit the society, resulted in the resentment and alienation of the society. To illustrate the impacts of the reforms initiated by Reza Shah on the Iranian citizens of various backgrounds, I propose to use a medical analogy as follows:

Reza Shah identified several illnesses and deficiencies in the Iranian society of the time, instead of proposing different therapeutic modalities for each problem, he selected only one regimen to cure them all, and that regimen was force. This approach eradicated some of the problems and stabilized or caused partial remission of a few more, with no provisions to prevent recurrences. Unfortunately in the great majority the treatment caused serious side effects. He judged the side effects were due to the subtherapeutic level of force; he increased the dose of force, thus increasing the side effects, creating a vicious cycle to the detriment of the patients. Good hearted and noble Iranians now were wishing a major change in the management of their illness and alleviation of side effects, which by now were worse than the disease. In addition Reza Shah, did not believe that the complaints were genuine, therefore not trusting the patients and thinking of malingering he began to punish them, sometimes violently without mercy. The Iranian people stopped complaining and the silence became the only sign of protest. Now the dictatorship was full blown. After abdication of Reza Shah the so-called Iranian army resisted the Allied invaders for a few days until the newly named Prime Minister, Foroughi, negotiated peace complying with the Allied forces. After lifting the dictatorial forces, political and social disarray returned, and the social illnesses were no longer in remission, and the opposing political forces, friends, enemies, and the public broke the silence and expressed their verbal assaults loudly against the now abdicated Reza Shah.

CHAPTER 36

American-Iranian Relationship

During the 19th century the Russian and British were two major nations competitively exerting influence in the northern and southern regions of Iran respectively .The American involvement was limited to missionary works by individuals, who began to travel to Iran, in the middle of the century, mainly for religious conversion purposes and teaching.

In the early 20th century some of the American educators, such as Dr. Samuel Jordan, the Principal of American High School in Tehran, reached prominence in Iran.

From this point on the relationship between Iran and the USA was influenced not only by the political internal climate of the Iranian government, but also by the desire and attitude of Iran's northern neighbor, the Soviets, and the controller of Iranian oil, the British. During WWII the influence of these two powers became more aggressive, and their relationship with Iran assumed a different meaning, they were facing a third, but a stronger competitor, the USA. Not only they had to compete with each other to protect their interests, but also to make every effort to prevent the USA from dominating the relations with Iran. The British were already enjoying comfortable and profitable oil concession, and their main concern was to safeguard their oil turf. The Russian did not have any concession, but they were determined to have one if the USA was awarded a concession. These two countries were like a jealous spouse, both believing that Iran should be faithful to them, and it must not even flirt with any other nation without their permission; otherwise they will take punitive action against it. Now the USA walks in, innocent, flirtatious, not prepared, extends the hand for negotiation, not aware that these pros jointly or individually will sabotage any meaningful relationship between Iran and the USA. The following events in succession influenced and altered not only the relationship between Iran and British and Soviets, but also the American and Iranian relationship.

Invasion of Iran during WWII

On June 22, 1941, when Germany invaded Russia, many Iranians unofficially were rejoicing the victory, because, they disliked Russians and British and they liked the Germans, some Iranians identified with Nazis, believing in their common so-called Aryan heritage, some were influenced by daily radio-propaganda of Nazis.

Before the invasion of Iran, several hundreds of German experts in various disciplines were employed and were working in various projects from mining to construction of factories for the military supplies.

The Allied considered Iran's railway connecting the Persian Gulf to the Caspian, an invaluable and faster corridor to transfer the military supplies to the Soviet Union. Reza Shah rejected the Anglo-Russian demand to use the railway as well as their demand to ouster the German nationals, who were a constant threat to the British controlled Iranian oil. Reza Shah declaring the neutrality of Iran valued the Iranian and German relationship, and he appeared to be a pro-axis king.

The Allies forces, that is the British and the Soviet invaded Iran during the period extending from August 25 to September 17, 1941. The Russians occupied the north and the British the south and west.

After a few hours fight in the South, the Iranian troops, predictably, were overwhelmed and their resistance fragmented, began to cave in. In Tehran, as in the past crises, a new Prime Minister, Mohammad Ali Foroughi, was appointed and martial law was declared. The army portrayed by Reza Shah as great one, instantly disintegrated. The military generals with the glittering stars on their epaulets and decorative medals on their chests no longer displayed themselves in public. All kinds of reactions and emotions expressed by the people; anger toward and disappointment of the Shah and army was prevalent. A general sense of humiliation was apparent. Hatred toward British intensified. It was also believed by some that capitulation of the army was planned secretly by the British agents in collaboration with some army generals loyal to the British. After the abdication of Reza Shah on September 16, 1941, despite his autocratic behavior of brutally silencing the opposing forces, a feeling of anger mixed with sadness prevailed among the Iranians. It was hard for them to observe their king forced to abdicate and a much disliked British Ambassador, named Bullard sitting in the British Embassy, acting as a de facto king, dictating policies to the Iranian government.

The purposes of invasion of course were to facilitate the defeat of Germany, and protect the Abadan's oil refinery by using the Trans-Iranian Railway for transportation. The Shah of Iran signed a Tripartite Treaty of Alliance with Allies, Russia and Britain in January 29, 1942, included in this Treaty was the right of the Allies to transport military personnel and equipment in Iran. Iran then was labeled a Persian Corridor or a Bridge to Victory.

The withdrawal of the Allied forces from Iran was set to no later than six months after the cessation of hostilities. Many Iranian politicians and landowners not sympathizing with the Allies or with pro-German tendencies were arrested and purged from the system. Meanwhile Iran declared war on Germany in September 1943 in order to be accepted to the United Nations. At the Tehran conference of November 1943, the Allies reaffirmed their commitment to Iran independence. At the end of the war the British withdrew their forces, but the Russians continued the occupation until May 1946.

A limited but a significant diplomatic representation between the United States and Iran started, when Louis G. Dreyfus, Jr., represented the United States in Tehran, during WWII from 1942-1944. Dreyfus and his wife, a nurse working as humanitarian person in poor section of Tehran, left an important legacy, portraying the Americans as kind, trustworthy and honest. Dreyfus position was a ministerial one, a rank lower than ambassador. A minister, the head of a legation, usually is assigned to a country with no significant or a specific interest.

The semi-official diplomatic relationship between Iran and the USA gradually but steadily progressed toward a serious official relation, and after the departure of Dreyfus, the next person representing the USA in Iran was Leland Morris, an ambassador, to address the needs of both countries. The Iranian government had been under pressure and Iranian independence and sovereignty threatened by the Soviet Union and the British, both eager to further and consolidate their sphere of influence in the northern and the southern regions of Iran. Iran needed a third strong nation to support it against these two major intruders. The rise of Nazis to power in Germany, at odds with the British and the Soviet was prompting some Iranian leaders including Reza Shah to seek Germany's support. The Nazi rhetoric was attractive to some Iranian youth, who, proud of their past Aryan heritage, became sympathizers or members of a pro-Nazi movement in Iran, called Pan-Iranism, and identified with Nazi ideology. Although, prior to the Allies occupation of Iran, many German advisers, consultants, business persons had been invited to Iran, the concept of Germany, as third major force and an ally of Iran did not take root in the Iranian society, because the majority of Iranians were not seduced by the German propaganda of supremacy. Therefore it was an appropriate time for the USA as a superpower and popular nation among the Iranians, to ally with Iran and engage in the implementations of strategies of mutual interest to Iran and the USA. The alliance with the USA was important to Iran for two major reasons: 1) to be able to control the aggressive attitudes of the Soviets and the British toward Iran and maintain the Iranian independence and sovereignty, 2) obtain economic aid, which also was important for the achievement of objective number 1. In addition Iran needed the USA to assist in industrial, economic, and military developments. Mohammad Reza Shah was particularly interested in the military assistance, probably to protect the Pahlavi dynasty from the internal adversary forces, rather than fighting the external invading enemies. The needs of the USA to have Iran as an ally included: to help Iran to resist the great powers influence in Iran, particular during the cold war. Obviously during WWII, the USA, like the other allies, needed Iran territory to facilitate the transportation of facilities needed during war across the Iranian land, to Russia; it was also necessary for the United States, to protect its interest in the oil industry in Saudi Arabia or even in Iran by cooperating with Iran, which had the strategic position in the Middle East. The importance and the level and the intensity of the implementation of the needs by both parties varied contingent upon the international events and the type of the government in Iran or the ideology of the American president of the time. For instance the Iran's need for the financial aid from the USA became more apparent after the nationalization of the Iranian oil; or when, the Russian government refused to withdraw from the Iranian territory, the Iran need for the American power became very desirous, and the Shah's request from America for military assistance and build-up augmented.

Reform and modernization of the Iranian financial system during and after the reign of Reza Shah was a top priority and the American assistance and advice was a welcoming event for the Iranian people. The

American involvement started with Arthur Millspaugh, PhD, and a former adviser to the Foreign Trade Office of the American State Department. Dr. Millspaugh, for the second time traveled to Iran in January 1943, by the invitation of Iran in an advisory capacity and was given a special authority to initiate the financial reform process in Iran. Although he had been in Iran from 1922-1927 with the same assignment, he did not achieve his objectives, because he failed to understand the Iranian socio-political state. He failed to identify the reasons that some groups were not cooperating with him because they wanted to protect their own self-interests, whatever they might be; others resented him for, what was perceived by them, as an intrusion into the internal affairs of Iran, but probably mostly because of his attitude. I was in high school at the time. Although we were considered to be novices in politics, many of my classmates, used to smile when they heard Millspaugh, they used to think that he was chakhan, meaning bragging, stating something convincingly but not true. Whether he was chakhan or not, it is not important, what is important is that he overestimated himself, and greatly underestimated his Iranian colleagues. He became a judge of characters, intelligence, honesty, and competence.

He was identified to prefer the British diplomacy, hated by the majority in Iran, therefore, inducing a negative feeling against America, which, at the time, was being portrayed as a nation against a dictatorial regime and injustice. Although Millapaugh managed to accomplish some reforms, he failed in his overall mission, and projected his failure to incompetent Iranians, calling them incapable of self-governance. After being dismissed by the Iranian Majles for incompetency and misjudgment, he returned to the USA. He wrote his second book about Iran called, Americans in Persia, published by the Brookings Institute, Washington, D. C., in 1946. The problem was that the American media and even the American government and even the presidents of the USA took these reports seriously and used them as a reference for the future policies, which unjustifiably led the USA in a wrong direction and negated the efforts of the USA to symbolize itself with freedom and justice.

The American oil companies' interest in sharing the oil industry in Iran did not materialize either. Although starting in 1920 Standard Oil Company of New Jersey followed by other American oil companies attempted to obtain an oil concession from Iran, it was not until 1943 when the American companies with the support of the State Department, started a serious negotiation with Iran. This negotiation alarmed the British and the Soviet and also contributed to the discussion among the Iranian leaders of the wisdom of granting the oil concession. At the time, in late 1944, Mossaddegh who had a strong position in the Majles, successfully supported the overwhelming passage of a law prohibiting the government from awarding the oil concession without the approval of the Majles. This law pleased England; but angered the Soviets prompting them to accuse Mossaddegh of being pro-British. The law although a disappointment for the USA oil companies, did not terminate the interest of the USA or Iran in continuation of productive relations. After all the interest of the USA was not limited only to the oil business, the USA had a diplomatic interest and was concerned about the influence of the Soviet in Iran and the proliferation of communism. The United State was also willing to provide economically profitable military support to the Shah to fight communism.

The Soviet Union did not withdraw the troops on March 2, 1946 per prior commitment and continued to remain in Iran and mingle with Iranian internal affairs and hindered the realization of the Iranian independence, which has been guaranteed by the Allied forces.

At the end of WWII the Soviet Union considered itself a superpower and tried to validate this status by not respecting its prior commitment to withdrawal, a practice not uncommon among powerful nations and people. In addition remaining in Iran provided an additional leverage to the Soviets in receiving an oil concession from Iran and supporting the group of politicians with the communism ideology. In 1946, the USA began openly to support the Iranians in their stand against the USSR and their demand for the troop withdrawal. The USA support of Iran is clearly documented, but it is not clear how much it contributed to the silent withdrawal of the Russians. The USA official involvement in the Iranian-Soviet conflict progressively increased, as time went on but it took a different form. The American Embassy as the official and important representative of the USA began to assert itself in strengthening the American-Iranian relationship. The Ambassador at this time was George Allen, who and the Shah had an amicable relationship and exchanged ideas and information frequently and often informally. Allen not only played tennis with the Shah, but also befriended the Shah's twin sister, Princess Ashraf, who played a very significant role in her brother's life and in his political directions and endeavors. Allen performed the role of a protector, an adviser, and even an agent of the Shah, influencing him in his personal and political decision-makings, including decisions relative to the United States. Ambassador Allen greatly assisted the Shah in materializing the support of the United

States for the Shah. This approach although seemingly could be considered a positive step toward the friendship of two countries helped alienate from the United States a group of Iranians leaders who did not have a friendly view of the Shah's autocracy.

They perceived the Ambassador and the Shah's relations a collusion to increase the authority of the Shah to dismiss Ghavam at the time, and for other purposes in the future.

The Shah welcomed this cooperation, which assured the delivery of military aid by the USA to Iran; prompting the Iranian nationalists to question the motives for the military aid at the time. What does the military propose to protect? The Shah, the Iranians, or the interests of the USA?

Some members of the American political mission in their eagerness to be recognized as an expert in the regional politics, did not limit their advice to the field of their expertise and their jurisdiction and, impressed by their own self-importance, ill- advised the Shah with a very unfavorable consequence. The next ambassador after the departure of Allen, advised or intrigued the Shah to appoint Ali Razmara, a highest ranking, French trained military man to become the prime minister. Irrespective of the outcome of this appointment the appointment of a military man to an executive power to act militarily in a nation looking forward for democracy and nationalism, seems a non-defendable concept. Razmara, became the prime minister on June 26, 1950 and was assassinated on March 7, 1951

This approach by the American political authorities relative to Iran was a wrong direction to the future, as the events will show. It also reflected a fundamental flaw in the American policies in Iran marked by lack of true experts and informed American authorities and conflicts and miscommunication among official representatives and unofficial envoys of the USA. The coordinated planning and effective implementation of the American policies with a meaningful analysis of the results needed much more appraisal and repair.

Starting then the Americans image began to change from a superpower and the just defender of Iran's independence to a secretive, deal making power similar to the United Kingdom, or even worse; The British although perceived manipulative and sneaky by the Iranians, were considered to be expert and knowledgeable in the internal affairs and culture of Iran.

The American leaders were having difficulty in integrating and reconciling their economic and political interests with their commitment to the highest political value and principles including commitment to the upholding of the sovereignty of Iran.

After the nationalization of oil in March 1951, there was a marked reduction in income from oil exports, the economic disarray was overwhelming. Eisenhower's administration not only refused to provide financial aid to Iran per the request of the prime minister of Iran, Mohammad Mossaddigh, but also in collaboration with the British looked favorably to the dismissal of Mossaddigh and reinstallment of the Shah. My graduating classmates had a little sarcastic tone in their voice when they used to say that four high-ranking military officers, the Shah, General Eisenhower, General Razmara, and General Zahedi, under the direction of her Majesty's government of England fought the Iranian democracy at the time.

Prior to and post nationalization of oil there were all sorts of meetings, by the Iranians, Americans, and British involved in the oil industry of Iran. Meetings were held in the US, in Iran, or in England, the participants, usually short of wisdom, addressed the wisdom of nationalization and its prevention or nullification; they verbalized the sentiments of their respective country claiming to support and assist humanity. In certain joint American-British meetings, the British authorities seemed to be in a confusional state, oblivious to the dramatic changes in history after WWII, the desire of all nations of the world for freedom and independence. They were seriously considering a military intervention against Iran to get the oil back and save humanity from disasters; the American authorities playing a moderator role, advised the British otherwise and reminded them of communist Russia watching Iran from the north; the British although suspicious of American intentions and interest in the Iranian oil, obliged. The Americans were ambivalent about nationalization of oil in Iran, on one hand, they considered nationalization the right of an independent country, on the other hand they were concerned about the spreading of the idea, to other countries such as Saudi Arabia, where America had its own interest.

In fall of 1951, Mossaddigh, addressed the Security Council of the United Nations, met with President Truman and Secretary of State Acheson. Mossaddigh in collaboration with the State Department prepared a proposal for a new contract between the AIOC and to be established a national Iranian oil company to give the purchasing power to AIOC. The British rejected the proposal, and they continued to persuade the United States for support to regain the control of Iranian oil and even share the expected profit with the United States. Meanwhile the American authorities also had begun to modify their policies regarding Mossaddigh's government and Iran, changing from cooperation to confrontation. The following factors contributed to this dramatic switch in the American plans toward Iran, changing its direction toward intervention in Iran and toppling Prime Minister Mossaddigh:

Fear of communism, concern about communist China, and conflict in Korea; the vulnerable state of the Mossaddegh coalition government; the interest of the United States in the available Iranian oil; and the influence of the British in the American foreign policy regarding Iran. Transition from the President Truman-Secretary of States Acheson to the President Eisenhower-Secretary of States John Foster Dulles government also facilitated the American intervention. The following play simplifies and summarizes the dismissal of a popular democratic prime minister of a sovereign nation in August 1953:

CHAPTER 37

Title of Play:
Boot (A Military Coup To Oust Mossaddigh)/
Ajax (The Same As Boot, Except It Is Considered
Countercoup, Blaming Mossaddigh For Coup)

ORIGIN: GREAT BRITAIN

Producers: 1. President Eisenhower, the executer of foreign policy of Dulles

2. Prime Minister Churchill, augmenter of Dulles fear of communism, and dreamer of colonialism.

Objectives: 1. Recoup of Iranian oil for British. Achievement: British Petroleum-AIOC received a large share of the Iranian oil; although the American companies also obtained satisfactory shares, they would have been able to receive the same or more without bruising the American value.

2. Containment of USSR communism. Achievement: Difficult to assess because USSR disintegrated due to it's intrinsic and genetic anomaly.

3. To overthrow Mossaddigh. Achievement: He was jailed for 3 years, then, was exiled to Ahmadabad, under house arrest for the rest of his life.

Directors: American CIA and State Department

Method: Overt and covert operation

Cast:
Actors
1. Secretary of State, John Foster Dulles, he was afraid of communism
2. Director of CIA, Allen Dulles (brother of John)
3. American Ambassador to Tehran, Loy Henderson
4. The Shah, Mohammad Reza
5. Head of CIA, Middle East operation and the coordinator of Operation Boot, Kermit Roosevelt.
6. British Foreign Minister, Anthony Eden.

Supporting actors
1. Undersecretary of State, General Walter Bedell Smith
2. CIA Director of Operation, Frank Wisner
3. Twin sister of Shah, Princess Ashraf
4. General Norman Schwarzkopf, former adviser to the Iranian gendarmerie
5. General Fazlollah Zahedi, to replace Mossaddigh
6. Others, Iranians and Americans: the Rashidian brothers intermediary Iranians, rich by wheeling and dealing and also liaison between the Shah and Roosevelt, and escalating opposition against Mossaddigh in Iran, paid for by the British and Americans.

Immediate benefit: The participants, particularly the actors felt great, they liked these sorts of things.

Long-range benefit: 1. The Shah and Princess Ashraf continued to exert their power, backed by the United States, enjoying the generous American financial and military aids. The United States received the shares of oil, but it could have received even more with negotiation after nationalization of oil without going through a coup.

Immediate risk: Innocent people casualties.

Long-range risk: An embarrassing act highly detrimental to the value, prestige, respect, and integrity of the American people, and the American-Iranian relationship; Iranian democracy was buried by the United States, carrying the torch of democracy.

The following may be considered as the contributing factors to this negative outcome:

Majority of actors and supporting actors were lawyers and generals and acted as such; they were preoccupied with winning without considering the long-range effect.

Lower echelon characters assumed or were given authority beyond their legal or competence limits, in turn these people used their personal feeling and opinion, rather than the official policies of their superiors to implement their plans; showing enthusiasm for their task, they influenced the higher authorities, who were not informed fully of the socio-political situation of Iran, at the time.

Great Britain, Shah, and his twin's sister influence on decision-making was unjustifiable.

The final authority, the American people were not informed of the situation properly.

Following the coup d'etat of 1953, starting late in 1953, there were many meetings under different titles, attended by American, British, and the oil companies representatives, and AIOC officials, held in the USA, and in Great Britain and Iran, to plan for the future of Iranian oil. In April 1954, these people began to negotiate with the Iranian government, eventually reaching an agreement that the National Iranian Oil Company (NIOC), be recognized as the owner of Iranian oil, but a consortium of the oil companies, including major American oil companies and AIOC (renamed British Petroleum or BP after the nationalization of oil) be given the exclusive authority to operate, the newly formed NIOC. The Consortium, directed by a Board, was charged with the management of operations, including exploration, refinery and sales. The proposal of the consortium was signed by the Minister of Finance, Dr. Amini in September and ratified by the Majles in October of 1954. Total revenue of the Iranian government amounted to 50% of the net profit of the oil company, the British Petroleum obtained a large share, followed by the American and independent oil companies. The compensation paid by the Iranian government to BP included $40 million.

The consortium markedly increased our much needed oil revenue, over the following years. The Abadan refinery was a vast institution, occupying 400 or more acres and employing more than 30,000 people.

The agreement also opened negotiations with other countries; in 1957, the Iranian government authorized NIOC to negotiate with the other countries outside the territory of operation of the consortium.

Although, this agreement, markedly improved the Iranian oil revenue, it was not welcomed by the Iranian people, and imposed a humiliating dark spot on the sovereignty of Iran, to be lifted in the future.

AMERICAN AID TO IRAN AFTER 1953

The cash value of the American aid amounted to more than a billion dollars over a period of several years.

The aids were of economic and military nature, both contingent upon the control over the affairs of the Iranian government. This aid was welcomed and very much appreciated by the Shah's regime and prompted them to ask for more. However it was the source of resentment for the majority of Iranians, not only because of the purpose of the aids, but also because of the manner of providing the financial aid. The Iranians, particularly the progressive sector, interpreted the financial aid as a political award, a behavior modifying method such as "sit! Good boy!" tactic, and a mal-adaptive compensation for good Iranian behavior. Furthermore it was utilized extravagantly by the governing rich, including the Shah and his supporters, not reaching the intended poor and the economical-socio-educational projects.

The people did not benefit from military aid, which was intended to control the USSR aggression, from the American point of view. From the Shah's perspective a strong military was of the utmost importance for the maintenance of the police state he and his supporters had established for their protection. The Shah personally was not concerned about the Soviets, he was maintaining a good relationship with the soviet, communicating and negotiating with them, and suggesting treaties. He was using his relation with the Russians as leverage in dealing with the West in general and the USA in particular.

In addition to economic and military aids to Iran, the American authorities and the Shah were interested in portraying the relationship with Iran as humanitarian and friendly, rather than a cold and calculated pure business alliance. Unofficial exchange visiting of the leadership of two countries was appealing to the Americans as well as to Shah and it seemed a good way to enhance the friendship appearance. Within a few years after 1953, the Shah's visits to the USA and his meeting with the president of the USA, were reciprocated by the American authorities' visits to Iran and meetings with the Shah.

Visitors to Iran within a few years after 1953 included the vice president, Nixon and his wife, the congressional delegates, Secretary of State, Foster Dulles, Secretaries of Defense and Treasury, and the President of the United States, Mr. Eisenhower. During these visits the beneficial effect of the friendship between two countries and the necessity of the American aids to Iran reaffirmed and the role of the Shah in achieving stability in Iran was acknowledged, and even admired.

These visits enhanced the friendship between the Shah and the American authorities visiting Iran, but alienated the majority of Iranians.

After President Kennedy assumed the Presidency, the American government attempted to change its policy toward the Shah. Instead of supporting the repressive rule of the Shah militarily and economically, the Kennedy administration began to discourage him from expanding military power and encouraging him to engage in a meaningful reform for betterment of the Iranian people. The reform was necessary to reflect the changes in the American policy advocating socio-economic reform throughout all nations, including the Middle East and Iran, for idealistic reasons. But for practical purposes the reform was urgently needed, because of official reports from Iran indicating the escalation of Iranian resentment against the Shah's regime, and the USA supporting him. The American authorities responsible for the foreign policy were getting progressively concerned about unrest in Iran in general and the leftist revolution in particular. The Iranians also had high expectations from President Kennedy, who was extremely popular among Iranians and he was considered to be knowledgeable about and sympathetic to the Iranian people as well as the protector of the American values. The new sentiment of the Iranians was in contrast to the feelings prior to 1953. The problem was clear to the Kennedy administration; the solution was a problematic one. The continuation of socio-economic aid seemed to be necessary according to authorities expert in Iranian affairs. But they demanded much more accountability and a much less dictatorial attitude from the Shah's regime. The Shah was advised and was willing to proceed with reforms. The American advisers provided a list of the items he should address or ignore, in order to be in harmony with the American policies and to ease the tension in Iran. The Shah partly encouraged by the American advisers and partly anxious and insecure about the Kennedy administration's support began actively to engage in the planning of a variety of programs and changes in his policies. His widely advertised the White Revolution, which officially began in January 1963, involving a variety of programs, including land reform, establishing a literary corps, the nationalization of forests, the industrial employee profit sharing, and the women's vote right.

The American authorities, including the Vice President Johnson, Secretary of States, some senators, congressmen, and advisers continued to visit Iran. They were sympathetic toward Iran, and directly or indirectly persuaded the Shah to enhance the implementation of his reforms. The Iranian representatives, including his Majesty visiting President Kennedy, continued to ask for more military-economic support from the USA. These diplomatic visits were not interpreted by the Iranians to be a good will gesture of the American authorities to upgrade the Iranian socio-economic status and promote their individual freedom; they thought these visits were intended to maintain the status quo and support the Shah's regime. During all these visits and communications, and discussions, it is easily recognizable that the personal relationship between the Shah and the American authorities at any level influenced their view of the Shah, diverting them from objectivity toward emotionalism.

Meanwhile the repressive attitude of the Shah was not altered. He dissolved the Majles, he declared martial law, he appointed the prime ministers and ministers, and then he dismissed them at his pleasure. He dissociated himself from his friends and isolated himself, exiled his co-workers. He claimed credit for the achievements of the others and blamed the others for his own mistakes or misjudgments. He gradually lost touch with the people and became more self-centered and introverted reaching to level of a paranoid and egomaniac personality. He surrounded himself with a limited number of people who were feeding the nutrition he needed, total obedience and reassurance that he was a benevolent king, supported by the Iranians for his modern and effective reforms. This behavioral pattern accelerated the dissatisfaction of the Iranians, overcoming their patience, manifesting as recurrent political protests, demonstrations, and riots, supported by various groups and classes of Iranians. These events, at times, prompted the Shah's regime to militarily intervene, and brutally attack and kill the people, whom the Shah's reforms supposedly were to protect.

The Shah used the term of White Revolution to contrast with red revolution, because the latter involves blood shed and violence, the former implies peace and indicates that revolution does not necessarily mean revolting against some establishments, it could be a peaceful reform, started on the top without changing the fundamentals. In his land reform plan, which involved purchasing the land, selling the land with a significant discount and with a very low interest rate on the borrowed money to purchase the land. The determination of the value of land was arbitrary and based on the real estate tax and did not reflect the actual value of the land. This way the farmers cultivate the land they own, rather than cultivating the land for the landlords, like a slave. Although a very noble and humanistic idea, since it was imposed without a solid analysis of the economic and cultural fundamentals, it did not achieve the intended goal and created the new problems. The landlords (the owner of the land), the religious leaders, intellectuals, the middle class were alienated and did not support the plan. Land reform and women's right to vote were interpreted by the leading clergy, not to be in line with Islamic law, prompting the Shah to criticize and confront the clergy and accuse them of fighting his reforms for self-interest reasons. The Shah called a referendum, which approved his reforms, but the people questioned the validity of the referendum.

The religious leaders, particularly Ayatollah Khomeini, were not intimated by the Shah's rhetoric and threats, continued to protest against this kind of land reform and women's suffrage, criticizing the Shah and his partners. The Shah attempted to militarily control the religious students' protest, which was taking an uprising form in the Holy City of Ghom, and silence the oppositions. By doing so, he created a vicious cycle, leading to stronger protest and uprising on the day of Ashura, in June 1963. The ensuing military intervention resulted in injuries and death of the chanting and grieving people. Ayatollah Khomeini was arrested and sent to Tehran for subsequent exile.

The Shah was planning to improve the living conditions of the farmers and receive their support by providing them their own lands to cultivate. The farmers, who were supposed to benefit from land reform, were also unhappy. They were not capable of utilizing the land, because they lost the supervision, financial supports, water supply, and necessary equipments previously provided by the landlords, who lost interest and had no incentive to assist the farmers. Many farmers were forced to sell the newly acquired land and move to industrialized large cities such as Tehran, to look for a permanent and secure job. This migration of the farmers added to the preexisting urbanization of the villagers that had begun after WWII. Many of them without skill and not finding a job, and unemployed added to the burden of unemployment and poverty in the cities and the consequences. By trying to implement his various programs, the Shah antagonized different groups of Iranians at different times, creating new opposition and directing the force of dictatorship toward them. The autocracy continued, only the targets were changing.

The shah's behavior perceived by the Iranians as arrogant, born of unlimited power, was reflecting his Fatal Power Syndrome.

The Shah thought his White Revolution, peacefully would guide Iran into modernity.

The Shah was perceived rightly or wrongly by the people saying that "I am the king of Iran land, Iran is mine, I can do whatever I want with it, I can tell all Iranians what each one should have or shouldn't have, If they protest against my decision I will shoot them with the guns I have amassed through the military aid of the USA.

Neither the USA, nor the Iranian authorities focused on the recent root of the Iranian current problem.

The 1953 coup d'etat reinstalled and supported the Shah to continue his maladaptive authority. If the USA did not interfere with the Internal affairs of Iran at that time and if the Shah's desire to control did not abrogate his moral judgment, probably Iran would have progressed in a different direction. The USA and the Shah's regime did not predict these outcomes, because they failed to recognize, the FPS afflicting many powerful individuals such as Mohammad Reza Shah Pahlavi of Iran.

The arrest and confinement of the most prominent and effective Islamic religious leader and nationalist, after his strong speech on June 3, 1963, the day of the martyrdom of Imam Hussayn and his subsequent exile to Turkey on November 4, 1964, led to a further exacerbation of symptoms of Shah's FPS, marking the beginning of a new chapter leading to a justifiable Iranian revolution.

After the assassination of President Kennedy on November 23, 1963, the Shah's anxiety and uncertainty regarding the American support of him subsided, and resumed more daring attitude toward repression, looking foreword to a close relationship with President Johnson.

CHAPTER 38

The University of Tehran or Tehran University (Daneshgah-e Tehran)

The University of Thran is evolved from Dar al-Funun or Dar ol-Fonun school. University of Tehran is also called Madar (the mother) University, indicating that it is the oldest University in Iran.

Dar ol-Fonun was founded as a polytechnic higher education school in Tehran by Amir Kabir (1807-1852) around 1850.

Amir Kabir, the great Iranian statesman and reformer was the Prime Minister of Nasser ad-Din Shah of the Qajar or Ghajar dynasty.

In 1934 during Reza Shah's reign, the University of Tehran was inaugurated and it incorporated the basic structure of Dar ol-Fonun.

The medical school of the new university was named Faculty of Medicine from which I graduated in 1953.

Several Years after the establishment of the Islamic Republic of Iran, in 1986, the medical school was reorganized and was named Tehran University of Medical Sciences (TUMS). The University includes many faculties including, the Faculty of Medicine, Faculty of Pharmacy and Faculty of Dentistry. TUMS is a part of Tehran University and within the same campus.

The University of Tehran, a highly advanced and prestigious institution, is the largest university in Iran, offering a variety of competitive undergraduate and graduate programs.

TUMS is a highly developed and internationally respected institution for scientific and clinical medical education and research, enrolling large numbers of students under the supervision of an outstanding, well trained, and well-qualified faculty. The medical school is affiliated with several teaching hospitals with most modern facilities, advanced technology and specialized services.

When I started medical school, the first year of the Faculty of Medicine was a transition period from the Natural Sciences, a college preparatory class of the last year of high school. In addition to studying the assigned curriculum, it was a year of orientation and adjustment, dealing with the anxiety of the new environment and culture. Around the end of this year social consciousness and responsibility began to take root and the environment compelled the students to determine their role and value in the community and choose the right position and direction and form and express their opinion and promote it.

In general there were several categories of students in my class. One group of students tilted toward Socialism-Marxism and identified with the Tudeh party's ideology. However only a few were hard-core believers. Many of them were amusing themselves with the ideology, because it sounded intellectual, sympathetic toward the poor and workers and fashionable at the time. Then there was an opposite group, the conservative students from rich and educated families in the leadership role. These students usually identified with the royal court and a few of them were considered to be anglophiles. Another group of students appeared to be socially detached and focused on the scientific studies and books. I belonged yet to another group of students interested in the current social, economic, and political events, but not affiliated with or be active in any organization with a fixed ideology. The sovereignty and independence of our country was of utmost importance to our group, vehemently opposing any treaty with or interference by any external force or any internal plan with a remote possibility of jeopardizing the rightful status of the country.

Promotion of the standard of living and securing individual freedom and civil liberty and the economic security for all Iranians were among our priorities.

Another group of students were members or sympathizers of the National Front. Their objectives in general were similar to ours, except our independent status allowed us to avoid the involvement in the dispute among the leaders of the National Front or follow their agenda blindly. The students sponsored and supported by the military and wearing the military uniforms did not form a special group, probably they politically belonged to the different groups of students as mentioned above but usually, understandably, did not verbalize their affiliation or ideology.

The schools of the University of Tehran, not only were the center of higher learning; they were also center for socio-political and ideological development and promotion.

The students of the University of Tehran had become the sensory fibers of the nation, sensing a variety of social stimuli, reacting individually or collectively and compelling various leaderships to take action.

Several of my classmates were literary and some pretending to be. It was a relatively common practice to discuss and analyze books as a conversation piece. Some classical books such as Les Miserables (1862) of Victor Hugo (1802-1885) of France and novels such as L'Ile des Pingouins 1908 of Anatole France, the pseudonym for Francois-Anatole Thibault (1844-1924), or Buf-e Kur (Blind Owl) or Bouf-e Kour (1937) of Sadeq (gh)-e Hedayet (1903-1951) of Iran, and East of Eden (1952) of John Steinbeck, were discussed with no concern of being listed as suspicious by the spying authorities of the time. The Grapes of Wrath (1939) of Steinbeck was quoted when the discussions were focused on the topics related to Socialism-Marxism ideology; discussing this book as well as Lev Tolstoy's (1828-1910) Voyna i mir (War and Peace, 1865-1869), or even Jack London's The Call of the Wild (1903), probably would have been a reason enough to place a watch label on the students.

During down turn of the Tudeh Party, the advocate of socialism, reading and discussing Maxim Gorky (Pen name for Aleksey Peshkov)'s Mother, would have been qualified you as a communist deserving to be jailed.

Medical school curriculum was a comprehensive one, starting with basic science, including anatomy, chemistry, physiology, and pathology. Clinical medicine was introduced in the second year. As the years progressed, the basic science was tapered down and the clinical exposure increased to that extent that by the sixth and last year the students had rotated through the major specialties of medicine. Although the sixth year program included didactic lectures, it was mainly an internship program, devoted to clinical medicine.

The selection of the internship rotation by the students was a competitive one and it was based on the student's performances during medical school as well as on the written examination prior to the internship. I received the privilege to select any rotation I preferred. The choice of the rotation was also influenced by the reputation and popularity and the academic status of the directors of the internship programs, usually the chairmen of the department of the chosen specialty in any institution. I selected an internship with Dr. Azizi, a renowned French trained Professor of Medicine, in Pahlavi Hospital. Then for my surgical rotation I rotated thru the Zanan (Women) Hospital with Dr. Saleh a professor of Obstetrics and Gynecology, a Syracuse University trained man. My final rotation was with Professor Shams, the most famous ophthalmologist of Iran at the time, the founder of modern ophthalmology in Iran. During the internship I began to feel like a doctor, even though the doctorate degree was only given after the internship. The healthcare personnel began to address us in a professional manner and in a polite tone. The interns, when on duty call, were served dinners and breakfast in a special dining room reserved for the interns. The semi-independent practice of medicine and the support of the people during my internship were so enjoyable that I wished the internship would linger on. My training in Tehran University was a fulfilling and a most enjoyable experience. The members of the faculty in the medical school or in the affiliated University Hospitals were highly qualified, enthusiastic and competent educators. Didactic lectures, small group discussions, individual supervision, laboratory and technical trainings, and bedside teachings were all well organized. Clinical rotations thru the hospitals, particularly during an internship, under the supervision of the expert clinicians were particularly rewarding.

To secure the patients safety and yet allow appropriate independence to the interns was well balanced, installing confidence in the interns, soon to become the physicians or surgeons.

The evaluation of the students was almost similar to the present evaluation system in the United States. The students were evaluated in their acquired knowledge, the application of it to the patients' care that is their cognitive and psychomotor skills, and the ability of the students to recognize their own limitations. The importance of an appropriate attitude and behavior and compassion in the practice of medicine was emphasized and it was a part of the evaluation. The evaluation methods consisted of the oral and written examinations and direct observation at the bedside and in the laboratories.

Prior to graduation and receiving the doctoral degree, during the last year of medical school, the students had to submit a thesis on a pertinent subject, to a jury consisting usually of three members of the faculty, for approval.

My Thesis was entitled "The Unusual Manifestations of Metastatic Malignancy of the Liver". It was dedicated, in addition to my mother and father, to my sister, who had died of a congenital heart disease when I was in medical school, and had mentored me graciously during my home schooling period. She was suffering from a cyanotic congenital heart disease (CHD); she was born with a heart defect associated with blue color of the skin and lips. At that time two major types of cyanotic CHD were considered to be the cause of my sister's heart disease: Tetrology of Fallot or Fallot's Tetrology (FT), and Eisenmenger's complex. In both conditions, because of a defect in the heart, unoxygenated blood bypasses the lungs and is shunted from a right chamber of the heart, carrying reduced hemoglobin, into the left chamber and mixes with oxygenated blood, increasing the concentration of reduced hemoglobin in the blood. Cyanosis is due to the abnormal accumulation of reduced hemoglobin. Etienne-Louis Arthur Fallot a French physician made an anatomical diagnosis of the defect at bedside and introduced the term of Tetrology, in 1888. Henry F. Gilbert, an American music composer, had FT; he was a patient of Dr. P. D. White one of the founders of modern cardiology in the United States. Victor Eisenmenger, a German physician, described the defect, which later on was named after him by other cardiologists. Several French and German trained cardiologists at the time could not concur on which of the two defects was responsible for my sister's incurable heart disease. She received palliative treatment for severe heart failure, including the application of leeches on her abdomen, a bloodletting procedure, and an accepted therapeutic modality of the era.

The dedication of my thesis was accompanied by superlative words of appreciation and gratitude. The usage of highly complementary words or gestures when addressing a letter to a senior or higher status person, or welcoming a guest or complementing anyone for any reason, is a learned skill, unique to the Iranian culture. Inability or unwillingness to use this skill may be construed as rude behavior and interfere with an appropriate and productive communication. Lack of familiarity with this behavior also may become troublesome by misinterpreting it as a flattering or ingratiating attitude.

CHAPTER 39

Army

After the completion of medical school, I preferred to meet my military obligation before deciding about the type of postdoctoral specialty and education in Iran or abroad.

Unless otherwise excused from the military, all medical students after graduation were obliged to serve in the military for a period of eighteen months. The first four months of this period was considered a period of orientation for a minimum military training including the use of firearms. The remaining fourteen months with a rank of a second lieutenant, the medical doctors were engaged in active duties.

Excluding the large cities such as Tehran and other provincial centers, there were several satisfactory openings in the different attractive regions of Iran for the military enrollment. I selected the city of Bojnourd to serve my military duty. As a medical student I had the opportunity to visit the city of Bojnourd and I was acquainted through my brother, the former chief of the Bojnourd branch of the Ministry of finance, with a few Khans, the regional tribal leaders. Bojnourd was located in the northeastern region of Khorasan (now, Razavi Khorasan) province in the eastern region of Iran. The center of Razavi Khorasan is the holy city of Meshed or Mashhad one of the largest cities of Iran, located 530 miles east of Tehran, close to the border of Afghanistan. The shrine of Imam Reza, the eighth Shia Imam, with annual pilgrims and tourists of twenty millions, is located in Mashhad.

In addition Bojnourd was famous for full-blooded Turkmen horses. I was trained on horseback riding during my childhood staying in Shahrak, and this assignment gave me the opportunity to renew my interest, as an equestrian, in riding the superiorly trained horses.

The people of Bojnourd and the surrounding area, in addition to Farsi, spoke a dialect similar to Azeri, my mother's tongue.

At that time traveling by bus was the most convenient way to go to Bojnourd. It turned out to be a cumbersome and a very unpleasant journey, because of heavy snow covering the narrow and mountainous roads.

On my arrival at Bojnourd an elderly army sergeant, as a medical assistant, and his gracious wife sheltered me in their cozy home, in a warm room with the fireplace on, and served me a most delicious Iranian meal. I whole-heartedly appreciated this warm welcome by a gracious sincere couple. It was the best remedy for my heart aching nostalgia of being away from close-knit family. The majority of the Iranian students during their higher education, including medical school, if not married, irrespective of age live at home with their parents. I was one of them and until that moment I had lived at home. Therefore saying goodbye, even though it was not a life long separation, was very uncomfortable.

I was assigned to the Bojnourd district of a military instillation called Ilkhy, which was charged with equine promotion and training. My military instructor for the technical military indoctrination was a very competent professional sergeant. I was the only physician of the unit. My duties included providing healthcare to the military personnel, members of the unit and their family, and also medical screening of the new recruits.

The medical problems I encountered were within my competence. The patients were genuine, cooperative, and pleasant. Co-workers, colleagues, and officers were gracious with respectful manners toward the medical profession. Civil employees (hamradiffs), having a specified military rank, or trained active military officers varying from lieutenant to colonel, all were educated, kind, competent, and dedicated to their military profession.

Our division, although a military unit was not related to a ground force military unit a battalion, located also in Bojnourd. The battalion had a tight organization and strict rules, and an active and vigorous military training. The battalion did not have jurisdiction over our unit, but part of our military training including my brief firearm introduction was supervised and certified by the officers working within the territories of the battalion. These officers of course were enjoying and also milking their short lasting authority of training a physician how to aim his gun toward a target.

In general these two military compounds functioned well and had a satisfactory working relationship. At times, however, some unexpected events would disturb the peace and harmony and cause disquietude among the military and civilian people.

For instance one day suddenly and to our amazement we heard that the head physician of the battalion unit was arrested by the military police and was transferred to Tehran, being accused by the army of being a member of a clandestine organization within the army, affiliated with Tudeh party with a socialism-communism ideology.

The doctor was an active duty captain with extraordinary skill and medical competence, and he was badly needed by his patients and the citizens of Bojnourd.

At the time there was no daily newspaper in Bojnourd, and probably there was no need for one. The news had already been widely spread, leading to speculation, rumors and a great deal of justifiable anxiety among people. Anxiety of possible secret police surveillance and false accusation was further worsened by the lack of trust of the judicial system of the time.

Simultaneously with this important news, almost a comic event occurred. A young officer, an active army second lieutenant, with a conspicuous ego, but miniscule intelligence and wisdom filed a complaint against one of our soldiers, working in our army unit medical clinic, accusing him for not saluting him in an appropriate manner, compatible with army regulations, when passing him on a street. Surprisingly this trivial event not only created a time consuming problem within our military unit, but also attracted public attention. It required significant time, energy, meetings, and corresponding with the highest-ranking officers to establish the pettiness and absurdity of the complaint. These infantile behavioral patterns displayed in an inappropriate time, although uncommon, are not limited in time and place, they are everlasting and universal and are seen in all communities and professions.

A variety of terms have been used to define this behavior, including nit picking, narrow mindedness, missing the forest for the trees, tunnel vision, and so on. For lack of a satisfactory term, I call this petty behavior PPT, a peculiar petty trait syndrome.

The afflicted persons not only are not capable of contributing to the community significantly, but they also delay and hinder the contributions of others. They focus obsessively on a very small subject and neglect the serious issues. This syndrome gains much more clinical significance, when the sufferer is involved in public safety work, including the practice of medicine.

A senior medical student in an upscale medical school in the United States was assigned to obtain a brief history from a patient with an acute myocardial infarction or heart attack, he devoted a good portion of his brief history to an athlete's foot the patient was diagnosed to have in the past. I believe this student was suffering from PPT syndrome, although not a scientific and approved term.

My service at the army was a fulfilling service. Beautiful scenery, fresh and clean air, spacious offices, pleasant friends in the work place, and supportive superiors, all were invigorating and conducive to an inner peace necessary for a quality medical practice.

I extended my practice hours to the afternoons and early evenings. The army permitted the private practice. I was also encouraged to do so by the leaders of the tribe and the community, which was in need of more physicians. In addition to the physicians of the army including me, there was another physician, the director of the Ministry of Health of the Bojnourd branch, specializing in public health and general practice. Engaging in general practice was a challenging task. I announced my practice by displaying a large sign above the entrance of my office, located in the commercial section of Bojnourd. No prior appointment was necessary or possible. The patients walked in with a variety of illnesses, ranging from mild conjunctivitis, earache to localized and systemic infections, including pneumonia, typhoid fever, malaria, and tuberculosis. I even was able to manage minor surgical problems such as small fractures or dislocation of a joint or even circumcision. The patients were appreciative, polite, cooperative, and very much likable. They were not demanding; I wanted to do my best to help them. When the patients were very sick, I attended them at their home, if feasible. Because of unavailability of laboratory tests, I relied, if time permitted, on a detailed and thoughtful history and a clinical examination to make an accurate diagnosis and proceed with the management, which, not uncommonly, were not totally available.

Lack of laboratory facilities and relying on clinical information improved my diagnostic accuracy and clinical judgment, which has helped me throughout my practice of medicine, reducing my dependence on laboratory data and expensive and potentially risky invasive diagnostic procedures.

When the diagnosis was not clear or the treatment was not available, the patients, if willing or could afford it, were referred to Mashhad or even to Tehran for the continuation of the medical management. I had no nurse, no technician, and there was no need to one. There was no record keeping or documentation system. The diagnosis was jotted down on the prescription form with prescribed medications and the patients were instructed to bring the forms on the next visit, if any. There was no set physician fee, and no set procedure for the collection of fees. The patients' payment was not considered a fee for the medical services provided, it only reflected the sense of appreciation of the patients. The amount of money paid was commensurate with the social and the economic status of the patients. My patient profile included, merchants, shopkeepers, farmers, landowners, tribal leaders, local government employees, housewives, school children, villagers and city dwellers; I had no charity patients.

One night I was requested to attend, as an emergency, the high profile general director of the Ministry of Education, visiting he Bojnourd branch of the ministry. To my surprise he was one of my old teachers from high school, concerned about his chest pain. I was not a cardiologist then, but I was confident that the pain was of muscular origin and of no significant consequences, manageable with two tablets of aspirin. The interpretation of pain was of a great comfort for both of us, in a relatively remote town, far away from our family. I was proud of the high achievement of my former teacher, and both of us aware of his contribution to my academic growth. Staying in Bojnourd and practicing medicine was one of the options I had considered for my future at the time. I still think about it.

I completed my military services and was evaluated on the ethics, behavior, competence, commanding capability, and military sprits, and I passed all with a good grade. At the completion of my services I also received a commendation letter from the Central Commander-in-Chief of our unit, in the Ministry of War in Tehran.

CHAPTER 40

Arsanjan

During my military service in Bojnourd, I had decided to pursue a postdoctoral education, preferably in cardiology either in France or in the USA. France seemed to be advantageous because I spoke French fluently and our medical textbooks were written in French, plus our medical school's training style and concept were patterned after French schools. In addition I could begin the specialty of cardiology directly without prior specialization the internal medicine as required in the USA. I preferred and selected the United States. After returning to Tehran in August 1955, I realized that also a year of internship is required prior to internal medicine training in the USA. But the internship would not start until July 1, 1956, so I had to fill the gap. It was not appropriate to return to Bojnourd for an additional several months of practice. Therefore I secured a position in the Imperial Organization of the Social Services, as the head of a medical clinic in the village of Arsanjan, nearby Shiraz, the city of Sa'di and Hafiz, the capital of Fars Province, the original Pars, homeland of Cyrus the Great.

The Mausoleum of Cyrus the Great is in Pasagadae, which is about twenty-seven miles from Persepolis. In 1971 a celebration of the anniversary of the Persian Empire, founded by Cyrus the Great 2500-year ago, started in Pasargadae, then moved to Persepolis, by Mohammad Reza Shah Pahlavi. Persepolis was cleaned, large tents were stalled, tree and flowers were planted, catering services by Maxim de Paris were established, and red Mercedes Benz Limousines were used to transport the guests. Festivities included the longest and most lavish banquet, fireworks, music, and the parade of the army at different periods of Iran. SAVAK provided security. Maxim provided the dinner menu. Kings, Queens, Princes and Princesses, Presidents, Prime Ministers were among guests. Emperor Selassie, and Vice President Spiro Agnew attended the celebration. The cost of the celebration ranged from twenty million to two hundred million. The celebration contributed to the fall of the Shah.

My new occupation started in the fall of 1955. Arsanjan and the surrounding areas were beautiful during autumn with vast natural landscapes, blue sky and colorful flowers on days and shining stars at nights, and the recital of Hafiz poems on days and at nights. The clinic was spacious, the living quarters modern and well furnished. A cook and a maid were assigned to the living quarters. A highly competent medical assistant helped me in daily practice. The patients' care and medications were free to all. One night I was visiting a very respected Shia cleric about ninety years old in his residence, sitting on a mattress, leaning his back against a large pillow. He was reciting the Hafiz poems in competition with his great grandson about ten year-old. In alternating turn, he recited one line of lyrics to be answered by his great grandson, by quoting another lyric line of Hafiz without repeating any line until one of them failed to recall a new verse. It was an inspirational experience, peace, love, and contentment filling the air. These were the moments I thought I was in heaven and tempted to stay in Arsanjan and practice medicine. Although +the practice of medicine in Arsanjan was enjoyable, it was different from that of Bojnourd. In both practices the patients were appreciative and treated the physician with respect; in Bojnourd they consulted me as their doctor; in Arsanjan they visited me as a physician working for the Imperial Organization Clinic and usually did not fail to extend their immense gratitude to His Majesty.

During my several months of stay in Arsanjan I had contemplated further about my future plan and I had become convinced to pursue my specialty training in the USA.

Therefore in the winter of 1956, I returned to Tehran to prepare for my long awaited journey. On arrival in Tehran, in addition to my self-study books, I enrolled in the official English language learning programs.

Meanwhile after preliminary research and consultation with my colleagues, I requested applications for an internship from several teaching institutions in the USA, mainly in the New York area. I received an application from Englewood Hospital, Englewood, NJ. After completion, I returned the application and shortly after I received a letter from the hospital, acknowledging my acceptance to their internship program. I obtained my passport with a student visa, ready to fly to Paris on my way to the United States, to start my internship on July 1, 1956.

Before the departure I followed a well wishing ritual that most Iranians undergo prior to a long journey. The ritual reflected the love, pride, and the support of the family, but it also was a source of sadness touching the soul and bringing on the everlasting painful nostalgia. The members of the family were gathered at the exit door of our residence in Tehran.

I kissed and hugged all members of my family and my mother, watching her smiling and crying at the same time, holding my face tightly between her two hands. It was a painful experience. My father held his holy book of Qur'an, the sacred book of Islam over my head, just under the doorframe, while I was getting out. He held the book until I reentered and exited once more; I kissed his hands and the Qur'an, not aware that I was saying my last goodbye to him. He died of a heart attack in Tehran, during my training at Chicago's Mercy Hospital. I moved toward the car ready to go to Mehrabad airport, while my mother was sprinkling rose water after me, and everyone wishing me a safe trip in Farsi or Azeri.

PART III

My Life In The United States Of America

CHAPTER 41

Internship in the USA

I stayed in Paris for several days. I felt at home and comfortable in Paris, being relatively versed in history, culture, literature, and the medical science of the French society. I was almost tempted to change my plan and secure a postdoctoral residency program in medicine. Soon logic prevailed and I departed from Paris to, then, LaGuardia airport.

I had a reservation in one of the YMCA hotels, in New York City, recommended to me by one of my friends in Tehran, who had traveled to the USA on several occasions. The hotel probably was suitable to my friend; but it was a depressing site for me. Leaving my comfortable home in Tehran, then beautiful Paris with a luxury hotel, and landing in that particular hotel, with a small and suffocating room, and not well kept facilities and bored and detached employees, was a judgment error. I wanted badly to go back, return to Bojnourd, to embrace my past life and the cozy environment; I was homesick, but determined to go on. The next day at the Englewood Hospital I met one of the administrators of the hospital, a well-dressed man, sitting behind a large desk greeted me with Howdy, rhymed almost with my first name Hadi. Before I could figure out what he was saying, he added "good" "good" followed by words uttered in rapid succession. It seemed he was contracting several words to one word or fast forwarding his conversation or trying to display staccato. Partly understood but mostly guessed, he was explaining my duties as an intern. My internship at the Englewood Hospital turned out to be an enjoyable experience. The living quarters provided by the hospital were well kept and comfortable.

The well-organized hospital and the surrounding area displayed an atmosphere of tranquility, solidness, and prosperity. The co-workers and nurses were supportive, gracious; however one of the nurses was more supportive and gracious or perhaps I wanted her to be, she is my wife and my soul mate now. It was not only love at first site, but it was also a first love. Although we did not verbalize, an inner melodic song was telling me that we were going to make the most important decision of our life. My mentors were composed of highly qualified physicians, surgeons, and capable teachers, mostly graduated from Columbia (P&S) and Cornell Medical Schools.

The medical staff included also physicians overwhelmed by their practice and in need of education themselves. My rotating internship duties seemed rather simple, with fewer responsibilities than those of my previous internship in Tehran University Hospitals. At times I felt overqualified for the assignments. For instance, at Englewood Hospital, I was permitted and honored to take care of a superficial skin laceration independently; in contrast in Tehran I performed an appendectomy under supervision, but independently. In Englewood Hospital we obtained history, performed physical examination, and reviewed the laboratory data of the patients, then reached a tentative diagnosis. The attending physicians reviewed, critiqued and co-signed our chartings. We attended a culturally, educationally, economically, and ethnically heterogeneous groups of patients, who were mostly gracious, appreciative, and intelligent. There were naturally rare exceptions. I was supposed to start an I.V. (intravenous) in a middle age morbidly obese woman, a part of scutt work the interns used to do at the time. She was distraught, not cooperative, and she was thinking that I was a Jew with a big nose. She was not anti-Semitic and her husband was a Jew. I believe she was my first patient in my practice suffering from severe xenophobia.

During my internship training I began to apply for a residency program in internal medicine, since the Englewood Hospital was not accredited for it. I wanted to secure a residency position in a hospital affiliated with a medical school in the East Coast or Midwest region. Several hospital required letters of recommendations from Englewood Hospital. The Chairman of the Department of Medicine at that time was willing to write, as he called, a superior recommendation letter. It was a very supportive recommendation letter, but in the letter he characterized me as a rather shy intern. The chairman not intentionally weakened the impact of his superior recommendation by using the word of shy. He probably and justifiably had had no time to delve sufficiently into my cultural background. In addition to his busy practice of medicine and his administrative duties, he needed time to keep himself well groomed and dressed with a demeanor of self-admiration, and tendency toward narcissism. In the Iranian cultural background, those days, to be reserved and quiet among the older and senior individuals was considered to be a virtue and being loud, voluble, and talkative was a sign of disrespect. Several years later, when I was being inducted to the fellowship of the American Heart Association, I met the chairman, who seemed rather reticent and quiet and seemingly shy at the time. I was tempted to tell him "come on man, who is shy?" I didn't, because he was my senior and former mentor, and I felt shy.

Some of the longtime nurses in the operating and delivery rooms had a territorial imperative attitude. The sight of an intern elicited in them a conditioned reflex response of fight compelling them to utter "don't touch, "be careful" with an air of super authority.

CHAPTER 42

Residency at Mercy Hospital, Chicago

From several available institutions I selected Mercy Hospital and Loyola University Clinics for my residency in internal medicine, starting July 1, 1957.

Madelyn and I said good-bye, but our affect was not in concordance with the occasion, when we were expecting a separation for a lifetime. Probably we knew our separation was a momentary one. On arrival to Chicago, I phoned and I asked her to marry me; I did not wait for an answer, it was clear, we set the date for September, we married in September in Englewood, among families and friends, at a dazzling ceremony hosted by Madelyn's aunt. Madelyn was born in Bayonne, New Jersey, but grew up in Englewood, New Jersey. Her father Edward Leonard was proud of his Irish ancestry and her mother Marion was of German and English origin and they resided in Englewood. The next day, after the wedding, we returned to Chicago, she started to work at Michael Reese Hospital as a nurse; there was no opening available at Mercy.

Mercy was and still is a catholic teaching and health institution, in Chicago, governed by the Sisters of Mercy. Presently called Mercy Hospital and Medical Center (Mercy), a part of the National Healthcare Facilities, is continued to be governed by the Religious Sisters of Mercy (R.S.M.) founded by Catherine McAuley in Dublin, Ireland in 1831. In addition to their religious vows of poverty, chastity, and obedience, and participation in the religious life, Sisters of Mercy are active in education, healthcare, social services, and promotion of welfare of the society.

The Sisters were granted a charter by the State of Illinois to found the first private hospital in Chicago in 1852. Mercy Hospital became affiliated with Rush Medical College in 1853 and became the primary teaching hospital of the Chicago Medical College in 1864, later to become the Northwestern University Medical School. The affiliation with Northwestern University continued until 1920. Mercy began its affiliation with the Stritch School of Medicine of Loyola University in 1920, and the affiliation continued for four decades.

Mercy Hospital was relocated to Chicago's South Side, 26th Street and Calumet Avenue in 1863, from its location at Van Buren and Wabash Avenue, thus escaping the Great Fire of Chicago in 1871.

The words of Mercy and McAuley are dear to us also because of Mother McAuley High School, governed by the Sisters of Mercy; both our daughters are alumnae of the school and received a solid education under the tutelage of the Sisters of Mercy. Denise has a doctorate degree in psychology from Loyola University, in Chicago, and she is a professor of psychology at Carroll College, Wisconsin. She married Dr. Steve Guastello, a professor of psychology at Marquette University in Wisconsin. Andrea their daughter is majoring in English in Marquette. Desiree, a valedictorian of the school, a graduate of the honors program of Northwestern Medical School, now a cardiologist and a Fellow of the American College of Cardiology, is practicing in Wisconsin.

Last expanded in 1869, the Mercy Hospital building was old but solid when I began my residency at Mercy. It was well kept with spacious rooms and corridors with a majestic appearance. The patients with insurance or capable of affording their hospitalization expenses were hospitalized in private or semiprivate rooms. The other patients were confined to the large wards, with several beds, separated by curtains, designated for men and women. Mercy had a large and busy clinic, delivering various medical specialty care to the surrounding community.

The famous historical Murphy Amphitheatre attested to the high level of teaching hospital status Mercy had reached in the Chicago area. Many of the renowned physicians and surgeons were also members of the faculty of Loyola University, Stritch School of Medicine.

They practiced jointly as a group or individually as a solo practitioner. A comprehensive training in internal medicine and its subspecialties were offered to the residents. My interest in teaching started early when I was in medical school. During summers I used to tutor the high school students in mathematics and natural sciences for financial support. But it was my participation in medical education, as a resident teaching the medical students and interns, at Mercy that enhanced my interest in teaching, which ever since has enriched my professional life. During my training at Mercy, the morning rounds with the members of the groups or individual physicians, not only were an educational experience, but also they had become enjoyable family-like rituals, part of our daily life.

Studying at home and self-learning equivalent to the home schooling of today, during my elementary school years was a learned behavior, which has stayed with me and helped me to upgrade my medical education at my convenient times.

The skill of self-learning, research, and the interpretation of medical literatures were promoted by some of the members of the teaching staff at Mercy.

The hospital had a high quality training program in the major specialties, and was an ideal place for training the medical students, rotating interns, and the residents of internal medicine.

In addition to the residents graduating from American medical schools, the residency program at Mercy at that time, included physicians graduating from foreign medical schools, including Argentina, Cuba, Germany, Greece, Iran, Ireland, Lebanon, the Philippines, Turkey, and others. A cohesive international group of physicians, all speaking English, but with different accents and a slightly different physical appearance.

This panoramic sight was reflecting the spiritual richness of the Sisters of Mercy at that time. However, some people probably lacking intellectual vision, were not able to appreciate it as a richness and instead of focusing on the individuals qualifications and aptitude, they unleashed their PPT (petty personality trait) syndrome, preoccupied with minutiae and trivia, and petty things, thus neglecting the essentials. These individuals constantly preoccupied with ethnicity, color, texture of hair, and the shape of the eyes, if unchecked may contribute to the creation of a mediocre, depressing and repulsive environment. As I have discussed as a part of my army experience in Bojnourd, the PPT syndrome has a worldwide distribution and is not uncommon in the American health system. After two years of training at Mercy, it was difficult to leave so many dear friends including the good Sisters, and my mentors behind and move on.

Madelyn was pregnant with our first baby, moving back to the east to be close to her wonderfully kind parents was advantageous; plus I was planning, if possible to obtain a fellowship in cardiology on the east coast, preferably in New York, Philadelphia, or Boston.

CHAPTER 43

Going to Philadelphia for fellowship

My third year residency in internal medicine was at Episcopal Hospital affiliated with Temple University, in Philadelphia. The quality and type of residency was similar to Mercy Hospital of Chicago. In addition to the difference in accent of the people, Episcopal Hospital was reflecting the east coast culture and the city of brotherly love of Philadelphia, and Mercy Hospital was mirroring Chicago and the Irish catholic trends and culture. Similar to the faculty of Mercy Hospital, the clinicians at Episcopal Hospital-Temple University were highly qualified, but probably with more inclination toward the academic medicine and didactic lectures with more emphasis on cardiology. Similar to Mercy there was no fellowship program in cardiology at Episcopal Hospital, so I had to search and move again.

From the several reputable cardiology fellowship programs in Philadelphia, where I had planned to remain until the end of my training in the USA, the program in the Philadelphia General Hospital-Graduate School of Medicine of the University of Pennsylvania was more compatible with my objectives. A dynamic program in cardiology with a faculty composed of high profile adult and pediatric cardiologists, physiologists, basic scientists, technicians, visiting professors, and consultants. The two institutions combined possessed abundant numbers of cardiac patients with various backgrounds, clinical facilities, well equipped diagnostic and experimental and research laboratories. The combined units were also a referral center for the evaluation of complex acquired and congenital heart diseases.

By the end of June 1961 I had completed my training and I was eligible to be certified by the American Board of Internal Medicine and after that by the American Subspecialty Board of Cardiovascular Diseases. I wanted to return to Iran and practice medicine there; after all that was my objective when I enrolled in the University of Tehran.

Now I had more responsibility, any major decision would have affected also my family; taking my wife and our daughter, now 2 years old, to Iran without an appropriate preparation did not seem to be advisable, therefore, I decided to return back to Iran alone.

CHAPTER 44

Returning to Iran

While flying back to Iran I was wrestling with a state of anxiety, which was bothering me. For sure I was missing the USA and my pleasant memories for the past 5 years, and most importantly my new family. I also was certain that I wanted to serve my beloved biological country. My cause of anxiety probably was the uncertainty of getting an opportunity to serve. The enthusiastic welcome of the members of my family at Mehrabad airport in Tehran, the delighted and joyful eyes of my mother, dressed in a black outfit, still mourning my father's death, riding again thru the streets of Tehran, all were soul lifting events, but also emotionally overwhelming. I felt after being away for five years, I was not simply returning home, but I was being reborn to utopia, surrounded by beauty, kindness, tenderness, and love. I was in heaven, staying with my mother in her new home, purchased by my father while I was in the USA. The house was located in southern Tehran, Shahpour Avenue, an old district, in those days modest enough and appropriate for my father with his religious status. The house was a walking distance from my father's religious center. All activities relative to the Islamic religion took place in the center or "masjed" under the leadership of my father. Daily prayer, sermons, and religious transaction were part of the activities. His Masjed was also in the vicinity of Tehran's grand bazaar. In every major city in Iran, there is one bazaar, spelled also bazar. Bazaars not only are the centers for trade, but they are also the centers of politics and they represent the conservative views and culture of middle class Iranians. They are linked strongly to ulema, yielding a political influence, capable of promoting or defeating major plans of the central government. They are usually vaulted long narrow labyrinths and corridors with shops on both sides. Architecturally beautiful high dome shaped ceilings cover the corridors. They are of varying size; the length of the corridors may reach several miles. The grand bazaar of Tehran is believed to be the largest one in the world.

The goods for sale consist of Persian rugs, jewelry, cloths, spice, furniture, shoes and a variety of other goods. Each corridor specializes in the trade of specific merchandize. Bargaining by customers is a part of the culture and requires a special skill. Some of my fondest memory of Iran revolves around my mother's skillful bargaining with the merchants at bazaar. Some bazaars have additional facilities such as bathhouses and restaurants.

After Reza Shah was deposed my father moved the rest of the family, including my mother, two sisters, and two younger brothers to Tehran.

At the time of his arrival to Tehran from Shahrak, my father had six sons and two daughters. Three sons older than me were Amin, who became the deputy minister of finance; Hassan, who became high-ranking officer of Gendarmerie in Iran; Mehdi, a member of the legal staff of the Majles. Two brothers younger than me were Ebrahim, an agricultural engineer and Aziz, who graduated from the military college and became a high-ranking officer of the army and received a doctorate degree in sociology.

My oldest sister Fakhri married in a few years and died of congenital heart disease. Badrieh Khanum (Badri), born after fakhri, married Ibrahim Vahebi (deceased), presently lives in Illinois with her children.

It took several years before my father was able to adjust to a new culture and community and organize his life. When he died I was in Chicago. I still feel the heart wrenching emotion and guilt, although his death was sudden. At the occasion of his death, a large number of his followers officially mourned and markets and shops were closed at his district. In his book titled "The Path of Truth" he discusses and analyses the fundamentals of Islam in a style similar to that of Sa'di's, the great Iranian poet. He skillfully by using verse, prose, and poem in Arabic and in Farsi languages expresses his beliefs and thoughts.

The next day after arrival to Tehran, I visited my father's mausoleum, a heart breaking experience, but an absolutely unwritten law of conduct in the Iranian culture.

In a few days, the pleasant dream was over and wide-awake I began to walk on the reality ground, looking for a place to live and practice medicine. Within several weeks the Iranian Ministry of Education approved my training credentials obtained in the USA and a permit was issued allowing me to practice medicine in the field of cardiology in Iran including Tehran.

Madelyn and Denise joined me in Tehran in early October. Their arrival was welcomed. They surprisingly and reluctantly witnessed a celebratory ritual of sacrificing a lamb, which is usually performed to express gratitude for the safe arrival of loved ones. This welcome was followed by dining festivities hosted by the members of our family.

According to the Iranian law, Madelyn and Denise both were Iranian citizens.

In civilized communities and families, cultural, language, religious, and nationality differences do not keep the people apart and even they might augment the matrimonial bond and commitment, we were surrounded by civilized people.

We had rented a house in an upscale section of Tehran. I used a few spacious rooms in the first floor as my office. The signboard at the door indicating that the practice was limited to cardiology. I filled out an application and submitted it to the Ministry of Health for a cardiology position in any hospital in Tehran, governed by the Ministry. Soon after, I was appointed as a cardiologist to Adham Hospital, in the heart of the southern part of Tehran. My work started in December 1961, after a brief orientation course in public health. The orientation lectures were held in a large conference hall, in the Ministry of Heath. Western style pictures, probably imported from the USA or Europe and donated or sold to the Iranian Government, by the advertising companies in collaboration with chain grocery or drug stores, were decorating the walls of the lecture hall. The pictures were showing red and succulent meat, fleshy chickens on expensive plates, and attractively uniformed prosperous looking women holding syringes with needles. Probably they meant to remind us to educate the patients in selecting an appropriate diet, taking their prescribed medications on time, and the importance and necessity of preventive immunization. The patients of the hospital that I was assigned did not need any instruction, I am sure, had they had food, they would have consumed it without any hesitation, because they were hungry. The instructors in public health were western educated elite Iranian physicians, good-hearted, neat but oblivious of the healthcare reality in Iran, they were misplaced. When I questioned the value of this pretentious orientation, I confronted a mixture of an angry and surprised look.

I also had submitted my resume to an organization founded by His Majesty, the Shah. The organization was supposed to assist the Iranians, trained in different fields abroad, in securing a meaningful position on their return to Iran. When I informed the director of the organization of my employment at Adham Hospital, he without any hesitation, checked an empty box adjacent to my name, implying the position was filled by the organization, receiving credit for it. Of course the organization had no input in my employment.

The president of the Adham Hospital, a medical doctor, and other medical personnel were gracious and supportive. My position was newly created; therefore, there were no existent cardiac facilities. Starting to build up a new cardiac unit with the appropriate manpower and facilities, at the time, seemed not plausible, but not impossible. I decided to begin a fact-finding journey and a feasibility study. Meanwhile the hospital, with insufficient resources and facilities, had to deal with urgent public health priorities and provide care for emergency patients. Naturally I got involved in these important priorities.

At the request of the president of the hospital I had started a lecture series in basic cardiology, but I changed it to a basic series in general internal medicine, after we encountered patients with undiagnosed streptococcal infection, sexually transmitted diseases, ruptured tubal pregnancies, attempted suicide and vitamin deficiencies.

Management of these patients although a rewarding experience, was not to my satisfaction and was often delayed; plus the emergency general practice was not in congruity with my training or my objectives.

On the brighter side my private practice began to flourish, but again most of the patients consulting me were free of cardiovascular ailments.

Even my own relatives with sincere and good intention indiscriminately, referred patients with problems not within my domain of practice, such as measles, degenerative joint disease, headache, disorders of the skin, and even opium addiction. During several months of private practice only one of my patients, who suffered from an acute gastrointestinal bleeding needed hospitalization. He was hospitalized in a small private hospital and I consulted a surgeon, a classmate of mine trained in the USA; for possible surgical intervention should the necessity arise. Small and relatively well-equipped private hospitals were being established in Tehran, mainly by American trained medical doctors.

I entertained the possibility of joining the faculty of Tehran University, Medical school. It probably would have been academically helpful, but without a significant effect on my cardiology practice. Therefore I tabled it for sometime in the future.

As I gained more experience by analyzing the medical practice state in Iran, and I crystallized my thoughts and clarified my options. I believed that the establishment of a comprehensive and modern cardiology in Tehran was not feasible as a short-range plan, but undoubtedly in a long time it would have become a successful practice and financially and intellectually rewarding.

I also could have continued the general medical practice for an undetermined period of time, hoping to eventually narrow my field of practice to the specialty of cardiology in the future, but uncertainty of the future with this option had a constant disquieting effect.

I could have forgotten my specialty training and restart the type of practice I had in Bojnourd, in Tehran or preferably in the smaller towns or even villages. This option at its best would have been considered to be missionary work, for which there was no need in Iran at the time and at its worst it was the acceptance of failure, of course not acceptable.

To establish a solid cardiology center with well-equipped modern laboratories, and qualified personnel, privately owned or governed by the Ministry of Health was another doable option, but it required a large sum of capital, political connection, and authoritative status with an entrepreneurship sprit, full time administrative work, and a very high level of conviction. I possessed none of them.

CHAPTER 45

Returning to the USA

The option of returning back to the USA for more advanced training or to practice as suggested by some of my American friends, became a realistic one, when unexpectedly I was notified by the National Heart Institute of the United States of America that my request for a post-doctoral fellowship in cardiology had been approved. It was pleasant and soul lifting news. I had forgotten that I had applied for a fellowship prior to my departure to Iran. Although naturally Madelyn was eager to return to the USA, she was also enjoying her Iranian life style. Even though I was facing some difficulties in organizing my professional life to my satisfaction, our private life style was peaceful and agreeable. In addition to the supportive and delightful members of the family, resources such as maids, cooks, and companions were available to assist Madelyn during her adjustment period.

I was indebted to David Lewis, MD, PHD, a physiologist and cardiologist of the University of Pennsylvania, and the Director of the Hemodynamic Laboratory at the Philadelphia General Hospital, for sponsoring my fellowship. In addition to advancing my technical and cognitive skills in diagnostic cardiac catheterization and hemodynamic studies, and addressing the problems at hands, I was engaged in investigational studies in the cardiovascular pathophysiology and electrophysiology and intracardiac acoustics with respect to the genesis of the heart sounds and murmurs.

Although the fellows abided with rules and regulations of the sponsoring institutions, they were privileged to focus on their chosen projects as submitted to the National Heart Institute, and in the hospital or medical school they were only responsible for the care of patients involved in their projects and no other duties assigned to them. The director of the division of cardiology at the Philadelphia General Hospital and University of Pennsylvania Graduate School of Medicine at the time and during my training was the renowned cardiologist, Samuel Bellet, MD, an internationally recognized researcher, scientist, and educator. Unfortunately I have not been able to emulate him in my clinical practice, educational, and administrative styles, perhaps that might be the reason I have not been able to achieve his eminent status.

Now I had more options, in addition to returning back to Iran, I could have continued my career in cardiovascular research, or I could have engaged in clinical practice in the USA. While contemplating and exploring the possibilities, I received a letter from one of my old mentors at Mercy Hospital in Chicago, encouraging me to consider returning to Mercy.

BACK TO MERCY AGAIN

Tabling all other options, I decided to join the medical staff at Mercy, to practice cardiology starting July 1, 1963.

I joined Vaughn Medical group, one of the two multispecialty groups at Mercy at that time, headed by Dr. Arkell Vaughn, a genuine and competent cigar-smoking surgeon. He was a past president of the Medical and Scientific staff of Mercy Hospital (1949-1952), an excellent promoter, proud of his group and his achievement. He also believed in the multipurpose efficacy of vitamin B12 injection in the management of his patients. The other group was the reputable Schmitz Medical Group, after Henry Schmitz, the founder.

Vaughn group had two offices located in the South Side of Chicago, one in the Bridgeport region, one of the political power centers in Chicago; the other office was located farther south, at 79th and Jeffrey Street, a better residential section at that time. The group managed a large number of hospitalized and office patients.

Both groups were influential in the affairs and the policies of the hospital.

The quality of practice by the members of both groups collectively mirrored in general the quality care in the Hospital. Although I was the cardiologist of the group, at the start I was unable to limit my practice totally to cardiology. For the organizational and traditional reasons within the group, I had to participate in on call schedule on a rotating basis. Fortunately adjusting from academia and Ivy League environment to fairly busy clinical practice was facilitated by the existence of quality education at Mercy Hospital.

During my residency training at Mercy, a few years back, we were assigned for a specific period of time to each group mentioned above. The consensus among the trainees at that time was that the Vaughn Medical Group's patients had more complicated illnesses and the Schmitz medical Group's educational style was more appealing with the inclination toward more sophistication.

Devoting a significant part of my time to medical education and learning upgraded my clinical skill with a positive effect on my teaching skill, promoting my professional image within the group as well as among my colleagues, co-workers, and the patients at Mercy Hospital.

In the graduation ceremony in June 1964, the House Staff awarded me with the first George O'Brien's Teacher of the year award.

Dr. O'Brien was the Chairman of the Department of Medicine, a reputable, high profile internist-cardiologist, Professor of Medicine at Loyola University, and an excellent teacher. I began to enjoy my fulfilling job despite hard work and a very modest income. June 1964 was also a special month for us because our son, Paul, now J. D. from Loyola University of Chicago, was born on June 8, 1964, at Mercy, delivered by Dr. Charles Smith. My mother visited us shortly after Paul was born and stayed with us for several months. She proved herself to be courageous, compassionate, and full of love. Several Sisters of Mercy made our life richer and her stay more enjoyable by their gracious attitude and kindness toward her. Their spirituality and faith nullified the cultural, religious, and language barriers.

I was surrounded by friends, encouraged, and supported by almost all. My relative success, not unexpectedly, was not received well by a very small number of my colleagues. I began to hear unfair criticisms initiated by them, concerning my nationality, medical school, ethnicity, and accent, the characteristics I could not and would not be willing to change.

They are always and everywhere, among all kinds of people, including intelligent, honest, and good doctors, who derive pleasure from the misfortunes of others or feel miserable and desperate by witnessing the success of others. Of course both sentiments are bad; it is difficult to determine which one is the worse. Unhappy people instead of advancing their own career, they dwell in magnifying their perceived deficiencies of the others. There might be many factors contributing to this unhealthy and devastating attitude, but probably one of the a plausible reasons may be the inferiority complex and lack of confidence of these people in their own ability to compete. They feel the best way to become noticeable is to work with the people less noticeable and competitive than they are. They turn off the lights; darken the room, to visualize their small candles.

Attending the patients at their home or making a house call was a policy of the group, in line with the trend of the community. The house calls were time consuming and really not cost-effective events and, at times, not free of risks. We visited patients with acute medical problems, exacerbation of chronic conditions, and the patients with disabilities, unable to visit the office. Majority of house calls occurred at nights when we were on-call, but not infrequently they were at scheduled times, we visited the patients at their home. Switching from the podium of teaching the graduate students at the University of Pennsylvania, discussing the electrophysiology of the heart, to making a house call in a crowded room in the third floor of an apartment building located in a Bridgeport neighborhood in Chicago South Side, on a patient with gouty arthritis, at the first glance seemed to be a very difficult task, but it was not. It was a great way to assimilate and become part of the people and their culture in Chicago and practice medicine among them.

To be identified as a cardiologist within the medical community, particularly among the high profile cardiologists in Chicago, it was necessary to modify the pattern and direction of my practice and strictly limit it to cardiology.

At the end of my third year contract with the group, I relocated my office to downtown Chicago and engaged in the solo practice of cardiology with more independence and more financial responsibility. Mercy Hospital was my primary and only private hospital affiliation. I initiated the process of affiliation with the faculty of Loyola University, Medical School and the professional societies.

I began to upgrade the cardiology services at Mercy Hospital, supported by Dr. John Hoesley, the chief of cardiology at the time. I also planned to initiate clinical research in cardiovascular disease.

In 1966, we established one of the first special units at the old Mercy Hospital for acutely ill patients, cardiac and non-cardiac, with potentially reversible conditions and named it Intensive Care Unit (ICU). I was the director of the unit and Sister Mary Paulette, the Supervisor. The unit was equipped with monitoring systems, defibrillators, and the residents, nurses and staff were especially trained. We planned to separate cardiac patients in the near future and establish a cardiac (coronary) care unit (CCU).

The events were encouraging and pleasant. The new building for Mercy was dedicated in November 1967, by the most Reverend John L. May, the auxiliary Bishop of Chicago, who was the Chaplin of Mercy Hospital during my training at Mercy.

In January 1968, the new Mercy Hospital was open for occupancy and the patients moved to the new location, at Stevenson Expressway and King Drive, Chicago, Dr. Robert Schmitz was the President of the Medical & Scientific Staff, at the time. The building was modernly designed, attractive, and impressive with lecture halls, conference rooms, spacious patients' rooms with an 517 beds capacity, and a well equipped, well staffed cardiac care unit in line with my suggestions based on the national trend of the time.

An integral part of the new hospital was a Diagnostic and Treatment (D&T) Center, with numerous examining rooms, pharmacy, Medical and Administrative Directors, thirty-six specialty clinics, and the voluntering members of the M&SS of Mercy. Since opening in 1921, in addition to offering quality medical care to the community, the clinic has been an excellent center for medical education.

Mercy Hospital activities also included basic scientific research by the members of the Research and Psychology Departments. The Research Department founded in 1969 was devoted to the advancement of medical knowledge. In addition to basic scientific research, the department carried out clinically applicable program in collaboration with the members of the medical staff. An active psychology center was offering assistance to children with learning disabilities and to their parents. Addressing the spiritual needs of the patients and their families a solid Pastoral Department directed by specially trained and expert priests and nuns has been an important part of Mercy Hospital.

The Sisters of Mercy have always been supported, for their good and humanitarian works, by prominent community business-civic leaders and organizations such as the Board of Advisors and Women's Board of Mercy Hospital. Members of Women's Board on those days usually were doctors' wives; by joining the Board they demonstrate their husband's loyalty to Mercy Hospital. Madelyn Dizadji was the president of the Board from 1979 to 1981.During my association with Mercy, Mayors of Chicago,

Mayor Richard J. Daley and Mayor Richard M. Daley have genuinely supported the Sisters in their humanitarian and ministry works. At Mercy Hospital's Dinner/Dance and Civil Salute on October 6, 1971, Mayor Richard J. Daley proclaimed, October 6, Mercy Hospital and Medical Center's Day in Chicago, honoring the Sister of Mercy for their vision and courage in assisting the victims of the Chicago Fire of 1871. The Mercy Dinner/Dance, sponsored annually by the friends of Mercy, started in 1968, is another way the people of Chicago extend their appreciation to the Sisters of Mercy for serving the community since 1852.

On the occasion of the 125th year celebration of Mercy Hospital and Medical center, in 1977, on behalf of the medical staff I made the following comment: "In achieving their humanitarian goals, the Sisters of Mercy have enjoyed the support of spiritual and civic leaders, the community in general, and competent and dedicated physicians in particular. Today's gathering attests to this fact."

After being certified by the American Board of Internal Medicine (Diplomate of ABIM) and specialty Board of Cardiovascular Diseases (CVD), I went through the required promotional changes in my affiliation with Cook County Hospital, Loyola University, University of Illinois, and Mercy Hospital.

By the end of 1970, I had been honored with Fellowships of the American College of Physicians, American College of Cardiology, American Heart Association, and the faculty rank of Clinical Associate Professor of the University of Illinois, Abraham Lincoln of Medicine, and the Chief of Cardiology at Mercy Hospital.

CHAPTER 46

Program Directorship and Affiliation with University of Illinois

In 1971, I was appointed the Program Director of the Department of Medicine at Mercy, a newly established position, in conjunction with our affiliation with the University of Illinois. Very briefly my duties in general terms consisted of development, implementation, evaluation, and maintenance of programs in undergraduate, graduate and continuing medical educations and possibly promoting clinical research, in Department of Medicine at Mercy and relative to the affiliation with the University of Illinois. My active participation in teaching and contribution to patients care in relation to education were also required.

Although many hospitals without training programs are able to provide quality care to their patients, undergraduate, and graduate medical educations were essential to promote Mercy as an academic institution and a provider of quality of care.

My philosophy in the practice of medicine has been on the premise that quality medical education and patient care are inseparable, striving to accomplish one ultimately leads to achieving the other.

Affiliation with Loyola University, Stritch School of Medicine had been of great value in the past. Loyola established a new Loyola University Medical Center, and a new teaching hospital in 1969. Mercy Hospital entered an affiliation with the University of Illinois, to participate in the undergraduate education program of the university and upgrade the residency program of Mercy.

The university of Illinois took a major step to extend its undergraduate clinical medical education programs to the hospitals in the Chicago Metropolitan area, with long-range objectives of establishing medical centers for training medical students, sort of local clinical medical schools, with a centralized basic science school. By doing so the University of Illinois would have been able to increase the number of the graduating physicians from the University of Illinois, retain more physicians in the state, and shorten the collective duration of medical training.

In Chicago, at the University's Medical Center Camp, the College of Medicine's traditional structure had been divided into the Abraham Lincoln School of Medicine (ALSM) a 3-year clinical school, and the School of Basic Medical Sciences, a one year program for the freshman medical students.

An affiliation agreement with ALSM was signed by Sister Mary Inviolata, R. S. M., the Chairperson of the Board of Directors of Mercy, at the time, and William J. Grove, MD, Executive Dean of the University of Illinois, College of Medicine. Sister Mary Ludmilla, R. S. M., was the administrator (later on the president) of Mercy Hospital and Medical Center.

My specific on-going activities as Program Director at that time at Mercy Hospital entailed the acceptance of the medical students, recruitment of interns and residents (house staff), securing qualified faculty members willing to teach, and dealing with the Accreditation Council for Graduate Medical Education, and the administration of Mercy hospital.

The objective of the program in internal medicine was to assist and inspire the trainees to expand their knowledge, and fully develop their cognitive and psychomotor skills to utilize the information obtained from a meaningful history and physical examination and pertinent laboratory data to formulate the most likely diagnosis and the most appropriate management plan. The paramount importance of judgment, compassion, and a sense of care for the patients and the proper attitude in the practice of medicine were emphasized.

The faculty consisted of the attending physicians of the patients contributing to the educational program by discussing the diagnosis, and his management plans for the patients with the house staff, and the volunteer and the salaried members of the faculty, who on daily scheduled hours, systematically participated in teaching, combining didactic and bedside discussions.

The recruitment of the graduates of the American medical schools took precedence over the graduates of the foreign medical schools, otherwise with an equal qualification. Foreign medical graduates, who possessed required or higher qualification were also searched for and recruited enthusiastically to enrich the cultural aspect of the program at Mercy Hospital.

The program director had also to address the occasional conflict among the parties involved in education. The interaction between the attending physicians, house staff, and medical students usually were harmonious and productive. Occasional conflicts over the diagnosis and management of the patients between the residents and attending physicians usually were not major ones and were managed through education and explanation. However, extremely rarely a major conflicting issue such as inappropriate and disturbing behavior of a member of the house staff or medical staff caused by drugs or otherwise required a disciplinary action, according to the by-laws of the Medical and Scientific Staff (M&SS).

Affiliation with the University of Illinois not only created an academic atmosphere at Mercy, but I believe elevated the standard of patient care. The presence of inquisitive and intelligent medical students influenced the attitude of the members of the medical staff, directing them toward more sophistication and excellence. The Joint Conference Committee (JCC) was composed of the representatives of six hospitals affiliated with the University of Illinois (collectively abbreviated Metro-6 Hospitals). The committee was chaired by the Chairman of the respective Department of the School of Medicine, established the policies of the affiliation and coordinated the affiliation affairs. The hospital members of the Metro-6 were, 1. Illinois Masonic, 2. Lutheran General, 3. MacNeal Memorial, 4. Mercy Hospital, 5. Ravenswood, and 6. Weiss Memorial hospitals.

To be effective as a program director participation in the ongoing activities of the school was indispensable. In addition to JCC, I served as a member of Student Appraisal and Faculty Promotions, Appointment and Tenure of the Abraham Lincoln School of Medicine committees, and Advisory Committee of the Department of Medicine of ALSM, Executive Committee of ALSM, and the Senate of the University of Illinois and other committees.

Deliberation in the meetings of JCC, at times, seemed apparently excessive, but focusing on details probably is one of the essential nutrients of academia and scholarship.

Joint meeting of the faculty of ALSM and Metro-6 were of value in filling the gap between academia and practicing physicians. Discussing the care of patients and medical education, the common denominator and objective of both groups, encouraged them to work in unison and cooperatively, rather than competing with each other in order to protect their turf.

The intensive preoccupation with research and experimentations, although necessary for the evolution of medical science, if unchecked and not balanced with patient care and medical education, may alienate and isolate the researchers individually and collectively from the medical profession, forcing them to lose sight of reality. If the trend continues in a given medical community, the investigative work might become inappropriate or even irrelevant, leading the researcher to be identified as a technician, or even act as a technician, when managing the patients.

Education is the major objective of the medical school. Yet in many institutions the promotion of the faculty is determined mainly by quality and not infrequently only by the quantity of the research works and definitely by the numbers of their publications in the referee journals. In these institutions the educational skill of the faculty, may play an adjunctive role, but it is not essential.

The University of Illinois leadership in the past, like many other institutions had attempted to remedy this problem. One of the attempts was to use modifiers such as "clinical professor", "research professor", "professor of clinical" to indicate the major interest and the tenure of the faculty member. Titles without qualification usually, not always, denote tenured, salaried-investigative rank; titles with qualification usually and not always, indicate non-tenured, non-salaried, and educational or patient care.

I have been honored with all three categories of clinical professor, professor of clinical medicine, and professor of medicine during my affiliation with the University of Illinois.

Because of my background in the postdoctoral fellowship of the National Heart Institute and engagement in the private practice and the activities in the medical staff affairs, I was able to fit in either discipline, academia or practitioner. However, I preferred to see them combined with a common denominator of education. Receiving the prestigious Golden Apple teaching award of the University of Illinois, from the student class of 1973, for the first time for the non-salaried physician, not only was a soul lifting experience, it supported my concept of integrating the academician and the practitioner of medicine. The award consolidated my devotion to teaching, I will cherish it always. I received numerous congratulations from both disciplines. But some members of the full time faculty, mainly engaged in research continued to defend their elite status in the medical community, considering the daily patient care and education less challenging and sort of a second-class task. They remind me of territorial imperative.

CHAPTER 47

Cardiology

Directing the internal medicine program facilitated upgrading education and the services in cardiology.

GENERAL CONSIDERATION

Our goal and objectives were to develop comprehensive and high quality cardiac services for patient care, medical education, and clinical investigation in a medical and teaching center with more than five hundred beds.

In achieving and maintaining our objectives, I systematically communicated with and attended the meetings of American College of Cardiology, American Heart Association, American College of Physicians, Directors of Adult Cardiovascular Training Programs, and the reputable medical schools and centers in the USA and Chicago. The existing services of the section of cardiology systematically evaluated and upgraded and new services were established. The section, which was changed to division after establishing a fellowship program according to the by-laws of the medical staff, included clinical cardiology; cardiac care unit; electrocardiography-vectorcardiography; hemodynamics laboratories; cardiac clinics; and subsequently echocardiography and nuclear cardiology. Each service had a director charged with clear objectives. The major objective was to develop, upgrade, and expand the units of cardiology and the personnel to provide high quality services and care. Our units welcomed qualified physicians to care for their own patients, perform the procedures, and participate in the educational programs. Monopoly of the unit deemed inadvisable, potentially limiting the competence of qualified physicians and the growth of the unit, eventually compromising the quality of care. The hospitals with the objective of providing care through their salaried physicians and surgeons preferred to limit the practicing privileges within the unit to a few physicians salaried by the hospital, encouraging the medical doctors to seek hospital employment or limiting their admission privileges or confine their practice to their clinic or office, leading eventually to two categories of doctors, hospital practitioners and office practitioners.

Cardiac (or Coronary) Care Unit (CCU) The original goal of CCU was to expedite the admission of the patients with myocardial infarction to CCU to prevent and manage the cardiac arrhythmias and cardiac arrest. I participated in emphasizing the importance of the patients transfer to the hospitals as expeditiously as possible, appearing on TV, writing in daily newspapers, and discussing at meetings with the representative of the Police and the Fire Departments of Chicago.

The CCU at Mercy was equipped with monitoring and audio-visual alarm systems, defibrillators and mechanical ventilators facilities, all in line with the Guidelines of the National Conference on Coronary Care Units of 1967.

There were lengthy discussions and debates over the confinement of patients to private rooms, vs. to a general ward with several beds, separated by curtains. The discussions usually shifted from the patient's privacy and safety to the affordability of payment. The beds in our unit initially were divided equally to private and ward beds. However, eventually the general ward was eliminated, when it was agreed that the care and the management of the patients in a non-private condition negatively and adversely affects the other patients.

The systems were operated by a trained and vigilant house staff and nurses interpreting the monitored parameters.

A comprehensive guideline for the management of patients was established. Qualified attending physicians or, when necessary, their consultants were responsible for the medical management of their patients.

Any attempt to curtail the admission privileges of the physicians or impose consultation arbitrarily, was discouraged. Every effort was made to assist the attending physicians through education, and if necessary discussing the appropriate management of the patients.

To familiarize the surrounding medical community with our CCU at Mercy Hospital and to demonstrate the value of CCU in the management of acute cardiovascular diseases we published the results of our experience at Mercy in several appropriate medical journals.

In conjunction with CCU, we organized, in collaboration with the Respiratory Therapy Department, a Cardiopulmonary Resuscitation (CPR) team. I chaired a multidisciplinary committee, which supervised all aspects of CPR, including the code for announcement, time of response, responsible personnel, duration and the result of CPR, and final diagnosis and suggestions.

A class was established to educate and certify the physicians, nurses and other individual volunteers in performing CPR.

A prior successful resuscitation of a gracious and respectable Mercy nun, who collapsed at the entrance area of the surgical suite at Mercy, contributed to the rapid development of CPR. The Sister was admitted to CCU after a cardiac arrest and resuscitation by me, she remained in a comatose state for a few days. During this period of time a few members of the staff, repeatedly reminded me of prolonging the dying period of a patient. The Sister gradually regained consciousness, to live a few years of quality life and resume her fulltime job and her religious obligations, and even discuss her views on death and dying with me.

The French philosopher Voltaire (1694-1778) has been quoted as saying, "Doubt is not a very agreeable state, but certainty is a ridiculous one." We were not promoting the positive outcome of CCU with an absolute certainty; neither were we constantly doubting it. The majority of the physicians, nursing staff, and the administration team, were supportive of the concept. But, as usually happens, there were a few doubters, who habitually survey the work of the others and doubt the outcome. These few doomsayers not only doubted the value of CCU with sadness and a question mark in their eyes and a sullen face, but also routinely questioned the value of any innovation or plan for improvement of patient care and were suspicious of the motives.

Their doubts were not deterrent to our goals, but they were time consuming and irritating. These people were not satisfied with simply verbalizing their sentiments; they wanted more, they wanted us to become doubtful like them.

The concern expressed by some was not totally unjustified; at times, the dying patients were receiving unjustifiable intensive treatment, which was prolonging the process of dying. These observations reinforced the concept that the management of the patients should be thoughtfully individualized and a multidisciplinary consultation might be necessary regarding the life support system. We initiated an educational program in death and dying, to define death and address the legal, ethical, religious, and emotional aspects of dying. The program consisted of lectures, seminars, individual consultations, and publication of articles and guidelines, all by multidisciplinary experts.

SURGICAL INTENSIVE CARE UNIT (SICU)

In 1975, a new unit, SICU was dedicated to the memory of Arne E. Shairer, MD, who died in a tragic auto-accident. Dr. Shairer, a cardiovascular surgeon, was the President (1971-1973) of M&SS of Mercy Hospital.

The distinctive features of the unit included the closeness of the location of the unit to the surgical operating room, the privacy and yet the visibility of patients relative to the central monitoring station, the convenience of transportation, the conference, on-call, and waiting rooms, all adding to the quality of intensive care of patients admitted to the unit.

An annual Arne Shairer Memorial Lecture was established to focus on the humanitarian and moral aspects of the practice of medicine at Mercy Hospital including Shairer ICU. The unit was a necessary supplement to the well-organized cardiovascular surgery program at Mercy, which was essential for the growth of cardiology.

FELLOWSHIP IN CARDIOLOGY

One of the most important achievements was the establishment of the fellowship program in cardiology for the first time at Mercy Hospital. Our fellowship program was small but we believed it was solid and closely supervised.

The goal of the program was to teach all of the basic disciplines prerequisite for the achievement of professional competence in cardiovascular disease. It was aimed at familiarizing the fellows in depth with functional anatomy, physiology, pathology, clinical manifestations, roentgenology, hemodynamics, non-invasive and invasive studies, pharmacology, and the management of the cardiovascular diseases. The fellows rotated through services of clinical cardiology, cardiac cathterization-hemodynamics, cardiac (coronary) care unit, and electrocardiography and research to achieve the objectives.

Although we received numerous applications and interviewed many for the fellowship, we selected most of our fellows from our graduating medical residents in internal medicine, including the chief residents. These residents, in comparison with the outside applicants with otherwise equal qualifications, were familiar with the systems of medical practice at Mercy, with a better interaction with other residents and the members of the medical staff. They were aware of the educational needs of the medical residents and the students, therefore more effective in the teaching program of the department. Since they had already been introduced to the educational program of the division, their orientation period in cardiology was minimum, thus they had more time available for the active training.

The fellowship program in cardiology, I believe, contributed to the quality of care, particularly in an emergency-urgency setting. However the program may have imposed additional stress on already financially stressed hospitals, by increasing expenses without contributing to the gross revenue.

As often it happens, there were a very few persons, who did not concur with our method of selection of fellows. The selection from our residents, they thought, will lead to inbreeding and will prevent the new sparkling ideas to shine in, as though Mercy was embedded in dark antiquities.

These people come from all walks of life, and they volunteer to express their opinions on every topic, and every event of life at any time and everyplace.

In a hospital setting, they may originate from the board of directors, from administration, medical and nursing staff, and from any other group. I remember, many years ago one of the Sisters of Mercy called them "Jack of all trades, master of none". I prefer to call them individually or collectively "All Knowledgeable" aka "big mouth". They talk in the: committees, board room, conference room, lecture hall, dining room, restaurants, opera houses, orchestra halls, I even hear them now.

They advise incessantly; Sadegh Hedayat, the most modern and famous Iranian writer of fictions and short stories, born in 1903 in Tehran, died in 1951 in Paris, compared some of the people in the "all knowledgeable" category to a toothpaste tube; squeezing the tube produces tooth paste, squeezing the "all knowledgeable" produces advice.

The core of our fellowship program was clinical cardiology, including electrocardiography and echocardiography and diagnostic invasive laboratory. The research was limited to clinical investigation, and writing a term paper, or review articles, for publication in suitable medical journals, particularly in Mercy Heart Journal, which was edited by me. The fellows were encouraged to familiarize themselves with the interpretation and analysis of the investigational data and reports, and improve their professional communicative skills. High quality basic scientific research although desirable did not seem to be feasible at Mercy at that time. A complex organizational structure occasionally might give birth to individuals who occupy superfluous positions created especially for them or established by an oversight. These individuals in order to justify their position and to appear visionary intrude upon their colleagues and co-workers ready to provide unwelcome advice. I had occasionally my share of these individuals, advising me of the existence of financial resources for scientific research, but hastily adding that they would not be able to collaborate because they were overwhelmed with their work. These occasions were sufficient to prompt me to meditate.

The fellows in cardiology had a through evaluation in the following aspects of cardiology:

In-depth and updated familiarity with the cause, diagnosis, pathophysiology, and therapeutic modalities of the cardiac problems.

Mature and explicit diagnostic and therapeutic plans.

Reliable and well-defined history and comprehensive physical examination.

The skill of application of knowledge to the patient care.

At the completion of the fellowship the fellows were expected to be highly competent in the interpretation and were encouraged to be proficient in the performance of the following procedural skills:

Electrocardiogram, echocardiogram, various forms of cardiac stress tests, insertion of cardiac pacemakers and catheters, right and left cardiac catheterization, and coronary angiography. If a fellow did not participate in the performance of any of the above procedures or participated but did not reach the level of competence, additional training were required prior to granting the privilege to perform such a procedure. The attitudinal qualities of the fellows, such as compassion toward and rapport with the patients, integrity, and professional relationship were emphasized during training and evaluated seriously. I believe in general we trained knowledgeable, skillful, and conscientious cardiologists at Mercy.

The evaluation of the competence of the fellows in patient's care and their capability of performing an invasive cardiac procedure is a difficult task. By holding different academic and administrative positions and attending courses at Harvard and the University of Illinois, I had gained additional insight into the educational endeavors and the evaluation of the performance and the character of the medical students and the postgraduate trainees, the members of house staff, and academia. I realized many of my colleagues in the medical practice and education, when evaluating individuals, mainly described the characters of the individuals and did not address the suitability and the performance of the individuals relative to the position they were seeking. One commonly noticed the phrases such as "working hard", "doing best", "pleasant", and "honest", in the recommendation and evaluation letters. A candidate might be all of the above but incapable of carrying on the duties he/she is being recommended.

The fellowship program at Mercy enhanced the image and the credibility of cardiology at Mercy, promoting its educational aspect, attracting well-qualified and trained cardiologists to the staff of Mercy. As time went on, nationally and internationally renowned cardiologists from the Chicago area and other parts of the United States as well as from abroad lectured at Mercy. Dr. Mauricio Rosenbaum, a world wide respected authority in the conduction system of the heart, from Argentina, visited Mercy, conducted a workshop, sponsored by the Chicago Heart Association, lecturing large audiences, discussing his area of interest, the anatomy and electrophysiology of the conduction system of the heart. The Division of Cardiology at Mercy, supported by the America Heart Association, Council of Clinical Cardiology, and/or Chicago Heart Association, sponsored and organized several other successful seminars and symposiums. In 1972, the Cardiac Clinic of the Annual Meeting of the American College of Cardiology was held at Mercy Hospital.

To share our experiences in different aspects of cardiology we also participated in medical workshops and lectures sponsored by the other hospitals and the Chicago Medical Society.

CLERKSHIP IN CARDIOLOGY

One of my favorite experiences in cardiology was the organization of a popular program in cardiology for senior students of ALSM, who would enroll in the program for a 2-3 months period to study the different aspects of cardiology. Later on with support of the University of Illinois this program was expanded and accepted the senior students from the schools in the USA and internationally. It was not unusual, at times, to have the students from Syria, Egypt, Germany, Poland, and Africa gathering together at the same time, discussing the cardiac problems as well as the practice of medicine in their respective countries.

Chicago Heart association (CHA)

For several years, I was active in CHA, an affiliate of the AHA at the time. American Heart Association (AHA) is a national health agency with a mission to reduce disability and death from cardiovascular diseases and stroke. Originally it was founded only by six cardiologists in 1924, among them Dr. Paul Dudley White, the late renowned cardiologist, one of the founders of modern cardiology in the USA.

In order to achieve its mission, identical to the mission of AHA, the CHA made public education one of its essential priorities. I was a member of several committees, including Coronary Care and Rehabilitation committees and the Chairman of the Health Education Committee, for which I became the recipient of the Golden Heart award of the CHA. There were several publications of CHA to promote public education and awareness in Chicago Metropolitan area. The contents of these booklets were excellent and accurate, but they were, it seemed to me, oriented toward very educated and wealthy individuals, who probably would not read them. These booklets reminded me of my public health orientation in Iran. I suggested to the staff that perhaps the modification and simplifying the contents of the booklets might serve the general public more effectively. I believe my suggestions were not received well by the staff. Later on I was surprised to hear from one of the more experienced doctors, that the cardiologists affiliated with CHA, at those days, worked under the direction of the staff, and their role in actuality is a symbolic one, and the members of the staff were not suggestions friendly.

A cardiologist friend of mine at that time jokingly told me that probably my Golden Heart award was intended to dissociate me from CHA, almost similar to the kiss of death in the Cosa Nostra society. I am profoundly glad that since then CHA has gone through major organizational changes and the awards of course are real and honorable.

Public Education

To increase awareness and familiarity of the community and the patients and their families with heart diseases, particularly in the prevention and the recognition of heart attacks and the significance of CCU, I organized regular monthly classes and meetings called "Healthy Heart," and "Heart

Alert" programs open to the public, employees, volunteers, and business firms, to discuss the related topics. The classes proved to be popular and probably modified the life style and behavior of some attendants or prompted them to seek professional advice. In addition, at the requests of Mothers' and Parents' Clubs I lectured in several schools in the Chicago area.

Starting 1980, I wrote a series of articles, for the public, titled "Heart Alert" in one of the Mercy Publications, Lifelines, for public education purposes, regarding the cause and diagnosis of myocardial infarction (heart attack), and angina. Other publications preceding LifeLines also published educational articles in cardiology; in chronological order they were Mercy Newsletter, Mercy Messenger, and Footnotes.

CHICAGO CARDIOLOGY GROUP (CCG)

The group was founded by Rolf Gunner, MD, MACP, the nationally renowned cardiologist, from the Chicago Metropolitan area, the objective of the group was to promote education and research in cardiology and expedite communication among the hospitals and medical centers with postgraduate education and training in cardiology. The directors of the fellowship training were invited to be the members of the executive committee of the group.

Our fellowship program received much recognition, after I was honored to be a member of the executive committee of the group from 1972-1988, and the Secretary-treasurer, the Vice chairman, and the Chairman from 1982-1988.

The prestigious Third Annual Scientific Seminar of CCG was held at Mercy, in November 1981. The topic of discussion was "Calcium Ion and the Calcium Channel Blocking Drugs". The members of faculty participating in the seminar, physicians with the highest credentials and leaders in the field of cardiology, were from the University of Chicago, Northwestern, Rush-Presbyterian St. Luke's, Harvard, and University of Kentucky Medical Schools. In addition to physicians of Mercy Hospital, about 300 cardiologists from the Chicago Metropolitan area and the State of Illinois attended the seminar.

CHAPTER 48

President of The Staff, And Change In The Direction Of Mercy

Around the time of moving to the new building and in the early 1970s, the organizational structure of the hospitals began to change; in the hospital setting, the relationship of the board of directors, the administration and medical staff was undergoing a revision. The legal responsibility of the board of directors for the quality of care provided by the medical staff was being discussed, emphasizing the need for the clarification of the interrelationship and establishing the authority of the board of directors. The Board of Directors of Mercy also underwent structural changes and established several committees in order to effectively address its new responsibilities. The redefinition of the authorities necessitated changes in the administrative structure of the hospitals, leading to changes in the title, size, duties, authority, and the attitude of the administrative staff, resulting in relatively oversized administration with a large agenda and a grandiose attitude. In January 1972, three new laymen members joined nine Sisters in the Board of Directors of Mercy Hospital, with Sister Inviolata chairing the meeting. However the dramatic change occurred in May 1973. A chart, showing an inverted hierarchy of authority, depicted the philosophy of the management at Mercy. In this chart the top administration, consisting of the board of directors and the chief administrator, was placed at the bottom of the chart, instead of on the top leading role, to indicate its role as a supporting base authority of the Mercy organization, overseeing the activities of all parts of the organization, within Mercy Hospital and Medical Center, including M&SS. The administrator, associate and assistant administrators title changed to president, vice presidents forming a cadre of experts to govern the hospital and achieve the corporate objective and provide the quality of care in line with the Management By Objective (MBO) Program, which started in 1972. The program identified Mercy as a not-for-profit organization, sponsored by the Sisters of Mercy, delivering comprehensive healthcare "in the spirit of Christianity and concern for the worth and dignity of the individual, and in a manner which furthers the ministry of the Sisters of Mercy with their traditional value." The objectives of MBO, which were described in detail, were to achieve a quality of care to meet the highest professional standards.

This change in attitude combined with the affiliation with the university of Illinois affected the medical education at Mercy. The Medical Education Department with a new director promoted the concept of quality medical care through medical education and the development of corporate responsibility for medical education at Mercy. Crowded agenda, large folders full with paper work and correspondence, numerous task forces, all advocated the new concepts in medical education. The means intended to achieve quality medical education, inadvertently were becoming the goal themselves. The Medical Education Office at Mercy was metamorphosing to and resembling a dean's office of a medical school.

To succeed in the educational endeavors and the promotion of the cardiovascular services, it seemed advisable to participate in the activities of the Medical and Scientific Staff. Starting in 1973 for next six years I was honored to serve as an elected Secretary-Treasurer, President and Immediate past President, each position for two years. These positions were emotionally and intellectually fulfilling. Although they increased my workload, they added more weight to my ideas and suggestions, making me more effective in implementing my concept in the healthcare and education, and even in coordinating my other responsibilities expeditiously.

The past presidents of the medical staff were men of high caliber and dedicated physicians and surgeons; Dr. John Murphy was the first president (1895-1916), who made the following statement in addressing the American Medical Association as its president at the turn of century: "Competency is attained and maintained only by zeal, indefatigable labor and continued efforts in self-education". On June 1916 the pope decorated Dr. Murphy.

Minutes of the medical and scientific departments and committees including educational activities were discussed and voted upon at the Executive Committee, which was chaired by the President of the staff and eventually was renamed the Executive Medical Board (EMB). The minutes and recommendation of the EMB must be approved by the majority at the general meetings of the M&SS, which was also renamed M&SS and Faculty (M&SS-F) to emphasize the educational responsibility of the membership and acknowledge the faculty. The basic membership of the EMB included the three elected officers of the M&SS and the chairmen of the departments, however over time the membership was extended appropriately to enable the EMB to deal with the changes in the practice of medicine and related educational activities. Three vice-presidents for Academic Affairs, Quality Appraisal, and Long-range Planning and three At-large members, all elected by the members of M&SS, were added to the EMB in order to meet the needs of the hospital.

Since, the president was elected by the members of medical staff, and acted on their behalf and their direction a fixed job description probably is not sufficient enough to describe his responsibilities. I believe the following comments, based on my communications and reports to the members of the staff and Board of Directors, indicate my thought process at the time, and since then, which in turn may reflect the direction I was pursuing in serving the medical staff and Mercy Hospital: The physicians at Mercy Hospital, silent and alienated by the jargon created by the so-called experts in the field of socio-economic aspects of medicine, demonstrate behavioral patterns indicative of preoccupation with this dimension of medicine. They evidence unhappiness with governmental intrusions into the medical care arena. They are bewildered by the platitudinous and a bit sophomoric solutions proposed for the sudden so-called "crisis in the health care delivery system." The abrupt insurgence of terms such as "quality accountability vs. cost accountability," "federally designated Health Service Areas (HSAs)," "rate review," "certificate of need," "consumerism," and "health care providers," have a profoundly irritating effect upon the physicians. The physicians major concern, while striving to familiarize themselves with abbreviated jargon, is the quality care of patients now and in the future. Different methods to improve patient care, all claiming to provide quality, with different motives, are being proposed. Some of them are sincere, some economically oriented and some belong to over-zealous individuals who would like to share the dividends of the giant medical industry. It has been an enormous task to determine which method is the best for the patient. Meanwhile the beneficiaries of the tort system, the trial lawyers are enjoying their humanitarian mission of helping some patients, and perhaps by hurting many, indirectly.

Facing these external forces, what are the health care providers on-going and long-range responsibilities? On their ongoing practice whether individual, group, or hospital based, the physicians must strive to keep equanimity, and continue to follow their humanitarian mission. They should continue to remain benevolent, diligent and devoted to their profession. The hospital administration must be compassionate and sympathetic toward patients, and the members of administration must be competent in the field of administration, and should fight the temptation to acquire overzealous authority for personal reasons, using unscrupulous means. The expansion of administration must not be equated with a better quality of care; the expansion might increase the cost without affecting the quality. Members of the board of directors must be selected based on expertise and credentials, independent thinking, and strength of character.

The members of the board of directors of the hospitals have a unique and special task in directing hospital affairs. They must interact with the most respected professionals, almost in all societies, the professionals accustomed to interpretation and identifying the behavioral patterns of the people individually and collectively. The members must also possess at least a rudimentary knowledge of a complex medical practice in general and the evaluation process of the quality care of patients in particular.

Inherited or fortuitously acquired social and community reputation and fame of a person must not be the sole criterion for appointment to the board of directors of a hospital. This practice on some occasions may be helpful in attracting new customers to the business corporation; but in a hospital setting the appointment of individuals lacking appropriate qualifications not only may prove to be embarrassing to the board, but it will be unfair to the appointees, who might not be aware of their short coming and accept the appointment with good intention and faith. These individuals presence in the board might misdirect the other members of the board, resulting in an unintentional deviation from quality care of patients, and creating a moral and ethical dilemma.

The board of directors, administration, medical staff of the hospitals must have a transparent and effective communication; using their expertise, they should work in unison, avoiding the non-productive and time consuming power play with each other. In facing adversity such as unjustified litigation, they should collectively try to remedy the problem, avoiding the adversary position. The hospitals must have a reliable mechanism to systematically, in accordance with their bylaws, address these issues and if necessary to remedy them.

The hospitals and medical centers must have a continuing medical education program to include training in the socio-economic aspects of the practice of medicine. These aspects of medical practice should also be included in the undergraduate curriculum of medical schools. These intra-institutional first steps measures are necessary to promote and maintain the quality of care, but by no means are sufficient to eliminate the problems we are facing in the practice of medicine. In long-range planning, the hospitals and medical centers must apply these intra-hospital policies to inter-hospitals relationship and work harmoniously with the other hospitals and medical centers to achieve quality care for all patients. Accepting their essential role in patient care, the doctors must demonstrate strong interest in participating in long-range planning for the future of the practice of medicine. As a member of professional organizations and societies and as an advocate for their patients they should demand accountability, competence, and performance from the leadership of their profession. The leadership must be prudent in delegating authority to non-medical doctor staff, whose interpretation of the problems might significantly differ from the medical profession. The professional organizations such as American Medical Associations, and American Hospital Association, and numerous professional, voluntary, and governmental organizations and insurance companies must work in collaboration to objectively identify the weaknesses in the practice of medicine in the United States and propose responsible remedies, with a reasonable and affordable cost to all patients and the nation. The proposals should reflect an attitude of care rather than regimentalizing the management of the patients. The proposals, void of political motives, should be addressed to the American people for implementation through their elected representatives in the governing body of the United States.

In reforming healthcare, providing healthcare to all, of course, takes priority, but it should be emphasized that providing care to all might not improve the quality of care, in contrast, it might affect the quality adversely by spreading the financial and man power resources.

Continuing medical education sponsored by the professional organizations, should also address the economic and financial aspects of the practice of medicine.

We must, always remember that the state of healthcare in the USA, reflects the true worth of the American people.

In the hospitals located in the Chicago Metropolitan area the elected president or chief of staff's responsibility and authority varied from a ceremonial and symbolic position, holding a gavel and chairing the meetings to a real leadership status with serious and important duties and sufficient authority invested on him by the bylaws and policies of the hospital.

The extent of the authority of the presidents of the staff depended also on the authority of the administrative staff of the hospitals, usually the presidents or chief executive officers and the board of directors of the hospitals, delineated by the bylaws of the hospitals.

However, it will be prudent to be cognizant of the possibility that in addition to the legal authority, the president of a hospital or a chairperson of a board of directors or the president of medical staff with an ambitious and strong personality may also usurp the authority of the other persons in the leadership position, elected or appointed, minimizing their authority and effectiveness, rendering the governing structure a futile, demeaning, and dysfunctional system. The Machiavellian oriented president or chief executive officer may even usurp the authority of the good people of the board of directors, unfamiliar with the healthcare system and medical practice, turning the hospital to a privately owned company run by one person, thus initiating the beginning of the end of a hospital. Probably it will not be unrealistic to assume that some hospitals administrative system in the past or currently have experienced these detrimental event. During my tenure, for more than 25 years, as a Program Director, Chief of Cardiology, President of Medical and Scientific Staff, Chairman Department of Medicine and various committees, I have witnessed on several occasions healthy differences of opinion between the administration and medical staff leadership at Mercy, both parties had the best intentions and were trying to ascertain the best answer and do their best for the institution and the patients.

The Sisters in the administrative and leadership positions in general usually were supportive of the actions of the members of the medical staff including the officers, the chairmen of the departments and the committees, within the bylaws of the hospital, and their support expedited the implementation of the hospital policies and objectives. But in life even a solid relationship between people and acts of goodness are not guaranteed. In a long-standing relationship it is possible that occasionally an amicable and supportive relationship be interrupted and change to an unpleasant confrontational state. In isolated incidences, it is possible that some members of the administrative staff, independently or encouraged by their co-workers or others in the leadership positions attempt to intervene in an unorthodox and bizarre way with the functions and the bylaws of the medical staff. These unnecessary interventions, if isolated and transient may result in a disconcerting state in the hospital and a brief disharmony among the doctors, but usually they are not significant enough to affect the quality of care and education. However, these disharmonies within the administration, if recurrent and frequent, may negatively reflect on the members of board of directors irrespective of the degree of their knowledge of the events, and they might become the source of speculation and rumors, detrimental to the credibility of the hospital, the board of directors, the administration, and the medical staff, and eventually the patients' care. It is advisable to be aware of the possibility of such conflicts and the various possible causative factors, and eliminate them in an embryonic stage before they affect the quality of care in a hospital setting.

Obviously the Sisters of Mercy are averse to having these events in the institution identified with and carrying their religious name. The good Sisters in addition to the customary authority of their position also possessed the religious authority. Their altruistic attitude and vow of poverty excluded materialistic gain as a motive to accept a leadership position. Their desire to serve and help the needy, as in a century and half ago, in Ireland, had compelled them to lead and get involved in competitive society. The Second Vatican Council of Pope Paul in 1962-1965, and the change in the women's social status probably were among the factors encouraging the religious orders to seek a more socially active role within the community.

We all know, even in a sophisticated and civilized society in all levels of life styles, including the corporate life, small or large, including the healthcare industry, occasionally a transient disruption in the ethical standard, detrimental to the institution may occur, which may not be identifiable easily.

Any sizable institution might have a few individuals in leadership or influential positions, who for one reason or another deviate from the acceptable standard behavior in the community. These individuals simply enjoy being bad with a tendency to dislike and possibly harm other people. The tendency to deviate from doing right, in these individuals, might be related to their genetic make-up or nurtured by their living milieu.

The precipitating factor for a particular bad act may be a financial or authoritative gain or reward. These individuals might possess a high level of misdirected intelligence. They may be well dressed, polite, with a courteous smile and even charm. In a hospital setting these individuals may originate from the board of directors, administration, and medical or nursing staff. They may have persuasive power over other people, particularly the submissive or unhappy ones. They are capable of persuading their co-workers and friends to adopt their behavioral pattern and form a small group, for simplicity reason the group collectively might be called Evil Cabal and any member of the group a Black Sheep. At different occasions individually or collectively these people may become combative, loud, insulting and demonstrate temper tantrums. Frequently the abrasive attitude of these individuals is followed by an angelic attitude, soft speech, agreeable demeanor and kindness. There are various interpretations for this bimodal behavior, depending on the qualification and the type of expertise of the interpreters.

A friend of mine, a political scientist assured me that the benign behavior demonstrated by the members of the Evil Cabal, individually or collectively, supposedly nullifies the effect of their preceding misbehavior, for preparation for the next assault, otherwise their repetitive and frequent harsh assault might become fatal to the victims.

One of my highly respected catholic priest friends related this intermittent antagonistically dual behavior to the coexistence of good and evil in the Black Sheep.

A late psychiatrist, a patient of mine, explained the Black Sheep behavior as a hate and love relationship between people. It sounded scientific, but I was not able to comprehend it.

A Sister of Mercy, whom I adored like my sister advised me not to dwell on the subject. She explained that the Black Sheep probably naturally possess unsophisticated and vulgar attitudes, which are contained and controlled by their community disciplines, but from which they emerge out intermittently. I concur with the Sister and I believe there is no need for a complicated explanation. There are usually no diabolically clever or ulterior motives behind these behavioral patterns, they are simply amateurish adolescent type behavior in an unimaginative Black Sheep, wrapped in a superficial education.

I definitely do not believe that an Evil Cabal or a Black Sheep existed at Mercy. But a few accused me of naiveté, believing strongly not only in the existence of the group, but also believing the group controlled and directed the hospital; these few did not have any convincing evidence, and I could not exclude the possibility of some degree of paranoia or a delusional state.

My preoccupation with various medical endeavors at Mercy Hospital did not allow time to dwell on these matters, which were not significant enough to affect the care of the patients.

During my tenure as the president of M&SS-F, and the representative of the medical staff in order to maintain or improve the quality care of the patients, suggestions were made, reflecting the opinion of the medical staff, to the administration, regarding the accommodations, amenities, and technical facilities in the hospital. We also systematically discussed the administrative and the nursing staff performance and duties and their attitude and mannerism toward the patients and the members of the medical staff. Suggestions also made pertinent to the membership of the board of directors of Mercy Hospital and Medical Center, to repudiate the unfounded notion held by some that catholic and Irish ethnicity were two major criteria for membership of the board, irrespective of experience and competence.

In order to improve communication among the board of directors, the administrative staff, and the medical and scientific staff, the Board of Directors concurred with my suggestion that the president of M&SS be an ex-officio member of the Board of Directors and its Committees at Mercy.

We focused mainly on the membership of the M&SS-F. The Bylaws, policies, and Rules and Regulations of the medical staff were upgraded to augment the degree of the participation of the members in the medical and educational affairs of the hospital.

Educational sessions were held to familiarize the members of the staff with the rules of orders in the meetings, to expedite their effectiveness.

To expedite communication between the officers of the medical staff and it's members, I published a newsletter called "Communication" to regularly inform the members of significant events and solicit their advice and input.

In collaboration with administration we addressed the quality, competence, and educational needs of the members of the medical staff and tried to remedy the deficiency if any, by recruiting the needed members based on credentials and resisted any possible political recommendation and pressure.

I have been humorously told that Mercy Hospital's policy had been to recruit the most competent physicians or surgeons as long as they were Irish and catholic.

The committees' structure, objective, and membership were adjusted to reflect the changes in the direction of medical practice in general and in Mercy in particular.

In the educational arena a vice-presidency position for Academic Affairs was established to reflect the academic activities at Mercy in line with the University of Illinois affiliation.

The following letter addressed to the members of the Medical and Scientific Staff-Faculty conveys my sentiments at the termination of my tenure as the president of staff: It has been my privilege, honor, and joy to serve as the President of the Medical and Scientific Staff-Faculty for the past two years. It has been an enjoyable, educational experience. I am grateful for your support, and the support of Administration, the Sisters of Mercy, and the Board of Directors during my tenure.

I have used Sir William Osler's statement as a guide for my activities, and I am confident the president who will be elected today will join me in this philosophical approach:

"I have loved no darkness,
Sophisticated no truth,
Nursed no delusion,
Allowed no fear".

CHAPTER 49

Corporate Medical Practice

I continued to serve Mercy Hospital as the member of different committees, among them, the Chairman of the Credentials and Bylaws Committees and the Vice-President for Academic Affairs.

During this period of time the healthcare system did not stand still and rapidly acquired different forms, within the hospitals, changing the relationship among the medical staff, board of directors and administration.

Medical doctors had enjoyed a unique authority and prestige. The members of the communities, when ill and vulnerable had been depending upon the unique skill of the physicians and surgeons, giving them a legitimate power, based on need, not related to politics, force, threat, wealth, religion or even persuasion. Within the traditional medical practice system there is no reason to change the authority of doctors, it cannot and should not be curtailed, as long as the authority is used in a civilized way in line with the laws of the community.

The authority of the doctors in a hospital setting, if not recognized may cause resentment among the administrative staff and the members of the board of directors, possibly leading to conflict. If the administration or the board of directors for any reason are not happy with the legitimate authority of medical doctors they try to usurp it. No special planning is necessary for usurpation however, because the transformation of the medical practice had been serving as a catalyst to modify the medical doctors image and erode their authority; eliminating them as individuals and incorporating them and gluing them, as a small part, to a large body of corporate practice.

During the decade of 1970s the number of medical doctors steadily increased, decreasing the number of patients visit per office. Setting up a private and solo practice became more difficult, requiring higher expenditure and longer hours. Younger physicians particularly women tried to avoid solo practice and gravitated to hospital and corporate practice. They preferred to limit the hours of daily practice in exchange for independence.

Healthcare insurance companies restricted hospital admissions. The federal government and state sponsored programs regulated and restricted reimbursements. The birth of new organizations such as HMOs reduced the need for hospital admission. A dramatic low occupancy census of the hospitals threatened their financial status. The hospitals tried to overcome and compensate for their loss, established satellites, local outreach offices, outpatients facilities, nursing homes, and other various subsidiaries.

To manage these facilities, the hospitals recruited young physicians and specialists, increasing the numbers of salaried physicians in the hospital, competing with the private practice of physicians of the community, at times, creating a collusion course. Some hospitals limited intra-hospital services, the others tended toward more diversification. In order to reduce the expenses and increase the revenue some hospitals contracted out part of their own services to the physician groups such as emergency, radiology, or cardiology services. For more consolidation the hospitals merged together and formed multi-hospital institutions for-profit and non-profit, and large-scale corporate enterprises. Healthcare began to become a giant industry, a medical industrial complex. The Sisters of Mercy Healthcare Corporation, a non-profit catholic multihospital corporation, and the largest non-profit by 1979, was founded in 1976 with 23 hospitals and 5,584 beds with the major authority usually invested in the local branches.The hospitals willing to and capable of adjustment not only survived but also expanded their services for patient care and upgraded their educational endeavors. The hospitals not accepting the direction of change decided to pursue their original missions, or not having visionary leadership kept their standing still position or lost their existence.

Physicians enrolled in corporate practice, particularly the younger doctors not familiar with the traditional professional practice, rapidly adjusted to corporate culture and they did not recognize or they didn't mind the loss of their autonomy and authority. Because of the business nature of corporations, in addition to quality assurance of care, the corporate practice also focused on the financial aspect of practice, setting some standards relative to the income generated by the physicians or expenditure incurred by them due to their mistakes or medical malpractice. The ethos of corporate conglomerates, because of their political and economic influences eventually permeated and modified the other medical practice systems.

In medical education the focus from cognitive skills was turning toward psychomotor and procedural skills; videotapes demonstrating endotracheal intubations were replacing in-depth discussions of pathophysiology of diseases. The training programs in the teaching hospitals have been adjusting their objectives to be suitable for the trainees intending to join and work for the hospitals, corporations, and other network practices of medicine in the future. The young doctors have been indoctrinated toward hospital related procedures and technically oriented superspecialties. The newly introduced generic titles such as healthcare providers, replacing doctors, nurses, and technicians, have been blurring the boundaries among different segments of the medical profession with a negative effect on the identity of the physicians within the system of traditional medical practice.

These changes are fundamental in nature and they will continue, and their final effect on the quality care of the patients remains to be determined.

CHAPTER 50

Chairman

In 1981, the members of the Department of Medicine honored me by electing me as the Chairman, lasting for several years. By this election, the members convey their trust, respect, and support of the elected person confirming his/her competence to address the affairs of the department. Receiving this vote of confidence I was delighted to serve. I was succeeding Dr. William Cernock, a highly respected gastroenterologist, who after several years of dedicated service did not wish to continue any longer as a chairman. Sister Mary Brian Castello, R.S.M. was the Chairperson, Board of Directors. Sister Sheila Lyne, R.S.M. was the President. Sister Sheila's numerous effective leadership positions in Chicago Metropolitan area include Commissionaire of Health during Mayor Richard M. Daley administration. The structure, function, and the meetings of the department were organized, the duties of the chiefs of divisions, sections and services of the department were delineated according to the bylaws of the M&SS-F and JCAHO, with the objectives of maintenance or improvement of quality care of the patients, effective education, and possible clinical research.

The quality of patients' care was evaluated through quality assurance and mortality and morbidity programs. Educational activities included weekly grand rounds of the department of medicine; I was the moderator. Nationally and internationally recognized guest speakers participated and discussed the medical topics of interest at these grand rounds.

The agenda of the meetings included the report of the program director, the chiefs, administration and nursing and house staff representatives. The minutes of the department were discussed at the meeting of the Executive Medical Board.

In addition to these duties I was invited by the board of directors to join a task force for the evaluation of the concept and feasibility of an appointed and paid chairman vs. the elected chairman of the departments. This possibility has been briefly considered in the past, but it was aggressively revived about a year after I was elected to the chairmanship position.

The task force, appointed by the board of directors, met in 1982 and began to address this issue. The task force considered the advantages and disadvantages of an appointed chairman and reached a conclusion that advantages of an appointed and salaried chairman exceed its possible disadvantages. In 1983, the board of directors approved the concept of an appointed, salaried chairperson along with a job description, the process of the appointment and the formation and composition of the search committee. The bylaws of M&SS-F changed to accommodate these changes. In a few years eventually the concept was implemented in the department of medicine and in 1988, an appointed, full time and salaried chairman was secured. Expectation from the new chairman and his modus operandi did not match; and after three years, Mercy Hospital was looking for another appointed chairman.

The concept and the process of the search were not limited to Mercy, and many medical centers were following a similar trend. When a new position in the leadership is available in a company, corporation, or any institution it is a common practice to debate the issue of recruiting an outsider, fresh with possible new ideas or select a known entity from existing talents within the institution. Perhaps it is fair to state the position should be filled with the most qualified person. If a member of the medical staff possesses the qualifications established by the board of directors and is willing to accept the available position, a search committee might be considered to be redundant. This is not to refute the concept of the appointed and salaried chairman or an appropriate search process. It is meant to emphasize that the remedy for any need or problem should be individualized and appropriate, in line with the highest legal and ethical standard. Although adherence to a set of rules and regulations may give the appearance of fairness and legality, in-depth analysis of it may label it a maneuver for justification of wrongdoing. Lack of rules and regulations is preferable to having them, but not following and disregarding them.

Over a period of many years the positions I had held at Mercy, did not form my image, to the contrary I believe my image at least for a short term popularized the positions I held.

At times a few doctors and their supporters were competing against me, believing they would be able to do a better job. I welcomed the competition by these qualified physicians to validate my own position. Had they won, they would have replaced my position, but not me at Mercy.

However, I believe, intermittently, there were a few characters, who malevolently did not want me at Mercy. The most hateful and foul language mail, intermittently I received confirm the existence of such characters and their hostility toward me over a period time. That hostile behavior or the vulgar letters to my family and me did not affect my positions and my goals, but initially somewhat temporarily disturbed my equanimity. One of my favorite books is Equanimitus, by Sir William Osler, containing his address delivered to the graduating students of the University of Pennsylvania, Medical School. By reading this book I had tried to temper my emotions using my wisdom, as suggested by Osler to the students, and also suggested to me by the late Dr. George O'Brien, former Chairman of the Department of Medicine at Mercy. As the years passed I developed immunity and resistance to those letters and maintained my inner peace.

These individuals had adapted the pattern of behavior of an Evil Cabal group and were its personification.

I was not aware of any particular attitude or action on my part to elicit the negative feeling of these individuals toward me; even if they had any reason, they never verbalized it.

It was possible that I was an innocent bystander, a target of their projection for possessing, the characteristics, they disliked. It is not uncommon for some individuals to mask their insecurity or even their lack of competence, by being aggressive, judgmental, hostile, and loud. Perceiving themselves talented and effective, these persons may be oblivious of their maladapted behavior and may possess a strong capability for rationalization and justification, thus avoiding guilt and possibly expecting awards.

The behavior of these individuals certainly has no reflection upon the order of R.S.M. The Sisters of Mercy, whom I have known or heard about, had been gracious, good hearted, benevolent, intelligent, and devoted to their mission; some of them have been among my most respected friends and advisers.

The Sisters of Mercy by their dedication to goodness, and by educational, healthcare, administrative and even political skills, have been enriching the lives of many, without their leadership in the future the continuation of Mercy with present set-up is questionable.

CHAPTER 51

Private Practice

Practicing in the field of cardiology in the magnificent location in the city of Chicago, one of the best metropolises in the world, serving the ideal patients was an enjoyable occupation. My patients were a representative of Americans with various socio-economic, occupational, educational, ethnic backgrounds. Most of them were from the Chicago Metropolitan area, and many from other States usually the relatives or friends of my patients in Chicago referred to me for consultation. I experienced the most soul lifting moments, when several patients from Iran consulted me. Patients with various types of cardiovascular diseases including congenital, rheumatic, hypertensive, and ischemic, heart diseases visited my office. The age ranged from very young-rarely younger than eighteen- to very old, one of my patients was over hundred. Some were very wealthy and a few very poor. There were many medical and non-medical doctors, nurses, attorneys, religious leaders, educators, homemakers, police officers, and businessmen and women among my patients. Being selected as a doctor of many medical doctors, including cardiologists, not only was an honor, but it also boosted my self-confidence and self-actualization.

The patients consisted of consultation patients referred by their primary physicians or surgeons from the Chicago Metropolitan area in general and Mercy Hospital in particular, and my private patients. Engaging in both types of practice was necessary. The consultation practice promoted and solidified my image as a cardiologist within the professional community, and serving my own patients with cardiovascular conditions fulfilled the need to be responsible for the well-being of the individuals during a long-term follow-up and gain personal experience relative to the prognosis and the efficacy of different types of management.

All of my patients shared one common denominator, my devotion and respect; they were truthful, loyal, and appreciative. I did not consider practicing medicine a regimentalized job, a segment of my life, separated from the other segments artificially; neither did I consider myself a healthcare provider; I was serving my patients to assist them in remaining healthy. My medical practice blended with my educational activities was a continuous endeavor, it was living a fulfilling life, and with my family life in the center, surrounded by my patients, friends, Mercy Hospital, my students, and my colleagues.

The following paragraph adapted from my lecture series, titled Core Curriculum in Cardiology (CCC) expresses my sentiment in caring for the patients. CCC lectures were a weekly discussions intended for the residents, interns and medical students, now they are available in a book format at Mercy Hospital:

" In caring for cardiac patients, the medical profession encounters patients with heart ailments of a varying nature and severity with diverse effects on different patients. This makes the individualization of care necessary and the management of the heart problem within the context of the individual patient's physical and emotional make-up extremely important.

The practice of medicine, although based on scientific concepts, requires intuition, judgment, compassion, and a sense of care for the patient. The care should not be organ oriented; the psychological and cultural background of patients, so variable from one individual to another, should constantly be taken into consideration. In the practice of medicine, the cardiac patients are justifiably concerned about their disease, life, home, family, and job, now and in the future. The patient is a human being with anxieties, depression, grief, sense of loss, sorrow, guilt, denial, and rich or unpleasant memories. In interviewing patients, therefore, questions must be appropriate to the individual patient, considering the aforementioned statements. Awareness of the patient's dignity and pride is an integral part of the interview.

There is a thin but distinct line between probing into the individual's private life and obtaining a pertinent and detailed history. Although the latter may be important for an accurate diagnosis, at times it may be irrelevant to the patient's problem and, more importantly, may prove to be offensive and traumatic to the patient."

A comprehensive history and physical examination was an essential tenet of my practice.

Adherence to this tenet reduces the need for laboratory tests, which in addition to increasing the cost of healthcare, may result in adverse effects in patients, particularly when the tests are invasive in nature or require the injection of contrast media.

As Dr. E. Braunwald, the professor Emeritus of Harvard eloquently stated: "there is a temptation in cardiology, as in many other area of medicine to carry out expensive, and occasionally uncomfortable or even hazardous procedures to establish a diagnosis, when a detailed and thoughtful history and a thorough PE (physical examination) are sufficient." I believe that medical schools, medical teaching centers, and medical profession should demonstrate a bit more enthusiasm in promoting this basic and essential part of the patient's care.

Lack of appropriate training in these basic skills is being transmitted to the future medical educators, who in turn lacking sufficient skill fail to train the new learners, creating a vicious cycle and eventual extinction of the art, prompting the medical doctors to rely more on the laboratory tests for diagnosis and the management of the patients, with unwanted consequences.

We Homo Sapiens Sapiens, have a strong tendency to utilize the skills with which we are most familiar in solving the problems, therefore the laboratory tests and procedures will become the major and eventually the only tool to solve the patients' problems, changing the direction of medical practice drastically.

With a bit of imagination and assistance from science-fiction literature a fanciful mind can picture the following scenario: The patients or their doctors type the symptoms of a patient into a search engine of a computer; the response will include the possible diagnoses and refers the patient to a diagnostic center (if pre-approved by the insurance company) in a location convenient to the patient.

In diagnostic center the patient undergoes several tests; after establishing a final diagnosis the patient is referred to a management center, where the patient receives medications or scheduled to undergo a procedure or surgery, which could be performed by a robot. In all steps of the scenario a healthcare provider such as a doctor, physician assistant, or a registered nurse, preferably a nurse clinician- practitioner, a technician, or even another robot specialist will be available to guide the patient. This scenario is not very far fetched considering that presently, at least in some clinics the patients undergo a cardiac examination while still dressed and the physician or a nurse examines the patient using the stethoscope over the patient's shirt and jacket hurriedly, then refer the patient to have a routine blood chemistry, an electrocardiogram, and an echocardiogram (ultrasound of the heart), all interpreted by the computer, establishing the final diagnosis. At this time one can not prophetasize the actualization of this fanciful scenario or predict its value compared with the current standard of practice, but one can strongly suggest that the medical profession must devote more time to the initial evaluation of the patient's history and physical examination and avoid unnecessary laboratory tests and procedures.

The medical profession should also control the temptation to justify and rationalize this misdirection as a progress, trying to receive a credit for it. The insurance companies and the government subsidized programs indirectly and not intentionally promote the overutilization of some of the laboratory tests and interventional procedures and surgery by an unjustifiably imbalanced reimbursement.

My training encompassed all aspects of cardiology, including the techniques and interpretation of cardiac catheterization, electrophysiological studies commonly performed during my training; but my major interest was in the clinical cardiology and cardiac acoustics. Although I had all kinds of opportunity to engage in invasive hemodynamic studies, I preferred to limit my practice to the area of my interest and educate myself with the new developments such as echocardiography, nuclear cardiology, CT scan and MRI.

Knowing that all organs within the body are interrelated and the dysfunction of one may lead to the abnormal function of the others, including the heart, I tried to keep abreast also of new developments in different organ systems of the body.

Many diseases may involve several organs of the body simultaneously. Seemingly an innocent lesion of the skin or a fingernail might be a clue to the existence of a serious cardiac problem. A small lesion in the lung detected by an x-ray examination, or and old scar in the groin region may clarify the cause of heart failure in a patient.

An unusual height or a webbed neck, or a pronounced curvature of the spine or a cataract of the eye may unravel a serious underlying heart disease.

Superspecialization and limiting the practice to one part of an organ of the body may be necessary and productive in a setting of scientific investigative work, to promote the progression in the field of medicine, but extrapolating it to patient care is a maladaptive pattern of practice and it is unjustified. The trend of limiting the practice to and focusing on a very small and isolated segment of an organ has been growing in the recent years in the every field of medical specialties. It is not an uncommon to know a highly intelligent person, a graduate of a prestigious medical school and many years of training in ophthalmology to limit his/her practice to intraocular injecting a specific medication for the treatment of age related macular degeneration; or a similarly trained cardiologist limiting his/her practice exclusively to inserting a balloon or a stent to the coronary arteries, and do nothing else.

This trend, creeping up in all specialties of medicine, needs a soul-searching contemplation and analysis. That is true that the technical skill aspects of these practices, usually improves in proportion to the numbers of the procedures performed, but eventually it reaches a plateau, and the learning curve can not be used as an excuse for the continuation of this very narrow practice. The performers of the procedures identified as a superspecialist by the community and within the center where the procedures are performed continue to utilize their super skills in an accelerated fashion and enjoy the financial rewards and professional recognition. The superspecialists, being a Homo Sapiens Sapiens, sincerely begin to believe that they are serving humanity and deserve all kinds of compensation. Of course in a free enterprise society this trend is not only acceptable but it may be admirable.

The superspecialist doctor now has become a supertechnician, unable to meet the demand of ever increasing numbers of patients, begins to recruit associates, who also strive to become supertechnicians, forming a group to perform the procedures. These technicians, particularly if working in a clinic setting with no private practice, adopt a mannerism, a pattern of attitude, not characteristic of a doctor we are accustomed to.

This expansion begins to overshadow the performance of other specialists who may be able to perform as well as a supertechnician, but they have not relinquished their broader style of practice in their specialty. The group of supertechnicians have now established a monopoly, albeit unintentionally and with a desire to serve. Now the doctor is performing as a technician and a vocation has taken the shape of a business and the patient has become a part of an organ and the community is changing to a supercommunity with a new life style, not worse, not better, just different. The leaders of the community now may contemplate training a new group of supertechnicians in a shorter period of time with much less expense and even with much less intellectual endowment and cognitive and psychomotor skills. The supertechnicians need no longer to be a doctor to take care of patients.

An excellent relationship with the patients does not automatically translate to a mutually harmonious and respectful communication with the members of the family of the patients. In my practice the vast majority of them were highly supportive of the patients and courteous toward the medical profession in general. The office staff usually addressed their questions and concerns and even their anxiety.

However, there were exceptions, very rarely a family member's behavior would tax my patience; It would not be difficult to understand when a freshman medical student inquires if his grand uncle, who has an staphylococcal infection involving the valves of his heart is receiving an adequate dose of antibiotics. But it would be difficult to maintain the equanimity when an intravenous drug abuser, in order to obtain the guardianship of his grandmother, requests a certificate to declare her incompetent in managing her financial state. Particularly when the grandmother is highly educated and competent, supporting her grandson and assisting him in recovering from his self-abuse and addiction.

I was not able to maintain my equanimity, even though I was able to control my facial demeanor when the adult children of my patients, although very rarely, wished to confine their parents to nursing homes. These members of the family were wealthy with impressive business titles, usually a member of a board of directors of a corporation, residing in an exclusive neighborhood in a mansion-like home. I had been taking care of their parents for more than a decade, they were old and had chronic, but stable cardiovascular ailments. Despite their age, they were alert, pleasant, and capable of living independently at home or with their children with some degree of supervision. The children owed their success and financial prosperity to the hard working and disciplined parents; they still were getting guidance and help from them. These patients would have felt isolated, abandoned, deprived and unwanted had they been confined to a nursing home, against which I advised strongly. A majority, but not all, stayed home or with their sons, lived a quality life despite their disabilities and added a new dimension of richness, a real one, to the monetary wealth of the family as they have been doing all the time.

I have missed my practice and my patients after I retired several years ago, but I must confess that the socio-economic aspect of medical practice was getting rather stressful and irritating. Dealing constantly with insurance companies, Medicare, Medicaid and their rules and regulations was time consuming and, I believe, rather undignified. The health agencies' and the hospitals' quality assurance and control programs indended to monitor the quality of care, it seems, were more interested in reducing the cost, rather than the risk to the patients.

I decided to continue my service by participating in educational endeavors. I continued my Core Curriculum in Cardiology at Mercy Hospital.

PART IV

Selected aspects of The Iranian Culture

CHAPTER 52

Poets of Iran and Avicenna

RUDAKI

During Samani dynasty's rule, Bukhara was identified as a cultural center for scholars and poets. Abdullah Jafar Ibn Mohammad Rudaki (b. c. 859, d. 940/941) was one of the scholars, born in Rudak, Khorasan (now in Tajikstan). He was a favorite court poet of Nasr II (914-934), composing poems in Persian with Arabic script, and regarded as the father of Iranian poetry. Of the large numbers of poems attributed to Rudaki, only small numbers have survived. The translation of Kalilah va Dimnah, or Damnah a modified version of the original Panchatantra book of India is one of the significant contributions of Rudaki to the Iranian and world literature.

Panchatantra (in Sanskrit: Five Chapters), an animal fable book to teach, metaphorically, wisdom. The original, probably written between first century B.C. and 55 A.D. in Sanskrit, is lost. However it was translated to Arabic by Abu Ibn al-Muqaffa (d. 760 A.D.) and was named Kalilah va Dimnah, after the names of two jackals in the book. Rudaki translated this Arabic version to versed Farsi poetry.

In one part of Chapter one (The Lion and The Ox) of the book, the intelligent and witty Jackals, accompanying their king, the lion, sense that the lion is fearful of a moo of a cow, they debate the wisdom of the low rank jackals getting involved with the powerful king, who is surrounded by high nobilities. They discuss the glory, wealth, and power that one may attain, although not permanently, by joining the inner circle of the king and endearing themselves to him, vs. obscurity and the comfort of contentment and frugality.

These animal fables will sound more familiar and current, if we change the lion king to a powerful political figure and the Jackals to people surrounding them.

FERDOWSI

spelled also Firdawsi (c. 935-c. 1020 or 1026) Abu al Qasem (al-Ghasim) Mansur, the great Iranian epic poet was born in the ancient city of Tus, Iran. He devoted thirty-five years for the creation of the world great and celebrated epic of Shahnameh or Shah-nameh (Book of Kings) published for the first time in 1010 A.D.

Sixty thousands couplet verses of Shahnameh tell the story of the Iranian kings, heroes, with their victories and defeats, and Iranian cultural values and religion, Zoroastrianism, from the mythical time until the Arab conquest of Iran (652 A.D.). Ferdowsi dedicated these high quality, legendry and historical poems to Sultan Mahmud of Ghazna of Ghaznavid dynasty. Shahnameh not only has eternalized the survival of the Iranian national epic, but it has been an undisputed instrument in reviving the pre-Arabic Iranian language. After almost 1,000 years, the patriotic Shahnameh enjoys a highly respectable position in the heart and mind of all Iranians and all other nations familiar and involved with the glorious dynasties of the Iranian past.

Sultan Mahmud's appreciation of the Shahnameh did not match the enormous task of Ferdowsi. Sultan did not understand or did not want to acknowledge the greatness of the work because of religious reasons and the persuasion and intrigues of the courtiers. Sultan was Sunni and Ferdowsi was a Shia. The great poet, hurtfully disappointed, satirized the Sultan and fearful of his revenge fled to Herat, then to Mazandran and eventually to Tus, where he died in 1020 A.D. or 1026 and is buried in his present Mausoleum.

The major part of Shahnameh is divided to three parts. The first and shortest part narrates and includes the story of creation, the kings, and the discovery of fire by Hushang. Hushang was the second king, the grandson of Kiumars, who was the first king and the first human in the world.

Hushang's father, the son of, the first king was killed by Ahriman, the devil, and therefore he became the king after the first king.

Part two is devoted to the heroes and the longest part; it is devoted to the Iranian men of distinguished courage, and their challenges and tragedies. The stories, with unusual clarity, are about heroes, including the bravest of all, Rostam, the son of Zal.

Part three, describes the Iranian empire after Alexander until the fall of the Sasanid dynasty and the invasion of Iran by the Arabs.

From the start Rostam is destined to face extraordinary challenges, and conquer ferocious enemies, and demons (divs). Rostam's mother, the princess of Kabul (now capital of Afghanistan), endured a prolonged labor, because of the oversized baby to be named Rostam. His father Zal, fearful of the mother's imminent demise summoned the Simorgh, who helped Zal to deliver baby by Caesarian section, and saved the mother's and child's lives.

Simorgh, probably Avestan (language of Zoroastrian Avesta) in origin, indicating a bird with some semblance to an eagle or falcon, was a mythical, benevolent, giant, and part mammal bird. According to legends Simorgh had lived a long life, perhaps immortal and possessed the knowledge and wisdom of all ages; some believed Simorgh was like phoenix to revive herself from the ashes.

Rostam as a hero had also his share of tragedies. The popular story of Rostam and Sohrab, illustrates this. Rostam kills a young brave man in a dual, unaware of his identity. Later on he finds out that the man he killed was his own son. To turn the tragedy to a calamity, the Iranian king of the time, Kaykavus, delays providing Noush Daru (healing medicine) to save Sohrab's life, fearful of the united force of father and son.

AVICENNA

Abu Ali al-Husayn ibn Abd Allah ibn Sina (980-1037), the great Iranian physician, scientist and philosopher of Islam during the Samanids of eastern Iran and the Buyid of central Iran dynasties.

Born and educated in Bukhara, Iran (now in Afghanistan), a child prodigy, by age of ten had memorized, all verses of Qur'an. By the age of 21, had mastered the Islamic law and medical science. After the defeat of the Samanids by Mahmud, the Turkish founder of Ghaznavid dynasty in Khorasan, Avicenna left the Samanids and his ardent supporters and began to travel the territories of Buyid rulers in central Iran for pursuit of perfection and excellence in the fields of his interest. He eventually reached Hamadan and joined its ruler Shams ad-Dawlah, a Buyid prince, who welcomed Avicenna as a court physician and in time awarded him the position of vizier, a high level and esteemed administrative and leadership post, but with an inherent risk of a downfall, a part of a maladaptive culture of the ruling Iranian dynasties of different times. During his stay in Hamadan Avicenna received his share of disfavor including a short time in prison. When Shams ad-Dawlah died in 1022, Avicenna facing and fearful of the continuous intrigues of the court moved to Isfahan, where he found tranquility, and completed his unfinished works. He authored 200 books in science, theology, philosophy, and medicine. His major works include the famous encyclopedic Book of Healing (Kitab ash-shifa) discussing, the basic and natural sciences, metaphysics, and philosophy; Canon of Medicine (Qanun fi at-tibb), unsurpassed in fame as a medical textbook. Avicenna's doctrine and ideas spread widely to the west and influenced the western culture. His Canon was selected as the source of classical teaching not only in the Iranian territories but as well in the western world for centuries, promoting Avicenna in the medical field to the highest position of the period. His work on the philosophy of Aristotle in the Farsi language distinguished him as the leading Islamic interpreter of Aristotelian philosophy. His religious ideology influenced Christian philosophers and theologians such as St. Augustine and the Franciscans.

Omar Khayyam (Arabic full name: Ghiyath ad-Din Abu Al-Fath Umar Ibn Ibrahim al-Khaiyami an Nishapuri)

He was born on May 18, 1048, in Nishapur, the Seljuki capital in khorasan (present Razavi khorasan Province), to a family of tent makers, thus the name Khayyami , meaning tent maker.

An Iranian, distinguished and renowned in poetry, astronomy, mathematimathics, philosophy, medicine, history, and jurisprudence.

He was an ideal brilliant man recognized and welcomed by Malik-Shah, the most famous ruler of the Saljuks, who also was interested in science, art, and literature.

Omar Khayyam was active, he traveled to Balkh, Samarkand, went on pilgrimage to Mecca, participated in reforming the Islamic Calendar, and building an observatory in the city of Isfahan, published a treatise on algebra, but his ever lasting achievement was the creation of his now world wide acknowledged, Rubaiyat or Robayyat or quatrains, 4-line verses, in which first, second, and fourth lines rhyme. Among the different translations of Robayyat, the English translation by Edward Fitzgerald has gained more popularity and acknowledgment, particularly in the west. Fitzgerald (b. 1809, d. 1883) was an English writer. He collected numerous quatrains of Khayyam, translated, rearranged, publicized under the title of "The Rubaiyat of Omar Khayyam" and published them. His translation was a dynamic and life long effort, adding, deleting, changing the format and wording over a period of more than two decades, with the first publication in 1859 and last in 1879, in four revisions published anonymously. The Fitzgerald translation, mostly is not a verbatim one, he takes a great liberty in the interpretation of the verses, at times expressing Fitzgerald's concept and thought process, rather those of Khayyam's. The use of phrases such as "A Jug of Wine, a Loaf of Bread-and Thou," by Fitzgerald however, reflect the essence of sentiments one perceives in reading Omar's verses in Farsi.

Khayyam's idyllic robayyat address and attempt to answer the complexities, and the mystery of existence; the purpose of transient and uncertain life, death, after life.

After an in-depth contemplation in all spiritualities and inability to obtain a logical answer, a skeptical Khayyam directs his focus toward simplicity, beauty, love, ecstasy, and the joy of life:

And if the Wine you drink, the Lip you press,
End in the Nothing all Things end in-Yes-
Then fancy while Thou art, Thou art but what
Thou Shalt be-Nothing-Thou shalt not be less.
Translated by Edward Fitzgerald

Khayyam if ecstatic with wine, be happy
In the company of the Beauty, be happy
Since nothingness is the end of universe all
Suppose you exist not, since you do, be happy.
Translated by H. dizadji

Happiness and joy used in the robayyat are not amenable to a simple interpretation. The words such as wine, beauty, and beloved may be purely literal or they may be allegorical, representing metaphysical existence of divine nature. Was Omar ascetic, living the life of a Sufi, in mystism, striving constantly for the sanctification of his soul or an epicurean, living in his garden, seeking sensual pleasures? Or was he simply trying to change his focus, not to dwell to find answers for complex questions of life that forever elude us? For now let's select the last option and be happy.

Khayyam died in Nishapur in 1131.

SANAI

Abu al-Majid Majdud ibn Adam (1050-1131), an Iranian Sufi poet during the Ghaznavid Sultans ruling. The writer of the Garden of Truth (Hadigeh al-Haqiqat), dedicated to Bahram Shah of Ghaznavid, died in Ghazna (now Ghazni in Afghanistan). He was the first poet to express the meaning of God, love, and existence of Sufism using ode, lyric couplets poetry, setting precedence for the future mystic poets.

NEZAMI

Elyas Yusof Nezami Ganjani (c. 1141-1203 or 1217), an Iranian romantic poet, born in Ganja (now yandzha, Azerbaijan. The author of the romantic epic poems, The Quintuplet (Kames) books of: The Treasure House of Mysteries (Makhzan al-Asrar), Khosrow and Shirin (Khosrow o-Shirin), Leyla and Majnoon (Leila o-Majnun), The Seven Beauties (Haft Paykar), and The Book of Alexander the Great (Sikandar or Eskandar nameh), written in rhymed couplets verses (Masnavi), inspired by his predecessors, Ferdowsi and Sanai. Nezami lived all his life and died in Ganja, during the Seljuqs dynasty.

ATTAR

Farid od-Din Attar (c. 1142-c. 1220), the mystical poet of Iran, born in Nishapur, a great Islamic traveling Sufi in search of perfection, continued the work of Sanai, wrote the allegorical tales in couplet (Masnavi) form of poetry, including the Conference or the Parliament of the Birds:

The birds, the seekers of truth, are searching for a spiritual leader (Deity, God) to guide them. All agree to look for the mystical Simorgh, reaching and facing him, they realize that Simorgh is them. Mawlana Rumi, influenced by Attar, later on expresses this theme of oneness:

How many words the world contains! But all have one meaning. When you smash the jugs, the water is one.

From the Sufi Path of Love by William C. Chittick.

Attar died in Mecca, Arabia (now in Saudi Arabia).

SA'DI

The great Iranian poet Sa'di (c 1184/1213-1292) was a contemporary of, Abu Bakr ibn Sa'd ibn Zang (1231-60) of the Salghurid dynasty (1148-1270). The Salghurids originated from Salghur Turkmen tribe, they ruled the province of Fars, as vassals of Seljuk, Khwarezmid, and Il-Khanid dynasties in succession. The dynasty, despite not being in a very stable position, was eager to promote the arts.

O brother, as the end is dust, be dust before thou art turned into dust.

(Sa'di, Story 41, The Morals of Dervishes, translated by Edward Rehatsek)

Sa'di's pen name is derived from Sa'd, the father of Abu bakr. His full name is Mosharref od-Din ibn Mosleh (Musleh) od-din Sa'di.

When Sa'di was a child, his father died. Sa'di was educated at the famous Nezamiyeh School in Baghdad. He traveled through the Islamic regions for many years, eventually returning to Shiraz, his birthplace.

A shining star in the Iranian culture and literature, Sa'di is the author of two Iranian classic books. The Bustan (the orchard, 1257) and Gulestan or Golestan (the Rose Garden, 1258). The Bustan, the stories written in verse elucidate and clarify the fundamental Islamic virtues. The Golestan, in addition to the Introduction (Dibatcheh) and the Conclusion has eight chapters. Each Chapter of Golestan contains many stories (Hekayats) told in prose style interrupted with short poems expressing a conclusion and reflecting the author's advice. Sa'di uses his unique styles of lyrics (Ghzaliyat, pleural of Ghazal), odes (Qasideh or Ghasideh), epigrams, and elegies, succinctly to express his philosophy and thoughts.

Sa'di begins the introduction of Golestan by praising God by the following statement (all quotes from Sa'di, written in Farsi are adapted to convey the meaning, not to translate word by word):

" Blessed we are for having air to inhale in order to sustain our life and to exhale to purify our being, a gratitude due to each." This gratefulness imparts more meaning, if said by a patient recovering from an agonizing difficulty in breathing due to acute heart failure.

In reference to the ultimate truth and love, he writes as a Sufi:

"A devout of the real truth after engaging in a spiritual contemplation was asked by his friend what gift he had brought back from the garden of flowers that he just attended. He replied that he had intended to bring armfuls of roses when he reached the garden, but the surrounding beauty and fragrance were so exalting and elating that he let go the hold of his arms.

He teaches the chanting morning birds to learn the true love from a butterfly, who has no more voice, cherished and burned for its beloved;

people singing of love and truth are pretenders, because the real lovers and possessors of truth are silent.

Sa'di writes about morality, piety, virtues, generosity and kindness vs. power, cruelty, and greed; kings vs. pious. He devotes stories to contentment, virtue of silence, love, strength and weakness.

His Hekayets metaphorically address complex issues encountered in life: the appreciation of safety of a boat in the ocean by a man who has experienced drowning; a reconciliatory lie vs. a destructive truth; you respect the privacy of their home then respect the privacy of their mind; a sinner by wearing a frock will not turn to a pious; a rose in the eye of an enemy is a thorn.

Real richness of mind and freedom of soul are achieved by controlling the temptations to accumulate the riches and power or secure the favor and support of the powerful.

Sa'di died in December 9, 1291, his tomb is in his mausoleum, in Shiraz, Iran.

MAWLANA OR MEVLANA (OUR LORD) RUMI Jalal ad-Din Rumi (c. 1207-1273) was born in Balkh, now in Afghanistan. In young age accompanying his family, threatened by Mongols, left Balkh, ruled at the time by Khwarezm Shahs, and after several years of travel including a pilgrimage to Mecca, arrived at Rum (Anatolia), ruled by the Seljuk Dynasty, eventually settling in Konya, the capital of the Rum. Rumi's father was soon acknowledged by the religious scholars in Konya, receiving the title of Sultan al-ulema the Sultan of knowledgeable. Jalal ad-Din was exposed to his father's teaching and influenced by the leading Sufis of the time, not only became well versed in the traditional Islamic divine laws (exoteric sciences) including jurisprudence, the Qor'an, but also in the Spiritual Path of Sufism (esoteric sciences). Rumi continued his father's teaching responsibilities after his death, in the traditional jurisprudence until he underwent a radical spiritual transformation to esoteric sciences, after coming upon Shams Tabrizi, a wandering Sufi, in Konya in 1244. Shams ad-Din of Tabriz mesmerized Rumi, transmitting his illuminated and divine spirituality to Rumi. The identification of Rumi with Shams Tabrizi was so intense that it led to the neglect of Rumi's family members and their intervention and the eventual departure or disappearance of Shams from Konya. After separation, Rumi much nostalgic, but encouraged and energized by his friends and disciples inspired to compose his lyric and epic poems to become the greatest Sufi poet of Iran, and his work to transcend the national and religious boundaries.

His highly recognized and admired works include Masnavi-ye-Manavi, Divan-e Shams (collection of poetry named after Shams-e Tabrizi), influencing, the ideology and literature of the entire Islamic world.

Masnavi (Couplets)-Manavi (Spiritual) of about 25000 verses of didactic anecdotes and tales address many aspects of esoteric teachings. Divan comprises about 40000 of various forms of individual verses, reflecting the state of mind in the ecstatic moments. In his poetry mawlana presents complex spiritual thoughts and divine love with unsurpassed clarity, beauty, and vividity simulating the sound of romantic music felt and understood by the readers. Mawlana's verses and music are permanent partners, he composes poetry to the sound of the flute and he dances to the recitation of his verses.

Fihi va fihi ("In it is what is in it"), a didactic prose form, contains the transcription of teaching of Rumi to his disciples.

After his death the order of Whirling (dancing) Dervishes, or Mawlawiyah order, a group of his disciples organized by his son Sultan Walad, continue the Mawlana's trend, dancing to a state of ecstasy. From his mausoleum, now a museum in Konya he continues to inspire the seekers of true meaning in life.

HAFEZ

Shams od-Din Mohammad Hafez Shirazi (1325/1326-1389/1390), Iranian poet, born in Shiraz, was educated in the Islamic religion, and he was well versed in Qur'an, and as the name Hafez implies, had memorized the whole sacred book of Islam. The most loved and adored Iranian lyric poet. Distinguished court poet, of the Muzaffarid dynasty of Shiraz (1335-1393); popularity of Hafez in the court of Mizaffarids was highly variable and intermittent, depending on the like and dislike of the rulers of the time.

His ghazals lyric poems of several couplets, express love, happiness, inner peace, and symbolic beauty, wine, and ecstasy.

If the belle of Shiraz, grabs a hold of my heart,
just for her Hindu-like mole, I would give
All of Samarkand, all of Bukhara
Translated by Clarence Streit

His fluent poetry with a musical tone reflects his Sufi theme, rejects hypocrisy and the pretenders of virtuosity, searching ceaselessly for the truth and striving for unity with the highest spirituality and God.

From the bier of Hafez, keep not back thy foot:

For though he be immersed in sin, he goeth to paradise.

Translated by Lieut. Col. H. W. Clarke, British (1891, Calcutta).

The collection of his poems called Diwan or Divan is one of the most popular books owned by the Iranian people. Divan is a loyal companion for the Iranians of all social strata, a friend of intellectuals seeking solace and inner peace from the complexities of life, a lyric to sing along with music, a poem to woo a beloved, a soothsayer to fight the sadness, a fortune teller for seekers of the right choice and right path, the path of Sufi.

Using Divan-e Hafez to predict destiny is a common practice among Iranians, similar to the practice of bibliomancy.

A person anxious to know his right choice for a specific task to be performed, closing his eyes, asks Hafez, the revealer of all secrets, for assistance, then opens the Divan at random to verses, the interpretation of which provides the answer for the seeker.

JAMI

Nur od-Din Abd or-Rahman ebn Ahmad (1414-1492), Iranian scholar and mystic poet. Born in a village near Jam (now in Ghor Province, Afghanistan) and a few years later moved to Herat (western Afghanistan) and lived there. The author of a treatise Lavayeh or Lava'ih (Flashes of Light) in prose about Sufism, and Haft Awrang (The Seven Thrones) in verses, influence by Nezami and includes Yusuf (Joseph) and Zulaykha.

CHAPTER 53

Iranian Calendar And New Year Compared With Islamic And Gregorian Calendar

A BRIEF DEFINITION OF TERMS

Year and month: The reported length of the year and month are variable because different parameters are used in the calculation.

The commonly used solar year, also called tropical or seasonal, is the time between two successive vernal equinox. In this system the solar year duration is 365 days, 5 hours, 48 minutes, and 46 seconds.

The vernal equinox is the time when the sun apparently crosses the plane of the equator, resulting in equal length of day and night.

Sidereal year, 365 days, 6 hours, 9 minutes, and 9.54 seconds, is the time required for the earth to complete one revolution around the sun, measured with relation to the fixed stars.

The lunar year of 354 days consists of 12 synodic months.

The approximate time required for the Moon to revolve once around the earth is a month.

The commonly used synodic month or complete cycle of phases of the moon (mainly one new moon to the next) is 29 days, 12 hours, 44 minutes and 3 seconds.

The time required for the moon to return to a fixed point is called sidereal month, and it is 27 days, 7 hours, 43 minutes, and 12 seconds.

It is evident that the length of the lunar year of 12 lunar months does not correlate with the length of the solar year. Therefore to maintain the lunar year calendar in harmony with the solar year and the seasons a periodic addition (intercalation) of days to the lunar years is necessary.

Originally the periodic intercalations were applied at random and usually retrospectively, but eventually as the reforms of the calendar system progressed a fixed intercalations, incorporated prospectively to the calendar systems, setting the number of days in the months and establishing leap years with more days than the usual or the common years.

Jewish and Islamic calendars are two examples of the lunar year calendar system.

The Iranian calendar one of the oldest systems of dividing time and studying chronology officially started 539 B.C., after the conquest of Babylonia. The Iranian rulers adopted the Babylonian calendar as the standard calendar of Iran. The Babylonian calendar was a lunar year system of 354 days and 12 synodic months, adjusted to the solar year calendar by a periodic addition or intercalation of an extra month or days.

This system continued until the Sasanid Empire, when about 226 A.D., a modified calendar of the Zoroastrian type replaced it. This new calendar consisted of 12 months of 30 days, plus 5 days, total 365 days, similar to Egyptian and solar year calendars of 365 days.

After the conquest of Iran by the Islamic power, the Islamic calendar replaced the Sasanids calendar.

Islamic calendar a lunar year dating system consists of 12 lunar months, the length of the year varying between 354 and 355, each month begins at the new moon, the length of the month alternating between 30 and 29 days, except for twelve, which receive 30 days in 11 years out of a 30 years cycle, making the total days 355 days for those years. In this system the named months are out of phase with the seasons, and the Islamic era is computed from the year prophet Mohammad emigrated from Mecca to Medina, July 15-16, 622 A.D.

During Reza Shah Pahlavi (reigned 1925-1941) Iran adopted the solar year system calendar, but kept The Islamic era of 622 A.D., abbreviated as A. H. S (after Hegira) vs, A.H.L.

This system is a modified form of the Islamic calendar with a solar year of 12 months, the first day of the first month, Farvardin, begins on March 21 at the time of the vernal equinox, starting from 622 A.D. of the Gregorian calendar.

The first six months consists of 31 days, the next 5 months of 30 days, the last month of 29 days, except in the leap year of 30 days. Leap years are every fourth year for seven episodes and five years for the eightieth episode, making the total cycle of 33 years.

The calendar system within the civilized nations has been in a state of flux; the most commonly used is a version of the solar year calendar, with constant months and seasonal relationship and fixed intercalation time.

The Roman republican calendar, before the Christian era, in about 738 B.C., probably derived from the Greek lunar calendar, the latter originating from the Babylonian system was a lunar year calendar not in phase with seasons, the beginning of the year falling on different days of the seasons, causing a significant confusion.

Then Julius Caesar, in 46 B.C. began to change it to a solar year calendar. The year had 12 months of 30 or 31 days, except for February of 28 days in common years (365 days per year) and 29 days in the leap year, every fourth year (366 per year). These changes were implemented in 8 A.D. In this system the overestimation of the length of the year by several minutes, cumulatively resulted in a significant shift in the days of the seasons.

Therefore Pope Gregory XIII, reformed the calendar and established a new system, named after him as the Gregorian calendar, in 1582 A.D.

A common year of 365 days and a leap year of 366 every 4 even years as well as the century years, only if they are exactly divisible by 400.

Today is September 1st, 2009 A.D. (09/01/1009) in the Gregorian calendar corresponding to Shahrivar 10 of 1388 A.H.S (06/10/1388) in the Iranian solar calendar, and to Ramadan 11, of 1430 A.H.L in the Islamic calendar (08/11/1430).

CHAPTER 54

Norouz

Iranian New Year called Eid Norouz (New Day), spelled also Norooz, or Nowruz, is the first day of the first month (Farvardin) of the Iranian solar calendar, corresponding to March 20-21, vernal equinox, and first day of spring.

The arrival of Norouz in 2009 was March 20, at 7:43:42 AM in New York time.

The basic celebration rituals are similar to those of ancient time, with addition or modification of some features or ceremonial acts over a period of centuries, based on local cultures and perception and interpretation of the historical events.

The preparation for the holiday, such as spring cleaning, purchasing new furniture, new utensils for cooking, and new outfits for all members of the family particularly for children, all begin long before the first day of spring; these changes in the life style are a prelude to the arrival of spring and rebirth of the nature. Based on the legends, the ancient Iranians initiated these rituals of preparations to welcome and share their prosperity with the spirits of their ancestors, coming from heaven to visit their offspring annually during the New Year.

The Iranians' everlasting admiration of their gardens of flowers, the aroma of colorful fruits, the singing of the birds, escalate in Norouz time. The spring flowers, sonbol (hyacinth) among them, beautify the windows of flower shops. Roasting nuts with their fragrance filling the air, and the salted Iranian pistachio and all kinds of nuts, spices filled in boxes and handsomely packed on the shelves, adorn the stores.

Vendors and shopkeepers display a variety of vegetables and colorful fruits, dried, preserved, and fresh, oranges from the north and dates from the south, pomegranates, melons, and particularly the Iranians favorite, dried or fresh apricot.

Several days before Norouz, the people with all sorts of backgrounds, fill earthenware pots with sifted earth, planted with seeds of wheat or other grains, watered and covered with a wet cloth, ready for germination. They wait for the seeds to grow to sprout out green.

A lighter part of Norouz festivities is a character called hajji Firouz, a charcoaled disguised face, wearing bright red lipstick and a colorful outfit, paroling, dancing, singing in the neighborhood. He plays his tambourine, heralding the arrival of Norouz, calling on people to participate in the events.

After these preliminary activities, chapter one of the Eid Norouz begins with bonfire festivities. At the eve of the last Wednesday of the year, in Farsi, Shab-e Chahar Shanbeh Soury, small bonfires, using bushes and wood, glow in the yards, alleys (kucheh) and streets. Girls and boys and even adults, eager and full of life jump over the fire while chanting, "your rosy glow be mine and my yellow hue be yours".

In some communities at Chahar-Shanbeh Souri, young people, particularly children, move from door to door, carrying pots and pans, banging on them with spoons, expecting to fill them with rice, eggs, and at the recent time, with chocolate candies and sweets, by the homeowners. Traditionally rice was intended for the poor, but chocolates probably are suitable for children. What does it remind us? Halloween of course.

The origin and the purpose of the fire festivity are not clear; it might be the remnant of the ancient Iranians fascination with fire. The legendary stories tell us that the bonfires were set up to guide the heavenly spirits on their visits to the earth during Norouz.

The ancient Celtics celebrated their New Year on November first at the beginning of a cold and dark winter heralding misery; the ancient Iranian celebration was at the end of winter, bright and colorful spring promising joy and happiness. In both occasions, the ghosts of the dead return to earth; in the Celtic version they were malevolent, they were coming to harm the crop; in the Iranian version they were benevolent, they were coming to enjoy the prosperity of their offsprings. Halloween probably is a derivative of Chahar Shanbeh Souri, or both are derived from another older tradition. For the Iranian, darkness and cold is over and light and joy are in horizon; the Celtic was concerned of and preparing for oncoming winter problems.

Norouz revives hope, hope for a better life. Cold and dark winter and all uncomfortable feelings associated with it are being replaced by fresh, clear, and warm days. All rejuvenating. It is a dream coming thru, sun is shining, fire is glowing at night, birds are singing, flowers are blossoming, green is growing, there is no ugliness, beauty is everywhere, sickness and misery are gone, health and happiness have come, the nature is being reborn again, it is Norouz, and Happy Norouz to you. Everlasting Iranian heritage hope and dream, an essential part of its civilization.

One of the essential parts of Norouz is the ceremonial Haft Seen display. A receptacle made of a picturesque tablecloth and embroided with prayer or poem, using it as a flat tray, called sofra, is spread over a Persian carpet, usually on the floor of the guest room, or in the modern era on the table. Seven (haft) items, starting with the Farsi alphabet sinn also spelled seen, equivalent to the English s are placed on the sofreh. Seven items usually are sabzeh (germinated wheat, sprout), sonbol (hyacinth), samanou (sweetened germinated wheat), seeb (apple), senjeed (a dry lotus fruit), seer (garlic), and sumagh (sumac) or serkeh (vinegar). These items collectively symbolize our wishes for the New Year: life, health, happiness, prosperity, and beauty. Additional items may also be placed on the sofreh, appropriate to the local culture and the religious faith. Most people place Qur'an, the holy book of Islam also on the sofreh. The sofreh might contain a volume of poems of the great Iranian poet Hafiz, or a goldfish or rosewater bowls and candles.

Members of the family gather around the sofreh, waiting for the exact time of Norouz (Tahvil), when the head of the family or his representative, or a senior member initiate the well-wishing, usually expressing the most commonly used phrase "eid (feast) shoma (you) mobarak (be blessed). Then depending on the family's financial state and the cultural background, he may dispense a gift of gold or silver or any other coins and candies and cookies to the younger members of the family, followed by kisses and hugs.

On Sizdeh Bedar, the 13th day of Norouz, all members of the family go to picnic, out of town, to a region in the surrounding areas with sprouting green grass and adjacent to a lake or river. Out there, plenty sunshine, fresh air, while singing, and dancing, they throw the sprout to the water and end the 13th day of eid Norouz. They enjoy these thirteen days, a dream or real ones, they do not care.

We, Madelyn and I, still celebrate Norouz in Chicago. We sit around Haft Seen table, in recent years accompanied by our three highly intelligent and healthy grandchildren, as Iranians say the noor (light) of our eyes, our souls (jans). They are David my raison d'etre, Daria, and Daniel. Their mother Dr. Desiree Dizadji is a cardiologist and their father Dr. Ofer Zikel is a neurosurgeon.

CHAPTER 55

A Brief Note On Iranian Cuisine

In the Iranian culture the extent of variation in the selection and courses of the meals served to group, depends upon the importance of the events requiring celebration and festivities as well as the seniority and status of guests to be honored.

Bread, side dishes, appetizers, salads, soups, main courses, desserts, all are placed on the sofreh or table and served simultaneously.

Bread (na'n or naan) has a most important and respectable position in the Iranian food menu. It is holy and a divine gift and it is treated as such. Of several types of bread, naan-e lavash, naan-e barbari, and naan-e sangak have become a part of life in Iran. Barbari is a flat loaf of bread, but relatively thick about one inch, leavened, made of flour with added corn meal, usually eaten fresh at breakfast. Lavash is thin, also oval or round in shape, about eighteen inches in size, usually made of wheat flower, may be kept for a longtime and consumed as needed. Both naan-e babari and lavash could be baked at home. Sangak, whole wheat bread is a flat and rectangular form of bread, two to three feet long, fifteen to eighteen inches wide at one end, tapered and much narrower at the other end, less than half inch thick. It is baked in large commercial ovens, constructed with building material, located in the bread making shops. The dough is stretched and spread on a flat rectangular wooden paddle of twelve and eighteen inches in diameter, using it's long handle it is placed on the scorching hot small stones or pebbles in the oven.

Rice is an essential part of the Iranian meal, practically available to all, after bread the rice is the core of all Iranian foods. It is produced in the northern provinces of Iran.

Simply cooked rice may be a part of the daily meal or in festive and formal occasions it may be cooked as a gourmet food, making it a jewel of the Iranian delicacies.

There are a variety of rice, cooked variably. From a simple smothered rice (kateh) and boiled and steamed rice (chelo) to a more complicated mixture of rice with the other ingredients (polo). Rice served with ground meat, stews (khoresh or khoresht), poultry, fish, vegetables, noodles, fruits, and saffron.

The most delicious part of rice, to some tastes, is the crusted brown-golden part formed at the bottom of the pot, after cooking, called tah-dig (literally bottom of pot). The cook could obtain, a thicker, more palatable and golden tah-dig by placing flat and thin bread on the bottom of the pot, underneath the rice during cooking.

Stew or koreshe (khoreshe or khoresh) is a mixture of various ingredients including all kinds of meats, poultry, and fish, a variety of vegetables and fruits, seasoned with aromatic spices.

Fresh herb stew (khoreshe-e ghormeh sabzi) and eggplant (badenjan or bademjan) stew (khoreshe-e bademjan) are among the most popular Iranian stews.

In addition to stews, red meat (mainly lamb and mutton), chicken, and fish are prepared in a variety of ways, to be served in different occasions. A whole lamb and chicken and fish may be served stuffed with numerous ingredients or meat and chicken may be charcoaled and served as brochette or shish-kabab.

Ground meat brochette, charcoaled using a flat skewer (kabob-e kubideh), served with rice (chelo-kabob) is suitable for all occasions. In addition to bread, rice, meat, chicken, and fish, a full Iranian meal, particularly in a festive occasion might include vegetables, fruits, yogurt, panir (feta cheese), cucumbers, tomatoes, onion, and eggplants and additional side dishes. These items might be served as appetizers, soups, salad, and desserts or as a main dish. Yogurt (mast) is a popular and inexpensive dairy product, available and consumed in most households in Iran. Plain yogurt might be a side dish, or a thirst quenching drink during hot summers, mixed with water or soda and salt (dough). It might be a part of main dish, if added to a plate of rice or to a plate of sautéed eggplant.

Aash or a'sh is a unique Iranian soup with plenty of nutritional ingredients to serve as a main course. A'sh-e mast made of water, meat, rice, yogurt, vegetables, oil, salt, pepper, spices, and mint flake for garnishing, is the jewel of the Iranian soups.

Of the stuffed vegetables (dolmeh), grape leaves stuffed with rice, vegetables, meats, spices, sugar, and lemon juice is a gourmet food, but practically available in every household.

A food appropriate for all occasions is kookoo, an omelet-like dish, a mixture of eggs and other ingredients such as meat, chicken, fish, vegetables, eggplant, and yogurt.

Included in side dishes are: Pickles (turshis), vegetables, fruits, and spices preserved in vinegar; pastries, cakes, pudding, and baklava (baghlava). Bamieh (ingredients including sugar, flour, lemon juice, and eggs) and zoulbia (ingredients including sugar, honey, lemon juice, and flour are popular Iranian sweets and they may be served as a dessert.

Halva (Arabic for sweet), a sort of saffron cake, an ancient Iranian side dish, and it usually is offered to friends and needy during mourning period or the other bereavement occasions. Sholeh zard, a saffron pudding is offered for a realized wish, or sort of pledge dish.

The type of the articles in a meal and side dishes served and offered usually is appropriate to the objective of the occasion and is in harmony with the surrounding atmosphere and decoration. The appropriateness is determined traditionally or common sense wise. For instance at a wedding, the bride sitting in front of a mirror with candles lit, and flowers abound, it is not appropriate to serve a sautéed eggplant, despite its delicious aroma. Instead a plate of sweet things, shirini, such as noghle (sugar-coated nuts), or baghlava, light cookies, or simply bread and cheese are served. These items reflect the wishes of the guests for a sweet future life for the bride and groom; and a sweet-savory rice dish (shirin polo) is the appropriate main dish at the wedding night.

After dinner or any other time, when sitting with the member of the family or guests, chatting or reading when one has a desire for snack, then one reaches for ajeel, a mixture of roasted nuts, seeds, and dry fruits, a delicious, nutritious and satisfying recipe.

At breakfast, lunch or dinner or at intervals, tea and samovar is the dear companion of Iranians from all walks of life. Samovar, a water boiler, consists of a metallic container in a barrel or cylindrical shape artistically designed, with a vertical central pipe. The water container is equipped with a chimney and a teapot holder on the top and a faucet at the bottom and handles on the sides. A solid fuel such as charcoal placed in the central pipe, heats the water in the container surrounding the pipe.

The scent of tea, the sight of the steaming samovar, elaborately designed with accessories, teapot, glass cups (stekan) with silver filigree cup holders, spoons, and sugar cube container are an ingrained part of the Iranian culture. The ensemble reflects the warmth and spirit with which Iranians welcome their guests.

Now if we add, lavash, a thin, flat, rounded or oval shaped bread (naan) usually baked at home in the mornings, to tea, feta cheese (panir), hot milk, honey, and boiled eggs, we will have an example of the Iranian breakfast (sobhaneh).

If one wishes for an elegant breakfast, particularly during winter months, the most delicious hot wheat porridge (haleem) will be available in the vicinities to purchase.

Compared with dinner, lunch usually is lighter, except on Fridays, the Iranian Sabbath day, particularly when the members of the family are united for a get together on the weekend, when the mother or grandmother prepares an elaborate lunch similar to dinner.

Coffee or kahve (ghahveh) is not an Iranian national beverage. Grounded coffee beans is strong and is consumed in very small cups usually in the official occasions, such as during funerals.

There are numerous coffee houses, all over Iran, but mostly tea is served in the coffee houses, indicating the historical consumption of coffee in Iran, before the popularity of tea.

Water is the most common cold beverage used in Iran, however, in addition to orange juice and other fruit juices pomegranate juice is a special drink in Iran. Sweetened and concentrated fruit juice (sherbet), such as lemon and cherry juices are often available to mix with water and ice, in most households.

Norouz dinner

Consumption of foods on the day of eid norouz is similar to the other days of the year, except the dinner served at norouz is much more glorious, ritualistic, and festive.

Norouz dinner, if wealth wise affordable, usually excels in quality and design the other festive or usual dinners. Each household attempts religiously to comply with the high standards of culinary art and practice set within the community. The artful mixing of ingredients and arrangement of the different portions of the dinner in a colorful and aesthetic format is a part of ceremony. The plates and dishes containing the main meal, appetizers, salads, soups, deserts are placed on the sofreh or table. The exhilarating aroma of the exotic herbs and spices, the captivating delicacy of the meals and the warmth and genuineness of the people sitting cross-legged around the sofereh or sitting in the chairs around the table is a pleasant and unforgettable experience, which one wishes for all Iranians, as a matter of fact for all humanity.

Although fish (mahi) is not among the most popular list of protein source in the Iranian menu, smoked fish is usually included in the Norouz dinner, combined with rice and herbs (sabze polo ba mahi). Sturgeon eggs, caviar (khaveyar), although a popular Iranian export and consumed locally, is not a delicacy in Iran.

YALDA

Winter solstice, December 21 or 22 with the longest night of the year, is the Iranian yalda night (shab-e yalda). The long night representing darkness is counteracted by staying awake and vigilant, with the candles and fire lit, the members of the family enjoy conversation and their winter fruits and ajeel.

ISLAM AND THE IRANIAN CUISINE

Since the Islamic lunar calendar is out of phase from seasons of the year, the Islamic holidays and festivities, using this calendar, are not seasonal. In general the Iranian culinary practices and the Islamic religion have a harmonious and compatible relationship. Those few items considered haram (not permitted), by Islam, such as alcoholic beverages and pork meat, are not consumed by majority of Iranians, followers of the faith; and in the preparation of foods the Islamic codes are adhered to.

IRANIAN KITCHEN

Is called ashpaz-khaneh, literally soup cook (ashpaz) house (khaneh). As the name implies, it was, at least during my schooling years, an independent place well equipped with culinary facilities, located in a convenient area of the house. The types of equipments were modernized periodically to keep up with industrial, economic, and cultural advances. The lady of the household (Khanum) was de facto chief executive officer of the ashpaz-khaneh and the mentor of her trainees, usually her daughters or close relatives. The objective was to prepare meals with highest quality and various quantity, suitable to the tastes of all members of the family, taking into the consideration each individual's idiosyncrasies and tolerance of foods.

It was an institution engaged in informal, low key, not pretentious, activities related to culinary science, art, practice, education, and research. Of course there were aids, and maids (kolfets), but Khanum was responsible for the over all performance of the kitchen. She supervised the purchase and the preparation of the groceries, at times numerous and in large quantity. She determined the type and precise amount of the needed ingredients, the duration and the intensity of the heating, to assure a nutritious, tasteful, and healthy outcome. Her students underwent a long period of training until they mastered their culinary skills, which were necessary as part of the curriculum vitae to become a lady of a new household and family.

Responsibilities of Khanum were not limited to the kitchen; she educated the members of the family about the Iranian heritage of hospitality and graciousness towards their guests, reminding them that guests are the gift of God. She would emphasize the importance of appropriate behavior at the table or sofreh, encouraging them to respect, not only the company, but also the food, the blessed na'n and panir.

My mother, Tahereh, whom we addressed as Khanum, avoiding her first name out of respect for her was the head of our culinary system. Being an Azeri, not only was she an excellent cook, she had her own recipes. She knew the ingredients of all dishes and she was able to modify them when necessity arose. She was the mentor of many relatives, but she specially trained my two sisters, Fakhri and Badrieh Khanum (Badri). We still enjoy the Iranian meals cooked by my only living sister Badri who lives in Lake County, IL.

Madelyn, my wife, is the Khanum of our household with all responsibilities. She was one of the favorite students of my mother when we lived in Iran or when my mother visited us in Chicago. She has mastered the art and science of Iranian culinary. One of Madelyn's favorite hobbys has been preparing Iranian gourmet dinners and sharing them with our friends. She has shared her Iranian cuisine recipes with the people at the request of Chicago Daily News.

My sister graciously is available for advice and direction when necessary.

REFERENCES:

1. The Constitutional History of Iran in Farsi
Ahmad Kasravi
Amir Kabir Publication
12th printing, in Farsi
Original printed in 1940.

2. Persia the Immortal Kingdom
Roman Ghirshman
Vladimir Minorsky
Ramesh Sanghavi
1971

3. On Human Nature
Edward O. Wilson
Harvard University Press
Cambridge, Massachusetts
London, England
1978

4. Religion and Politics in Contemporary Iran
Shahrough Akhavi
State University of New York Press
1980.

5. The Rise and fall of the Shah

Amen Saikal
Princeton University Press
Princeton, New Jersy
1980.

6. Answer to History
Mohammad Reza Pahlavi
Stein and Day/Publishers, New York
1980.

7. Iran: The Untold Story
Mohammed Heikal
Pantheon Books, New York
1981.

8. Paved With Good Intentions
Barry Rubin
Penguin Book, New York
1981.

9. Going to Iran
Kate Millett
Coward, McCann and Geoghegan, New York
1982.

10. Iran, Between Two Revolutions
Ervand Abrahamian
Princeton University Press
Princeton, New Jersey
1982.

11. The Social Transformation of American Medicine
Paul Starr
Basic Books, Inc., New York
1982.

12. History of Iran in Farsi
Hassan Pirnia and Abbas Eghbal

Heidari Publisher
Third printing
1983.

13. Muhammad, his life based on the earlier sources
Martin Lings
Inner Traditions International, Ltd.
Rochester, Vermont
1983.

14. History of Iran for twenty years
Husein or Hosayn Makki
First volume, fourth printing 1984.
Second volume, fifth printing 1983.

15. An Historical Geography of Iran
W. Barthold, translated by Svat Soucek
Princeton University Press
Princeton, New Jersey
1984.

16. Iran Under the Ayatollahs
Dilip Hiro
Routledge and Kejan Paul
London and New York
1985.

17. The Mantle of the Prophet
Roy Mottahedeh
Simon and Schuster, New York
1985.

18. The Book of Absent People
Taghi Modarressi
Doublday and Company, Inc.
Garden City, New York
1986.

19. Food of Life
Najmieh Batmanglij
Mage Publishers, Inc.
Washington, D.C.
1986.

20. Shiism and Social Protest
Juan R. I. Cole and Nihhi R. Keddie
Yale University Press
New Haven and London, 1986.

21. Witness
Mansur Rafizadeh
Former Chief of SAVAK
William Morrow and Company, Inc.
New York
1987.

22. The Blindfold Horse
Shusha Guppy
Beacon Press, Boston
1988.

23. The Eagle and the Lion
James A. Bill
Yale University Press
New Haven and London
1988.

24. Islam in Practice
Reinhold loeffler
State University of New York Press
1988.

25. Islam
The Straight Path
John L. Esposito
Oxford University Press

New York, Oxford
1988.

26. The Shah's Last Ride
William Shawcross
Simon and Schuste
1988.

27. The Turban for the Crown
Said Amir Arjoman
Oxford University Press
New York, Oxford
1988.

28. Iran and the World
Shireen T. Hunter
Indiana University Press
Bloomington and Indianapolis
1990.

29. Education for Judgment
Edited by C. Roland Christensen, David A. Garvin, and Ann Sweet
Harvard Business School Press, Boston
1991.

30. Majestic failure
The Fall of the Shah
Marvin Zonis
The University of Chicago Press, Chicago
1991.

31. Daughter of Persia
Sattareh Faman Farmaian with Dona Munker
Crown Publishers, Inc.
New York 1992.

32. A History of God
Karen Armstrong

Alfred A. Knopf, New York
1993.

33. History of the World
J. M. Roberts
Oxford University Press
New York, 1993.

34. Blood and Oil
Manucher Famanfarmaian and Roxane Farmanfarmaian
Random House, New York
1997.

35. Influencing Attitudes and Changing Behavior
P. G. Zimbardo, E. D. Ebbesen, C. Maslach
Addison-Wesley publishing Company
1997.

36. The Last Great Revolution
Robin Wright
Alfred A. Knopf
New York
2000.

37. Persian Mirror
Elaine Sciolino
The free Press
New York
2000.

38. A Concise History of Iran
Saeed Shirazi
PublishAmerica, Baltimore
2004.

39. An Enduring Love
Farah Pahlavi
Mirmax Book
2004.

40. Eternal Iran
Patrick Clauson and Michael Rubin
Palgrave Macmillan, New York
2005.

41. The Shia Revival
Vali Nasr
W. W. Norton and Company
New York. London
2006.

42. Mirror of the Unseen
Jason Elliot
St. Martin's Press, New York
2006.

43. Treacherous Alliance
Trita Parsi
Yale University Press
2007.

44. A History of Iran
Empire of the Mind
Michael Axworthy
Basic Books, New York
2008.

45. A History of Modern Iran
Arvand Abrahamian
Cambridge University Press
New York
2008.

46. Destiny Disrupted
Tamin Ansary
PublicAffairs, New York, 2009.

About The Author:

H. Dizadji, MD was born in Iran, a graduate of Tehran University, Medical School, he has practiced medicine in Iran and the United States.

He is a Professor of Medicine, University of Illinois at Chicago, and a Fellow of the American College of Cardiology, American Heart Association, and American College of Physicians. He lives in the vicinity of Chicago.